Franz Brosch

Integrated Software Architecture-Based Reliability Prediction for IT Systems

The Karlsruhe Series on Software Design and Quality

Volume 9

Chair Software Design and Quality
Faculty of Computer Science
Karlsruhe Institute of Technology

and

Software Engineering Division
Research Center for Information Technology (FZI), Karlsruhe

Editor: Prof. Dr. Ralf Reussner

Integrated Software Architecture-Based Reliability Prediction for IT Systems

by
Franz Brosch

Dissertation, Karlsruher Institut für Technologie (KIT)
Fakultät für Informatik,
Tag der mündlichen Prüfung: 29.06.2012
Erster Gutachter: Prof. Dr. Ralf Reussner
Zweiter Gutachter: Prof. Dr. Alexander Pretschner

Impressum

Karlsruher Institut für Technologie (KIT)
KIT Scientific Publishing
Straße am Forum 2
D-76131 Karlsruhe
www.ksp.kit.edu

KIT – Universität des Landes Baden-Württemberg und
nationales Forschungszentrum in der Helmholtz-Gemeinschaft

KIT Scientific Publishing 2012
Print on Demand

ISSN 1867-0067
ISBN 978-3-86644-859-9

Abstract

The ever-increasing demand for IT support within businesses, communities and everyday life has raised the complexity and distribution of modern IT systems, as well as the amount of included software, to levels never known before. In this situation, assuring the reliability of an IT system – namely, its ability to deliver service as expected to its users – constitutes a major challenge. The reliability of an IT system during its run-time depends on its software implementation, its usage and its underlying hardware infrastructure.

Approaches to *architecture-based software reliability prediction* (ASRP) constitute a means to anticipate the reliability of an IT system before its operation. They build upon an architectural model capturing the software components together with their interactions and reliability characteristics. Evaluating the model – through analytical solving or through simulations – yields the expected operational reliability of the system under study. Being model-based, such approaches allow for early reliability assessments already during design stages, guiding design decisions and helping to identify critical parts of the architecture with respect to reliability.

However, existing reliability prediction approaches are limited in their applicability because they implicitly "hard-code" or neglect several factors which influence a system's reliability: (i) the reliability impact of imperfect hardware resources, (ii) the system's ability to recover from local failures and to prevent them from reaching the system's boundaries, and (iii) the system's usage profile and its influence on the control and data flow throughout the architecture. Neglecting these factors leads to inaccurate prediction results; implicit "hard-coding" of information strongly reduces the reusability of the models and the support they can give in evaluating different design alternatives.

This thesis proposes PCM-REL, a novel approach to *integrated software architecture-based reliability prediction for IT systems*, which explicitly considers the reliability-relevant factors discussed above, offering

- a combined consideration of software and hardware reliability impacts by modelling both software components and hardware resources with their specific failure potentials, and by providing an integrated analysis method taking into account these potentials;

- a consideration of fault tolerance capabilities by modelling how service execution can recover from local failure occurrences, carry out failure-handling behaviours and avoid the occurrence of system failures;

- explicit modelling of a system's usage profile and the influence of input parameters on the service execution through the concept of parameter dependencies.

The approach is realized based on the Palladio Component Model (PCM), which offers a design-oriented modelling language for component-based software architectures. While the PCM traditionally allows for performance predictions based on the created architectural specifications, the thesis adds capabilities for reliability modelling and prediction by extending the PCM modelling language with reliability-specific constructs, and by providing an automated analysis method – based on a *discrete-time Markov chain* (DTMC) model – for the reliability evaluation of architectural specifications created in terms of PCM-REL instances. Compared to related ASRP approaches, PCM-REL offers a significantly improved decision support for software architects during system design, improved reusability of the created model artefacts and support for a distributed component-based development process.

ii

The thesis includes two major case studies to validate the PCM-REL approach, giving evidence of

- the feasibility of the included abstractions of the provided modelling language;

- the feasibility of deriving input estimates for the required reliability annotations;

- the validity of the Markov analysis itself;

- the significance and robustness of the obtained prediction results in the light of uncertain inputs.

The first case study features a prototypical system implementation and compares prediction results with measurements. The second study relates to an industrial system and allows for demonstrating the estimation of reliability annotations based on existing information sources. Together, the two studies provide comprehensive evidence for the validity of PCM-REL.

The approach and its contributions have been described in the Transactions of Software Engineering (TSE) journal [BKBR11] (currently accepted for publication and available in an online pre-print version) and further peer-reviewed publications [BZ09, BKBR10, BBKR11].

Kurzfassung

Der ständig steigende Bedarf an IT-Lösungen in Wirtschaft, Gesellschaft und Alltag hat die Komplexität und Verteilung moderner IT-Systeme auf einen nie dagewesenen Grad ansteigen lassen. Angesichts dieser Tatsache stellt die Zusicherung der Zuverlässigkeit eines IT-Systems – d.h. seiner Fähigkeit, eine Dienstleistung wie von seinen Benutzern erwartet zu erbringen – eine große Herausforderung dar. Die Systemzuverlässigkeit zur Laufzeit hängt von der Software-Implementierung ab, ebenso wie von der Systemnutzung und der zugrundeliegenden Hardware-Infrastruktur.

Ansätze zur architekturbasierten Vorhersage der Software-Zuverlässigkeit stellen eine Möglichkeit dar, die zu erwartende Zuverlässigkeit eines IT-Systems schon vor seiner Laufzeit abzuschätzen. Sie basieren auf Architekturmodellen, welche Software-Komponenten, deren Interaktionen und Zuverlässigkeitsaspekte erfassen. Eine analytische oder simulationsbasierte Auswertung dieser Modelle liefert die gewünschte Abschätzung. Mit Hilfe solcher Methoden ist es möglich, Zuverlässigkeitsbetrachtungen bereits in frühe Phasen des Systementwurfs miteinzubeziehen, um so Entwurfsentscheidungen zu unterstützen und kritische Bereiche der Architektur zu erkennen.

Allerdings sind bestehende Ansätze für Zuverlässigkeitsvorhersagen insofern eingeschränkt, als sie wesentliche zuverlässigkeitsrelevante Aspekte einer Systemarchitektur implizit in das Modell "hartkodieren" oder gänzlich vernachlässigen. Diese Aspekte beinhalten erstens die Beeinträchtigung der Systemzuverlässigkeit durch fehlerhafte Hardware-Ressourcen, zweitens die Fähigkeit des Systems, intern auftretende Fehler selbständig zu behandeln und vor seinen Benutzern zu verbergen, und drittens das Benutzungsprofil des Systems und seinen Einfluss auf den Kontroll- und Datenfluss innerhalb der Architektur. Eine Vernachlässigung dieser Aspekte führt zur Verfälschung der Vorhersageergebnisse; eine implizite Abbildung der Informationen im Modell verringert dessen Wiederverwendbarkeit erheblich, so dass die Auswertung verschiedener Entwurfsalternativen nur sehr eingeschränkt unterstützt wird.

Die vorliegende Arbeit führt mit PCM-REL einen neuartigen Ansatz zur integrierten Zuverlässigkeitsvorhersage für IT-Systeme basierend auf ihrer Software-Architektur ein, der die oben diskutierten zuverlässigkeitsrelevanten Aspekte wie folgt berücksichtigt:

- durch eine kombinierte Betrachtung von Zuverlässigkeitsbeeinträchtigungen durch Software und Hardware, bei der sowohl Software-Komponenten als auch Hardware-Ressourcen mit ihren spezifischen Fehlerpotentialen modelliert und durch eine integrierte Analysemethode bei der Vorhersage berücksichtigt werden,

- durch die Betrachtung von Fehlertoleranzmechanismen, bei der die Behandlung lokal auftretender Dienstausführungsfehler durch ausgleichende Maßnahmen zur Verhinderung von Systemfehlern in die Modellierung mit aufgenommen wird,

- durch eine explizite Modellierung des Benutzungsprofils des Systems sowie der Auswirkung von Eingabeparametern auf die Dienstausführung, ausgedrückt durch das Konzept der parametrischen Abhängigkeiten.

Der Ansatz basiert auf dem Palladio-Komponentenmodell (PCM), das eine entwurfsorientierte Modellierungssprache für komponentenbasierte Software-Architekturen bereitstellt. Während der PCM-Ansatz traditionell die Systemmodellierung und Modellauswertung hinsichtlich der Systemperformanz ermöglicht, fügt die vorliegende Arbeit die Fähigkeit der zuverlässigkeitsorientierten Modellierung und Zuverlässigkeitsvorhersage hinzu. Dazu erweitert die Arbeit die bestehende PCM-Modellierungssprache

vi

um zuverlässigkeitsspezifische Konstrukte und stellt – basierend auf einem diskreten Markovkettenmodell – eine automatisierte Analysemethode zur Verfügung, welche als PCM-REL-Modellinstanzen bereitgestellte Architekturspezifikationen hinsichtlich ihrer Zuverlässigkeit auswertet. Im Vergleich zu verwandten Arbeiten bietet PCM-REL eine wesentlich verbesserte Entscheidungsunterstützung für Software-Architekten beim Systementwurf, eine erhöhte Wiederverwendbarkeit der entstehenden Modellartefakte, sowie die Unterstützung eines verteilten komponentenbasierten Entwicklungsprozesses.

Die vorliegende Arbeit beinhaltet zwei umfassende Fallstudien zur Validierung von PCM-REL. Die Fallstudien geben Anhalt dafür,

- dass die in der bereitgestellten Modellierungssprache beinhalteten Abstraktionen für die Zuverlässigkeitsvorhersage nicht ungeeignet sind,

- dass die als Eingaben für das Verfahren benötigten Zuverlässigkeitsabschätzungen machbar sind,

- dass die Analysemethode selbst valide ist, und

- dass die Methode signifikante und im Hinblick auf unsichere Eingaben ausreichend robuste Vorhersageergebnisse erzielt.

Die erste Fallstudie stellt eine prototypische Systemimplementierung zur Verfügung und vergleicht die erhaltenen Vorhersageergebnisse mit Messwerten. Die zweite Studie behandelt ein industrielles System und demonstriert die für die Eingaben benötigten Zuverlässigkeitsabschätzungen basierend auf realen Informationsquellen. Insgesamt geben die beiden Fallstudien umfassenden Anhalt für die Validität von PCM-REL.

Der Ansatz und seine Beiträge wurden in einem Artikel [BKBR11] im Journal "Transactions of Software Engineering" (TSE) und in weiteren von Experten begutachteten Veröffentlichungen beschrieben [BZ09, BKBR10,

BBKR11]. Der TSE-Artikel ist gegenwärtig für die Veröffentlichung akzeptiert und in einer vorläufigen Online-Version verfügbar.

Acknowledgements

I am deeply thankful for so many people who have guided, supported and encouraged me during the last four and a half years. The help of these people was very fundamental and important to me throughout my dissertation project.

First, I want to thank Heidi, my wife, for her great love and support. Heidi always encouraged me to go on, kept me grounded and endured even my most stressful periods of work with admirable patience. A very big thank you also goes to my parents Christine and Stefan Brosch, who have given me their full and unconditional love ever since my birth, and who kept encouraging me throughout the dissertation.

In many respects, my supervisor Ralf Reussner paved the way for my dissertation. Not only did he invite me to join an inspiring team of researchers, but he also taught me the principles and standards of good research. Furthermore, he gave direction to my dissertation with thematic help and advice. I also thank Alexander Pretschner, who was willing to act as a second referee for my thesis, and who provided me with highly insightful and valuable feedback towards the final dissertation stages. A further thank you goes to Steffen Becker, who – at the early dissertation stages – gave me additional supervision and guided my introduction to foundational topics such as component-based software engineering, model-driven software development and the Palladio Component Model.

Throughout the whole dissertation process, my most faithful and inspiring discussion partners and publication co-authors were Barbora Bühnová and Heiko Koziolek. They had a great impact on my work and my thematic progress, and I very much enjoyed all of our discussions. I am especially thankful for the regular meetings I had with Barbora during the months of her stay in Karlsruhe in 2008/2009, which helped me to shape my topic and its focus.

An important milestone with respect to the credibility of my thesis approach was the Astaro Security Gateway (ASG) case study. I am deeply thankful for the efforts of Dietrich Rebmann, who helped me to establish contact with the Sophos (formerly Astaro) company, and who greatly supported me throughout the study. I also thank Micha Lenk from Sophos for his additional support, as well as Marcel Gehrlein for giving me permission to conduct the study and to include its description in my thesis.

Furthermore, I thank the students which I had the pleasure to supervise. They supported me in various ways. In particular, Igor Lankin developed concepts for predicting the reliability of fault-tolerant software systems in his diploma thesis, Daniel Patejdl contributed to the realization of my thesis approach in terms of an Eclipse-based implementation, and Desislava Demirova helped me to investigate the Markov theory foundations required for the dissertation.

A big thank you also goes to Lars Grunske, who made it possible for me to join the Centre for Complex Software Systems and Services at Swinburne University of Technology (Melbourne, Australia) as a visiting scientist for seven weeks in 2010. This stay was a very special experience for me, and I greatly enjoyed the discussions with other Ph.D. students whose topics were close to mine, especially Indika Meedeniya and Aldeida Aleti.

I also want to thank my current and former colleagues at the software engineering department of the Research Center for Information Technology (FZI) and the Chair for Software Design and Quality at the Karlsruhe Institute of Technology (KIT). It would have been very hard to keep dissertation progress going without the very motivating and inspiring atmosphere that these great colleagues provided. In particular, I thank Klaus Krogmann and Samuel Kounev for their great encouragement and thematic support during our discussions, which often enough emerged spontaneously and were driven by a shared passion for our research topics.

As department heads at FZI, Steffen Becker, Mircea Trifu and Klaus Krogmann provided me with solid funding and a stable work environment which constituted a framework for my research. Moreover, several colleagues greatly supported me as team members working for industrial and research projects, ensuring that, even at peak times, I still had freedom to advance my dissertation. In this regard, I want to thank Christian Bartsch, Zoya Durdik, Giovanni Falcone, Thomas Goldschmidt, Henning Groenda, Jens Happe, Benjamin Klatt, Martin Küster, Christof Momm, Christoph Rathfelder and Mircea Trifu (hoping very much that I did not forget other names to mention).

Another special thank you goes to Christoph Rathfelder, Barbora Bühnová, Heiko Koziolek and Klaas Andries de Graaf for reviewing parts of my thesis and providing me with very helpful feedback.

Finally, and even though this may seem unusual, my biggest thank you goes to my Lord Jesus Christ. It is my deepest conviction that He has created me and made me all that I am today. It is ultimately through Jesus that I had all the power and strength that was necessary to accomplish this dissertation.

Contents

1 Introduction

This thesis proposes PCM-REL, an approach to integrated software architecture-based reliability prediction for IT systems, which explicitly considers software and hardware failure potentials of a system under study, included fault tolerance capabilities, as well as the system's usage profile and the propagation of input parameters. This chapter motivates and introduces the approach and its contributions from a high-level perspective. The chapter starts by motivating the need for architecture-based software reliability prediction (Section 1.1), formulates a problem statement (Section 1.2), discusses existing solutions, their shortcomings and the corresponding thesis contributions (Section 1.3), briefly describes the realization and validation of the proposed approach (Section 1.4), introduces an illustrating example (Section 1.5) and gives an outline of the remaining chapters (Section 1.6).

1.1 Motivation

IT systems are steadily growing in size and complexity, in response to the expanding demands of businesses and communities for IT support. The systems possess potentially complex architectures of interconnected and hierarchically composed software components, and they are often based on IT infrastructures with physically distributed computing nodes. They require the interoperation of their constituent software, hardware and network parts, and they provide a potentially heterogeneous set of software services to their users. The development and engineering of such systems presents significant challenges, which are tackled by the software engineering discipline through providing corresponding processes, methods and tools.

1

One of the most fundamental characteristics of an IT system beyond its pure functionality is its *reliability* – namely, its ability to deliver its intended services to its users. Formally, the IEEE Standard Glossary of Software Engineering Terminology [IEE90] defines reliability as "the ability of a system or component to perform its required functions under stated conditions for a specified period of time". A system service should meet the expectations of its users, conducting all required processing steps, achieving valid computational results, delivering all expected outputs, and not producing any unwanted side effects. If a system deviates from its intended service, it exhibits a *failure*. As a quality attribute, reliability is especially important if a system's provided services are mission-critical, with failure occurrences implying high reputational or financial losses, environmental damage, or even loss of life. The critical role of reliability is demonstrated by numerous historical and current IT project failures, which involve reliability problems of the developed IT systems. One such example is the case of the Sainsbury's food retailer attempting to introduce an automated supply chain management system in 2004 to manage its stocks [Mes04]. As the system failed to properly trigger the flow of merchandise from the company's depots and warehouses to its stores, Sainsbury's was forced to hire approximately 3 000 additional clerks to stock its shelves manually. The overall loss resulting from the failed project was estimated to more than USD 500 million. As another example, a defective computer-assisted dispatch system introduced at the London Ambulance Service in 1992 was held responsible for several losses of life due to significantly delayed assigning of ambulances [Fin93].

Out of the various efforts to attain and assure IT system reliability, this thesis focuses on the problem field of *architecture-based software reliability prediction* (ASRP) [Gok07, GPT01, IN08]. This problem field is motivated by the observation that the achievable reliability levels of many IT systems are essentially determined by the fundamental architectural decisions made during the design stages of those systems. This is especially true for systems with complex software architectures, such as business information systems or industrial control systems. As a consequence, system design activities, which precede the actual development for initial system creation as well as system evolution, should be enriched by systematic consideration of reliability aspects. Approaches in the field of ASRP support software architects, who face principal questions such as the following ones: *Which design alternative (out of a given set of possible alternatives) promises the highest system reliability? What are the expected reliability impacts of individual failure potentials contained in the system's architecture? Which architecture parts or service execution steps are most critical (namely, most likely to cause failures)? Does a planned architectural change have an effect on the expected reliability of the system? If so, is the effect positive or negative? Out of a given set of possible architectural changes, which one promises the greatest reliability improvement?* Such questions are answered by ASRP approaches through evaluating an architectural specification of a system under study in terms of a *system model*, enriched by probabilistic annotations representing the system's failure potentials. Based on these inputs, the approaches quantitatively predict the reliability of the final system. Multiple design alternatives can be evaluated and ranked according to their reliability by conducting individual prediction runs for all alternatives. Being based on a system model rather than the system itself, the approaches can already be applied at early design stages, when the system is not yet available and ready for observation of its actual reliability.

While ASRP approaches do constitute a promising means for a more systematic consideration of reliability aspects throughout system development processes, they also face significant and partially unsolved challenges with respect to their practical applicability. To this end, modelling languages must be provided that adequately capture the different reliability-influencing factors of a system and its environment, such that relevant design decisions can be reflected in the system models, and input estimates

3

for the required probabilistic model annotations can be feasibly determined. Moreover, the reliability evaluation of the models must take into account the individual specified failure potentials, reflecting their specific natures, their interplay and their influence on the system's reliability as perceived by its users. This thesis focuses on a specific set of factors which are insufficiently captured by existing ASRP approaches, namely hardware-related failure potentials, fault tolerance capabilities of a system under study, as well as the system's usage profile. The following sections introduce the tackled scientific problem, the state-of-the-art of existing ASRP approaches and the contributions of the thesis in greater detail.

1.2 Problem Statement

Motivated by the discussion of the previous section, the central problem tackled by this thesis is to predict the reliability of IT systems with component-based software architectures, taking into account relevant reliability-influencing factors in a comprehensive way, and supporting the corresponding design decisions. To solve this problem, an approach shall be developed that provides an architecture modelling language and a method for analysing a system's architectural specification to obtain the prediction results.

The goal of comprehensive reliability modelling and prediction includes the challenge of adequately representing the individual failure potentials of a system under study, as well as evaluating their quantitative impacts on the system's reliability. The failure potentials may relate to each of the software, hardware or network dimensions. Software implementations can be flawed due to programming errors, specification errors or natural limitations of the implemented computational procedures. Hardware resources exhibit limited availability due to physical degradations and wear-out. Network connections can be affected by various phenomena such as communication overload, transmission protocol errors, physical interference of transmission lines or unavailability of transmission devices. Moreover, failure potentials can be introduced in a system by utilizing imperfect system-external services. However, existing failure potentials do not necessarily lead to failures perceived by the system's users. A flawed implementation part may never be visited by the system's service execution, an unavailable hardware resource may not be required, a failing network link may not be utilized, and an imperfect system-external service may not be invoked. Moreover, the system may include capabilities to tolerate certain failure potentials and to recover from local failure occurrences during the service execution, preventing them from reaching the system's boundaries.

The reliability impacts of existing failure potentials significantly depend on the overall software architecture, including the system's internal structure of interconnected software components with their interfaces and behaviour, as well as the allocation of software components to a hardware resource environment, the utilization of system-external services and the system's usage profile. These factors determine the potential points of failure within the architectural control flow, as well as the probability that they are actually visited by the service execution upon a certain system service invocation. The additional consideration of the system's included fault tolerance capabilities allows for determining points of recovery in the control flow including their reliability-improving effects. The envisioned reliability modelling language shall capture all these aspects, and the analysis method shall take them into account in order to achieve an integrated reliability evaluation of the system under study.

1.3 Existing Solutions and Thesis Contributions

As discussed earlier, the thesis is situated in the problem field of architecture-based software reliability prediction (ASRP). Approaches in this field constitute the closest related work with respect to the targeted problem of comprehensive reliability modelling and prediction. They build upon a model of a software architecture, which – in its prevalent form – represents the involved software components and the transfer of control between them during the service execution; existing failure potentials are expressed through independent failure probabilities associated with individual visits to components. Based on such a model, the approaches predict the reliability of the software architecture as the probability that the service execution is successfully completed, without any failure occurrence triggered by a visited component.

When comparing the state-of-the-art in the ASRP field with the problem statement given earlier, several limitations of existing ASRP approaches become apparent, which significantly limit their applicability to software development processes in practice. By overcoming these limitations, this thesis achieves its main scientific contributions:

- *Combined consideration of software and hardware failure potentials:* Most ASRP approaches focus purely on software failure potentials, thereby neglecting the reliability impacts of imperfect hardware resources. As a consequence, predictions tend to be over-optimistic, and the introduced inaccuracies may lead to wrong design decisions, if such decisions relate to the overall architecture of an IT system rather than its software parts only. While a few ASRP approaches do consider hardware failure potentials, they do not provide an integrated analysis combining both dimensions [ST07a, ST06], or they have a less differentiated view on the hardware layer [Gra05]. In contrast, the thesis offers a combined consideration of software and hardware failure potentials, taking into account the specific nature of the failure potentials of both dimensions, and deriving an overall system reliability value as the result of an integrated analysis method.

- *Consideration of fault tolerance capabilities:* Typically, ASRP approaches assume that each local failure occurrence during service execution inevitably leads to a system failure perceived by the users, even though many systems exhibit fault tolerance (FT) capabilities allowing for autonomous failure recovery. This assumption either leads to over-pessimistic prediction results, or it forces modellers to implicitly encode FT capabilities into correspondingly decreased software failure probabilities, providing insufficient model expressiveness and decision support with respect to FT. Some approaches take a step forward and offer basic FT considerations limited to specific FT mechanisms and failure situations (such as [CG07b, GL05, ST06, WPC06]). This thesis offers a significantly advanced consideration of FT capabilities, explicitly modelling how certain parts of the service execution can recover from failure occurrences by carrying out failure-handling behaviours. These capabilities enable software architects to comprehensively evaluate different FT mechanisms and their effect on the system's reliability.

- *Explicit consideration of usage profiles and the propagation of input parameter properties:* The success probability of service execution depends on the execution paths taken through the architecture, which in turn depend on the sequences of service invocations of a specific usage scenario, as well as the properties of the input parameters of each invocation[1]. Existing ASRP approaches generally provide only implicit means to account for a system's usage profile and its influence on the service execution. Hence, the usage influences are "hard-coded" in the architectural models, which strongly reduces the reusability of the corresponding model artefacts. This is also true for a few advanced approaches (such as [CSC02, GPHG+03, PDAC05, YCA04]), which explicitly model some usage aspects but hard-code other aspects. In contrast, this thesis provides an explicit representation of a system's usage profile with all its relevant aspects, including

---

[1]The term "property" refers to any characteristic of an input parameter that may influence the process of service execution, such as the value of an integer parameter, the size of a list of data objects, or the encoding of a string parameter.

7

the input parameter properties of service invocations and their influence on the service execution. Thanks to this contribution, software architects can easily evaluate architectural candidates under varying usage profiles.

1.4 Realization and Validation

In order to realize the envisioned contributions, this thesis proposes PCM-REL, an approach to *integrated software architecture-based reliability prediction for IT systems*, which builds upon the existing *Palladio Component Model* (PCM) [BKR09]. The PCM provides a design-oriented modelling language for component-based software architectures, enforcing a strict separation of modelling concerns along the lines of multiple envisioned developer roles in a distributed component-based development process. The modelling language includes a repository model for the specification of software components, a system model capturing component instances and their interconnections, a resource environment model specifying computing nodes, hardware resources and network connections, an allocation model mapping software components to computing nodes, as well as a usage model capturing the system's usage profile. While traditional applications of the PCM are in the area of software performance prediction, the thesis extends its capabilities to realize comprehensive reliability modelling and prediction. To this end, the thesis develops a methodological basis for integrated IT system reliability prediction, extends the PCM meta-model by corresponding reliability-specific modelling constructs and develops an analysis method based on *Markov chains* [Tri02] for the reliability evaluation of architectural specifications created in terms of PCM-REL instances.

The thesis includes two major case studies, which serve to give evidence of the feasibility of PCM-REL's included modelling abstractions, the feasibility of deriving input estimates for the required reliability annotations, the validity of the Markov analysis itself, as well as the significance and robustness of the obtained prediction results in the light of uncertain inputs. The first case study is based on the audio hosting example as introduced in the following section; it features a prototypical system implementation and compares prediction results with measurements. The second study relates to an industrial system with SMTP processing functionality and allows for demonstrating the estimation of reliability annotations based on existing information sources. Both studies support the claim for the validity of the approach.

In conclusion, PCM-REL fulfils the criteria defined with respect to the targeted scientific problem; it overcomes central weaknesses of existing ASRP approaches, and it constitutes a comprehensive and validated solution for supporting software architects through integrated reliability prediction for IT systems.

1.5 The Audio Hosting Example

This section introduces an exemplary application scenario for PCM-REL, which serves to illustrate reliability modelling concepts throughout the thesis, and which provides a basis for one of the case studies conducted for validation purposes. The example focuses on *MediaServ*, a fictive company that offers various hosting solutions for media files such as images, audio or video files. MediaServ pursues two types of business models. As a software provider, the company offers software components to third party service providers, which use the components to build and promote their own hosting services. Additionally, MediaServ acts as a service provider itself and offers a hosting service to end customers. Figure 1.1 gives an overview of these scenarios.

MediaServ provides solutions for different kinds of media hosting use cases, ranging from repositories for online media shops and portals to storage facilities for limited user groups or communities. The required instal-

9

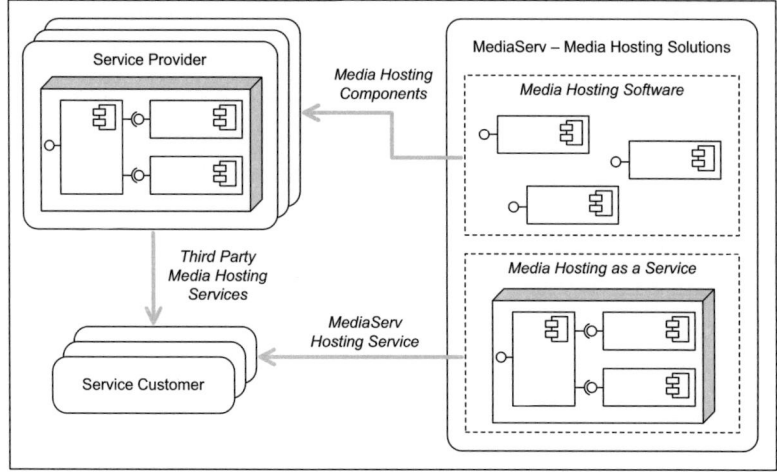

Figure 1.1: Media Hosting Solutions Offered by MediaServ

lation sizes and expected functionalities vary accordingly. A new development project of the company aims at a lightweight *audio hosting service*, providing a centralized storage for audio files, corresponding up- and download functionality and user management enabling restricted data access and individual audio collections per user account. A web-based front end allows for user registrations and transfers of individual files and file collections. The service also includes processing capabilities such as the adaptation of audio compression levels.

The hosting solutions developed by MediaServ exhibit a non-perfect reliability. Even though the company applies rigorous quality assurance to its development processes, a certain probability of failure always remains. Software bugs in the developed components may lead to failures during the execution of MediaServ's and third party hosting services. Additionally, unavailable hardware resources and transmission failures of network connections may lead to failures on the service level. Depending on the established service usage contracts, MediaServ may be held responsible for failures of its hosting service, as well as third party service failures caused by MediaServ's software components. Hence, reliability is an important factor for the company to consider. However, the impact of the different failure potentials on the overall service reliability is not trivial to determine, as it depends on the underlying software architecture and the service usage profile.

MediaServ attaches importance to the reliability of its offered hosting solutions. The company uses PCM-REL for reliability modelling and prediction throughout the system design stages. The application of PCM-REL allows MediaServ to anticipate the expected reliability of its planned audio hosting service, to assess the reliability impacts of individual failure potentials contained in the architecture, and to select out of a range of possible design alternatives the most reliable one.

1.6 Contents and Outline

This section gives a brief overview of the contents and structure of the thesis. First, Chapter 2 introduces the existing foundations upon which the PCM-REL approach builds. The discussion covers basic concepts related to IT systems and reliability (Section 2.1.1), the overall scientific context of reliability engineering and software reliability engineering (Section 2.1.2), as well as the directly related field of architecture-based software reliability prediction (ASRP, Section 2.5). Further relevant areas of discussion include existing methods for specifying and estimating software and hardware failure potentials (Sections 2.2 and 2.3), an overview of the area of fault tolerance (FT, Section 2.6) and a brief introduction to Markov chains and their underlying theory (Section 2.4), upon which PCM-REL and many ASRP approaches build. In addition, Section 2.7 introduces the PCM as a conceptional and technical foundation for PCM-REL.

Chapter 3 builds upon the foundations given in the previous chapter and develops an own PCM-REL methodology, based on an integrated perspective on IT systems (Section 3.1) which combines the perspectives of the hardware-oriented and software-oriented reliability communities. The discussion is complemented by putting reliability prediction into the context of an envisioned reliability-aware system engineering process (Section 3.2). Further discussions cover the adoption of PCM methodology by PCM-REL (Section 3.3), as well as the degrees of freedom that PCM-REL offers for reliability modelling (Section 3.4).

Chapter 4 focuses on the modelling capabilities of PCM-REL, which extend the PCM meta-model by reliability-specific concepts and modelling constructs. Section 4.1 introduces the notion of an overall behavioural view, which combines all specifications of user and system behaviour, and which serves as a basis for defining the concepts of a successful run through a usage scenario, the potential points of failure and points of recovery in the control flow, the occurrence of failures-on-demand and their propagation throughout the architecture. Section 4.2 further introduces the differentiation of multiple failure-on-demand types, and the following Sections 4.3 to 4.6 deal with the specification of failure potentials related to software, hardware, network and system-external services. Section 4.7 describes the specification of capabilities for failure recovery, and Section 4.8 shortly introduces PCM-REL's tool support for reliability modelling.

Chapter 5 describes the Markov analysis method provided by PCM-REL for the reliability evaluation of its architectural specifications. In order to cover all relevant aspects for integrated IT system reliability prediction, PCM-REL develops novel ways to apply existing Markov theory, and it includes a space- and time-efficient algorithm for transforming a PCM-REL instance into a discrete-time Markov chain. Section 5.1 gives an overview of the involved concepts, before Sections 5.2 and 5.3 go into the details of evaluating the potential hardware states of a system under study, as well as its behavioural specifications. Section 5.4 adds a consideration of the method's complexity, and Section 5.5 shortly describes the integration of automated evaluation capabilities in PCM-REL's tool support.

Chapter 6 reports on two major case studies that serve to validate the PCM-REL approach. Against the background of the overall state-of-the-art in the validation of software reliability predictions (Section 6.1), the thesis sets up its specific validation goals (Section 6.2) and develops a plan how to achieve these goals through the case studies (Section 6.3). Sections 6.4 and 6.5 then describe the studies. The first study is based on the audio hosting example. It demonstrates PCM-REL's reliability evaluation capabilities and compares the obtained prediction results against a simulation, as well as measurements conducted on an implemented prototype. The second study examines the Astaro Security Gateway (ASG) as an industrial IT system. The study focuses on the SMTP processing functionality of ASG installations. It derives an architectural specification including input estimates for reliability annotations from existing information sources and conducts a reliability evaluation to answer relevant system design questions. Section 6.6 briefly reports on further case studies and validation experiments conducted for PCM-REL.

Chapter 7 provides an in-depth review of the PCM-REL approach compared to its related work. Three Sections 7.1 to 7.3 specifically focus on the three main contributions of PCM-REL, namely the combined consideration of software and hardware failure potentials, the consideration of an IT system's fault tolerance capabilities, as well as the explicit consideration of usage profiles and the propagation of input parameter properties. The discussion mainly focuses on, but is not limited to, related approaches in the field of ASRP. Section 7.4 then summarises the innovative features of PCM-REL and sets them in relation to existing efforts and results specifically in the ASRP field.

Chapter 8 concludes the thesis with a short summary (Section 8.1), an overview of completed and ongoing research efforts related to PCM-REL (Section 8.2), an examination of future work potentials (Section 8.3) and a final assessment and outlook (Section 8.4).

2 Foundations

The PCM-REL approach presented in this thesis builds upon a significant amount of existing knowledge and methodology in several areas related to IT systems and their reliability characteristics. As a foundation for the presentation of the approach itself, this chapter provides overviews and discussions of all relevant aspects which form the context of the approach. More concretely, Section 2.1 explains basic reliability concepts and presents existing approaches in the area of hardware and software reliability analyses. Sections 2.2 and 2.3 then discuss the state of the art in deriving hardware and software reliability estimates, which are required for the application of PCM-REL. An introduction to Markov chains as the underlying formalism of PCM-REL is provided by Section 2.4, and the field of architecture-based software reliability prediction (ASRP), to which PCM-REL belongs, is introduced by Section 2.5. Section 2.6 gives an overview of fault tolerance in IT systems, and Section 2.7 concludes by presenting the Palladio Component Model (PCM) as the conceptional and technical foundation of PCM-REL.

2.1 IT Systems and Reliability

This section provides a high-level overview of the scientific context of the PCM-REL approach. Section 2.1.1 discusses foundational concepts and terms of IT systems with a special focus on reliability, before Section 2.1.2 introduces the problem field of analysing hardware and software reliability, to which PCM-REL presents an integrated solution.

2.1.1 Basic Concepts

Although there is ongoing discussion about notions and terms in the field of IT systems and reliability, Avižienis et al. [ALRL04] have defined a set of core concepts as part of a widely accepted *taxonomy of dependable and secure computing*. The thesis takes part of their definitions as a terminological foundation. The authors introduce a *system* generically as an entity that interacts with its environment delivering *services* through well-defined *service interfaces*. The system may be recursively composed of *components* which are systems themselves. A *service failure* is any deviation of the system's behaviour from its intended functionality, as perceived by a system user[1]. *Errors* are defective parts of a system's state which may lead to service failures. *Faults*, in turn, constitute the adjudged or hypothesized causes of errors. *Reliability* is associated with the ability of a system to provide service free of failures. It is one out of several *dependability attributes* next to availability, safety, integrity and maintainability. While the scope of the taxonomy provided by Avižienis et al. is very broad, the thesis focuses on *IT systems* as computer-based systems comprising software components, hardware resources and network connections. PCM-REL measures system reliability as the probability that a *system usage scenario* comprising a series of service invocations is completed without any *system-level failure-on-demand* (see Section 4.1).

Apart from the basic definitions given above, the taxonomy also includes a classification of service failures that illustrates the broad range of possible deviations from the intended system functionality. In case that a service includes the provision of data to its users, deviations are classified as *content failures* if the provided data is not as intended. Any service that involves actions within specified time frames may suffer from *timing failures* if actions are conducted too early or too late. *Halt failures* result from a complete cancellation of service delivery; *erratic failures* are temporary

---

[1]The term *failure* may be used as an abbreviation for *service failure*.

service disruptions that usually occur at unpredictable points in time. Depending on the question if a system can detect a service failure and notifies its users about it, the failure is either *signalled* or *unsignalled*. A further important criterion is the severity of the consequence of failure for the system's environment ranging from *minor failures* up to *catastrophic failures*. Based on the confined scope of the thesis, PCM-REL allows for specifying custom types of failures-on-demand (see Section 4.2) induced by software, hardware or network. The possible range of those types is comparable to the range of service failure types described here.

The taxonomy further categorizes the efforts to attain dependability and security into four major groups:

- *Fault prevention* aims to reduce the number of faults introduced in a system. The range of measures includes following best practice for system design and implementation, as well as improving the quality of the engineering process.

- *Fault tolerance* summarizes all built-in capabilities of a system to avoid service failures in the presence of faults. It involves error detection (identifying the presence of errors) and system recovery (removing the errors and possibly identifying the error-causing faults and reconfiguring the system so that they cannot be activated again).

- *Fault removal* aims to reduce the number and severity of faults. During system development, a wide range of measures may be taken to identify and eliminate different kinds of faults, including static software analysis, theorem proving, model checking, symbolic software execution and various software and hardware testing methods. During system operation, faults may be removed through corrective or preventive maintenance.

- *Fault forecasting* aims to estimate current or future dependability and security characteristics of a system under study, such as the number of existing faults or the expected frequency and severity of service failures. Available analysis methods can roughly be classified as being qualitative (e.g. Failure Modes And Effects Analysis), quantitative (e.g. Markov chains, stochastic Petri nets) or mixed (e.g. reliability block diagrams, fault trees).

Each of the four categories has its own importance, even if the focus is narrowed down to reliability as one specific dependability attribute. PCM-REL as a reliability prediction approach belongs to the fourth category. While the first three categories aim to decrease the likelihood of service failures as far as possible, approaches in the fourth category acknowledge the fact that in virtually all cases a certain potential of failure remains, and they make estimates about this potential and its consequences.

2.1.2 Hardware and Software Reliability Analyses

The scientific context of the PCM-REL prediction approach is determined through the reliability-tailored fraction of the analysis methods introduced in Section 2.1.1 under the aggregated term *fault forecasting*. While various methods have been researched extensively and are widely accepted, they do not necessarily focus on software or on the software part of IT systems. Most approaches that have gained a certain level of industrial acceptance by now are more generally tailored towards industrial products with mainly electronic components or parts. The approaches focus on the physical wear-out effects of individual parts and on the various states of degraded service – referred to as *failure modes* – of a whole product or system resulting from the failure of its individual parts. Hence, their reasoning is based on a primarily hardware-oriented perspective. Target metrics of interest may be qualitative (such as identifying the different failure modes of a system) or quantitative (such as estimating system failure rates or frequencies of occurrence of critical failure modes). Available analysis methods include the Failure Modes And Effects Analysis (FMEA) and its extension for consideration of criticality (FMECA), fault trees, reliability block diagrams, Markov-based analyses, reliability growth analyses and others. Each method comes in a number of variations, and often a combination of multiple analyses is applied to a certain system under study. A number of standards exist describing how the methods can be applied [Aut08, Int04, Int06a, Int06b, Int06c, Int06d, Uni06]. Both commercial tool suites and consulting services are offered for conducting the analyses, and they are used mainly by automotive, aeronautics, telecommunications, medical and electronics industries. The term *reliability engineering* has been coined to denote the systematic consideration of reliability aspects throughout design and production processes (see [Bir10] for a comprehensive overview).

The ever increasing amount of software in modern products and systems has led to a situation where the failure potential of many systems is significantly influenced by both their software and hardware portions, or even dominated by software. Determining reliability characteristics of such systems, which have been termed *software-intensive systems* [WH07] or *software systems*, presents a severe challenge to reliability engineers [Ham92]. On the one hand, there exist similarities between the logical composition of software components and the physical composition of electronic parts. In both cases, individual components or parts may fail, and failures may have effects on other parts as well as the whole system, leading it into states of degraded service. On the other hand, while electronic parts can be characterised through basic failure models (see Section 2.2) and failure rates can be feasibly determined for them, software components are significantly more difficult to handle. They do not fail due to wear-out but due to the activation of their comprised software faults. Fault activation patterns may be complex and unique for each individual component. Moreover, component reliability heavily depends on the usage of the components, which in turn depends on the system's usage in non-trivial ways. Even minimal changes in system usage (such as a changed input parameter value of a service invocation) may lead to a completely different control and data flow throughout the system, activating different software faults. Hence, the aggregation of component reliabilities to a system-level reliability metric is far less intuitive than for hardware-dominated systems.

In spite of these differences, there have been efforts to reuse hardware-oriented analysis methods for software systems, resulting in software-specific or combined hardware-software analyses (see [PA02] for an example of FMEA tailored towards software and [LN97] for an overview). However, such efforts remain limited in their applicability to systems with rather basic functionality and static control and data flow. For more complex software, the abstractions are either too simplistic or the analysis effort gets out of hand. Even the enumeration of potential failure modes of software systems may be hard to achieve in a comprehensive and consistent manner (for example, Vijayaraghavan identified more than 700 individual failure modes in e-commerce systems [Vij03]). The only analysis methods that have undergone a major evolution towards software-specific application are reliability growth analyses. In their software-specific form, these methods focus on the process of testing software systems or components and removing detected faults. *Software Reliability Growth Models* (SRGM, see [Ape05] for an introduction and [SGNG10] for a most recent overview) map the increasing reliability of the systems or components under test to parametrized statistical functions, allowing for estimations how the reliability growth will continue during further test activities, and when given reliability goals are expected to be reached (see Section 2.3.1 for a detailed discussion). Traditionally, SRGMs have been applied at the system level, thereby avoiding the consideration of individual software components and their reliability impact. Authors such as Musa [Mus04] have much focused on the SRGM approach and have coined the term *software reliability engineering* to denote the software-specific evolution of reliability engineering with SRGMs as a central ingredient (also see [Lyu07] for a more recent overview). The IEEE Standard 1633 "Recommended Practice on Software Reliability" [IEE08] follows this pattern and focuses mainly on SRGMs.

However, the applicability of system-level SRGMs to modern highly distributed component-based software systems is limited. SRGM analysis results cannot be reused across a family of similar systems, as the individual reliability impacts of the changed components are unclear. Moreover, the application of SRGMs requires the installation and execution of the complete system under study. Hence, SRGMs cannot easily be used to make comparisons between several system design alternatives, especially not at early design stages, when the system is not yet ready for execution. To this end, another family of analysis methods has emerged within a field of research called *Architecture-Based Software Reliability Prediction* (ASRP) throughout the thesis (see Section 2.5 for further details). Approaches in this field explicitly take into account the *architecture* of a software system, namely its internal structure as a composition of software components. They model the transfer of control between components and provide a means to express system-level reliability based on individual component reliabilities. Still, the approaches face the challenge of estimating the failure rates of the individual components. To this end, they can employ component-level SRGMs and other estimation methods (see Section 2.3).

While ASRP approaches constitute a major step forward in analysing the reliability of component-based software architectures, their practical applicability is still limited due to missing support for expressing hardware failure potentials and fault tolerance capabilities, as well as implicit usage profile encoding in the employed architectural models (see Chapter 7). This thesis proposes PCM-REL to overcome these weaknesses and to provide a comprehensive approach to integrated IT system reliability prediction.

2.2 Hardware Reliability Estimation

This section gives an overview of existing failure models and reliability estimation techniques for hardware resources in IT systems such as hard disk drives and CPUs, based on results from the reliability engineering domain. The discussion provides a foundation for the modelling of hardware resources and their reliability in PCM-REL (see Section 4.4).

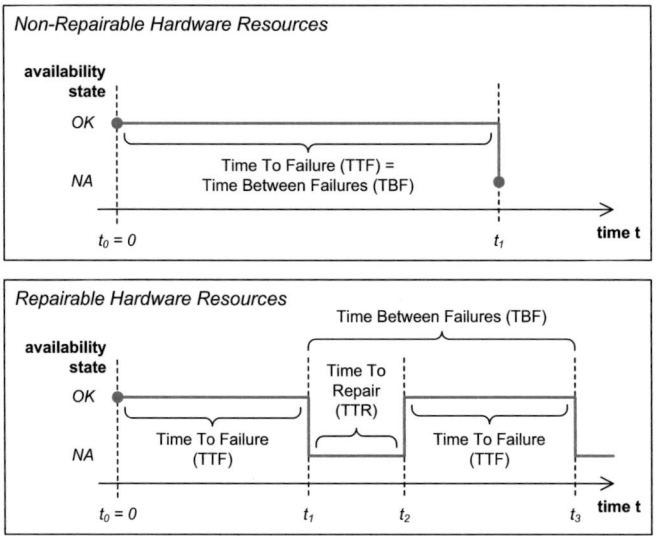

Figure 2.1: Hardware Resource Failure Model

Typically, a hardware resource is modelled as having two basic service levels or *resource availability states* which may be termed *OK* (fully available – the resource serves all requests) and *NA* (not available – the resource does not serve any request). The main reason for a resource becoming unavailable is physical wear-out. Although the model is coarse-grained and does not account for intermediate service levels, it is a widely established abstraction chosen for individual resources. As Figure 2.1 shows, *non-repairable resources* have a lifetime measured from the start of operation t_0

to the first failure t_1. In contrast, *repairable resources* switch between intervals of uptime (such as $[t_0, t_1]$ and $[t_2, t_3]$) and downtime (such as $[t_1, t_2]$). A switch back from *NA* to *OK* is often achieved through replacing a broken resource with a functionally equivalent one, rather than actually repairing the existing resource[2]. The length of a resource uptime interval is referred to as *Time To Failure* (TTF); the downtime interval length is called *Time To Repair* (TTR). The *Time Between Failures* (TBF) refers to the time span between two consecutive switches to *NA*. The notions of TTF and TBF may also refer to the lifetimes of non-repairable resources.

Based on the described failure model, the reliability of a hardware resource is characterised through statistical measures such as its expected TTF, TTR and TBF values – also referred to as *Mean Time To Failure* (MTTF), *Mean Time To Repair* (MTTR) and *Mean Time Between Failures* (MTBF, which constitutes the inverse of the resource failure rate). For repairable resources, a *Steady-State Availability Av* denotes the expected fraction of uptime measured over the infinite time interval $[t_0, \infty)$:

$$Av := \frac{MTTF}{MTTF + MTTR} = \frac{MTTF}{MTBF} \tag{2.1}$$

To model the availability state progression of resources over time, TTF and TTR values are typically assumed to follow an exponential distribution with expected values equal to MTTF and MTTR. The exponential distribution is chosen because it readily lends itself to analytical evaluations, even though it is not the most accurate abstraction [SG07]. Alternatively, Weibull, Gamma and Lognormal distributions have been used to characterise the TTF and TTR values.

The problem of hardware resource reliability estimation can be narrowed down to estimating MTTF and MTTR values. Based on these estimates, MTBF and *Av* values can be readily determined. The estimation of MTTR

---

[2]Hence, a repairable resource model often reflects the usage of a series of non-repairable resources with replacement intervals after each resource wear-out.

values is relatively straightforward as resource repair and replacement follows a controlled process rather than physical indeterminism. A TTR may include several aspects such as the time to detect a resource failure, the time to conduct the repair or replacement, and the duration of required re-initializations. These aspects can be determined for most IT systems and application scenarios to derive MTTR values. For the estimation of MTTF values, several sources of information are available. First, hardware vendors conduct internal studies of their products and publish MTTF values denoting their expected lifetimes. Vendor estimates are based on data gathered from customer reclamations and conducted service jobs, as well as *accelerated stress tests*, where "stress" refers to environmental characteristics such as voltage, temperature, humidity, physical vibration and mechanical forces [Yan99]. Second, vendor-independent studies have been conducted evaluating empirical resource failure and replacement data, especially for hard disk drives [PWB07, SG07]. These studies calculate *Annualized Failure Rates* (AFR) over a large population of functionally equivalent resources, from which MTTF estimates can be derived. Third, IT system or infrastructure providers can estimate MTTF values for their hardware resources based on their own experiences gathered during system operation.

As an alternative to direct resource reliability estimation, existing reliability engineering techniques (see Section 2.1.2) can be used to assess complex hardware resources based on their constituent parts. For example, an MTTF estimate for an array of hard disks may result from a reliability block diagram that models the internal structure of the array and contains MTTF estimates for the individual hard disks. Such an analysis may be performed as a preliminary step providing input to PCM-REL resource environment models (see Section 4.4).

2.3 Software Reliability Estimation

This section discusses strategies for software reliability estimation, with a special focus on determining failure rates or failure probabilities of software components. Such estimates can be used as an input information for approaches to architecture-based software reliability prediction (ASRP). Software reliability is modelled stochastically because – although software fails *systematically* (in contrast to *randomly* failing hardware) – software failures are *uncertain* from an engineer's point of view [Lit05]. "Systematic" means that the same failures will always result from the same set of circumstances. "Uncertainty" relates to the nature and frequency of those circumstances and includes several aspects. First, there is *missing knowledge* about the faults contained in the software, as well as their activation patterns. Second, reliability models include probabilistic *abstractions* from the actual system behaviour to reduce modelling complexity. Third, the system usage presents a source of *indeterminism* as the exact nature, sequence and timing of system invocations by users is unknown in advance.

Reliability estimations for software components are significantly more difficult than for hardware resources, for reasons outlined in Section 2.1.2. However, the need for corresponding methods is steadily increasing, and an own field of research has emerged around the issue. While this thesis does not focus on the problem of software reliability estimation itself, the application of PCM-REL does require deriving input estimates for the modelled software failure potentials. To this end, an exemplary estimation process was conducted as part of a PCM-REL case study, which is documented in Section 6.5. Here, the discussion focuses on major families of software reliability estimation methods, including software reliability growth models (Section 2.3.1), software defect prediction models (Section 2.3.2) and others (Section 2.3.3).

2.3.1 Software Reliability Growth Models

Software Reliability Growth Models (SRGM), which have been briefly introduced in Section 2.1.2, are one of the most successful families of analysis methods within the software reliability engineering discipline [Lyu07]. Beyond system-level black box testing, they can also be used to determine failure rates of software components as an input to Architecture-Based Software Reliability Prediction (ASRP) [GPT01]. The following discussion introduces the basics of SRGM approaches and reflects possibilities and challenges of their application.

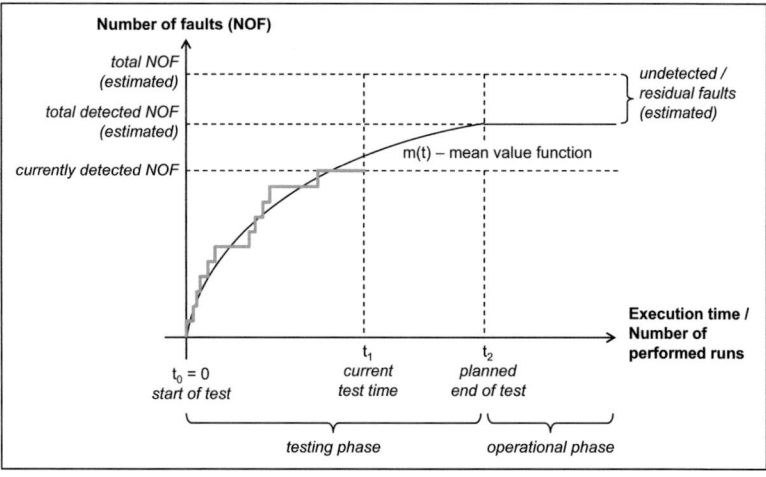

Figure 2.2: Software Reliability Growth Modelling Scheme

Figure 2.2 depicts the general SRGM scheme. SRGM approaches observe a software system or component under test and record how the number of detected faults increases during the test. The test time may be measured in terms of system or component execution time (for continuous applications) or as the number of performed test runs (for terminating applications). At any point in time t_1 during testing, a parametrized statistical *mean value function $m(t)$* can be fitted to the existing history of fault detection since test start t_0, and this function can be used to predict the further progression of the testing process. Such information allows for estimating the total detected number of faults at the planned end of test t_2. More importantly, many SRGMs include an estimation of the total number of faults comprised in the system or component under test at t_0, thereby indicating the remaining or *residual* number of faults during the operational phase (namely, after t_2). Corresponding to the different test progression types one may encounter in practice, various different mean value functions have been proposed by several authors (see [SGNG10] for an overview of the most important ones). The proposals are generally based on the assumption that the rate of fault detection decreases over time, leading to mean value functions with decreasing slopes. Moreover, most SRGM approaches share the common assumptions that each detected fault is removed instantaneously (or alternatively, testing stops upon fault detection and is resumed after fault removal), and that fault removal activities do not introduce new faults into the system or component under test.

Beyond the essentially static information about the number of existing faults comprised in systems and components under test, SRGM approaches also reason about their dynamic reliability characteristics, namely their failure rates. Assuming that each failure occurring during the test corresponds to the detection of one new fault, the fault detection history also indicates all times between failures in $[t_0, t_1]$. From this information, a *failure intensity function* $\lambda(t)$ may be derived that indicates the system or component failure rate at time t. Failure intensity functions directly follow from mean value functions through derivation (namely, $\lambda(t) = \frac{dm(t)}{dt}$) and are expected to decrease over time. Through determining $\lambda(t)$, the expected failure rate at the planned end of test t_2 can be predicted. Alternatively, t_2 can be dynamically chosen to fulfil a given failure rate requirement. It may also be possible to anticipate a system's or component's operational failure rate as being the one expected at the end of test, namely $\lambda(t_2)$. However, such an estimation is only credible if an overall field usage profile of the system or component at the operational phase can be determined, and if *statistical testing* is applied – namely, if test inputs are randomly selected according to the field usage profile.

SRGM approaches have been pointed out by several authors as a possible means of gathering input information for ASRP approaches [Eve99, GPT01, GWTH98]. SRGMs may be used to estimate current or future failure rates of software components which already exist and have undergone a certain amount of testing. A very recent case study by Koziolek et al. [KSB10] on a large industrial control system illustrates this usage of SRGMs. On the other hand, successful usage of SRGMs is still challenging. Apel [Ape05] lists open issues directly related to SRGM research, including the problem of choosing between the various proposed SRGMs and characteristic mean value functions for concrete use cases[3], as well as the lack of empirical validation (especially regarding long-term prediction quality). Moreover, it is often not feasible or possible to apply SRGMs in practice without violating their underlying assumptions [BKH09, Woo97], thereby weakening the significance of their prediction results. In particular, if SRGM analyses are based on standard unit tests and their failure reports, it may be difficult to gain meaningful results from their application. Time stamps of bug entries usually refer to calendar time instead of execution time, test inputs are generated to locate as many faults as possible (and not to represent an identified field usage profile), fault removals may not be instantaneous, and new faults may be introduced during removal activities. If, on the other hand, SRGMs are applied under strict conformance to all their underlying assumptions, their practical applicability is limited. For example, they can only be used to assess relatively low reliability levels (such as failure rates of 10^{-2} to $10^{-4}h^{-1}$ [BF93, GPT01]); otherwise, the testing effort gets out of hand.

If system test runs are used to derive component-level reliability estimates, additional issues need to be considered. For example, to evaluate

---

[3]However, a recent work of Sharma et al. [SGNG10] tackles this issue.

failure rates of components as the ratio between their overall invocation counts and successful invocation counts, it must be determined how often each component is invoked in each test run, and which component is to blame in case of a failed test run. Moreover, a potentially large number of test runs must be conducted so that a statistically relevant amount of successful and failed invocations of each component can be observed. If, on the other hand, SRGMs are applied to each component in isolation, care must be taken to test each component according to its individual usage profile within the overall architecture (which means that component-level usage profiles need to be determined prior to the application of SRGMs).

A body of work exists to improve SRGM approaches and tackle their issues (see [Lyu07] for a summary). Still, successful application of SRGMs in practice requires care. The use of SRGMs as an input to ASRP has been demonstrated by Koziolek et al. [KSB10], but needs to be further investigated with respect to the challenges discussed above.

2.3.2 Software Defect Prediction Models

The notion of *Software Defect Prediction Models* (SDPMs) captures a wide and heterogeneous field of efforts related to estimating the amount of faults or *defects* comprised in software systems or components. Widely established target metrics are *defect count* (number of defects) and *defect density* (number of defects related to code size). Defect prediction approaches use various kinds of artefacts emerging from specification, design, implementation and test stages as possible sources of information. The most important factors that have been assumed to influence the amount of defects in software include the following:

- *Size and complexity*: The amount of software defects is expected to generally increase with the size and complexity of the system or component under study. Measures of code size include the number of *Lines Of Code* (LOC), code segments or machine code instructions. Examples for code complexity metrics include Halstead's *Volume, Difficulty* and *Effort* metrics [Hal77] (correlated with the number of operands and operators in the code) and McCabe's *Cyclomatic Complexity* [McC76] (correlated with the number of decision statements). As an alternative, *Function Points* (originally defined by Albrecht [Alb79]) measure the amount of functionality offered by a system or component and examine requirements and design specifications rather than code.

- *Test-related factors*: At any point in time during the testing stages, an existing test history may be exploited to estimate the total or remaining number of defects. Metrics of interest include the number of already detected defects (differentiated according to test iterations, test approaches or associated function points) and the already achieved *test coverage* (which may refer to statement coverage, branch coverage, code sequence and jump coverage, see [VM94]). Another metric of interest is the *testability* [VM95] of a given system or component (namely, the likelihood that potential defects will be detected through test), which is determined through static code analyses.

- *Process quality*: Software is expected to generally contain less defects if created following a high-quality development process. A process quality model that has been used to derive defect density estimates is the SEI Capability Maturity Model (CMM) [DS97].

Many earlier works on SDPMs tried to derive straightforward general formulae for the number of defects based on existing sets of empirical data from software development (see, for example, [CW90, Gaf84]); however, the validity of their results is questionable. Fenton et al. [FN99] have identified substantial flaws in such works including incorrect use of statistical analyses with misleading results, as well as a tendency towards oversimplification by focussing on a partial subset of the relevant factors only. Nevertheless, research in this field is very active until today (see [CD09] for a recent review). More advanced prediction approaches have been developed using Bayesian networks [FNM+08], Capture-Recapture models [BEFL00] and other formalisms. Machine learning and data mining techniques are increasingly employed to derive defect estimations from code metrics data [MGC07, MGF07].

While the wealth of existing SDPMs can in theory be used to derive input information for ASRP approaches, there is no straightforward relation between the number of faults of a software component and its failure rate. The latter depends on the likelihood that existing faults will actually be activated under a certain component usage profile. In contrast to SRGMs (see Section 2.3.1), SDPMs do not define the process of gathering data in such a way that it provides information about both faults and failures. This is a major obstacle against the use of SDPMs for architecture-based software reliability prediction – in fact, it is a weakness of SDPMs as such [FN99], limiting the significance of their prediction results. Moreover, a recent study by Zimmermann et al. [ZNG+09] suggests that reusing defect prediction results across multiple software development projects may be invalid, even if these projects stem from the same domain or employ the same underlying development process model. Still, SDPMs are an extensively researched means guiding decisions in software development processes, and further research efforts may close the gap towards usage for reliability prediction.

2.3.3 Further Approaches to Software Reliability Estimation

Beyond SRGMs and SDPMs, various further efforts have been made to estimate failure rates of software systems and components. At late testing stages, a *validation test* or *operational test* may be conducted to assure required reliability levels [MMN+92, MIO90, LW97]. The system or component is tested as if executed in the field – namely, according to its field usage profile. By applying frequentist inference [Cox06], upper bounds for failure rates can be deduced with certain levels of confidence from a certain amount of failure-free execution. For example, 4603 successfully executed independent test runs give a 99 percent upper confidence bound on a failure rate of 10^{-3}. Methods and tools from *model-based testing* (MBT) [UPL11, Pre03, PPW+05] can be applied to support and partially automate the testing process[4]. For example, the *J Usage Model Builder Library* (JUMBL) [Pro03] automatically generates test cases according to a usage profile specified in terms of a Markov model, and it determines reliability estimates and confidence levels from a set of executed test cases and their results. As of today, the potentially very high testing effort associated with such methods constitutes a major challenge and essentially limits their applicability to cases with relatively low reliability requirements [GPT01].

Component reliability models are a further means specifically tailored to component-level reliability estimation [CRMG08, CMRK10, Imm06, TW99]. Markov models are used to indicate different component states between which a component switches forth and back over time according to specified transition probabilities. Typically, the states are grouped into two categories, where one category corresponds to normal operation and the other one to failure. Cheung et al. [CRMG08] identify several sources of information that can be used to construct component reliability models, including existing component specifications, expert knowledge, component use case descriptions, simulations and existing functionally similar components. Applying Markov theory allows for determining reliability characteristics of a component such as the component failure rate or the fraction of time in which the component provides normal operation. Approaches to component reliability modelling seem promising due to their flexibility. Being model-based in nature, they do not necessarily require a component to already be implemented and executed under test, and they are not re-

---

[4]In general, the main goal of MBT is to support the identification of faults in the system, or to verify that certain parts of the system's behaviour conform to its specification. A model captures the system's intended behaviour; it serves as a way to specify the possible system inputs, as well as the relation between inputs and expected outputs.

stricted to assessment of low reliability levels. On the other hand, there is no straightforward general way to construct the models, and the problem of stochastic estimation is not resolved but rather decomposed to a set of intra-component properties. When used as an input to ASRP approaches, care has to be taken so that each component reliability model reflects the individual usage profile of the component within the architecture. Further research regarding component reliability models would be valuable to facilitate a more wide-spread use.

Further attempts to derive component reliability estimations from various influencing factors have been summarized by Palviainen et al. [PEO11] under the term *heuristic reliability evaluation*. Considered factors may include component maturity levels, size and complexity metrics (as also used for software defect prediction, see Section 2.3.2), testing and operational data from existing similar components, reputation of or experiences with component vendors (in case of externally acquired components), level of experience of involved software developers (in case of in-house development), and others. However, the results of such estimations are typically only valid within specific project contexts and cannot be easily transferred across development projects or companies. Palviainen et al. [PEO11] consider them as weak compared to component reliability models and test-based approaches.

2.4 Markov Chains for Reliability

This section gives a short introduction to *Markov chains*, which are used as a modelling formalism by many approaches to architecture-based software reliability prediction (ASRP), and which also constitute the underlying formalism of PCM-REL (see Chapter 5). The discussion is limited to aspects relevant in the context of the thesis; for a detailed account, see [Tri02]. A Markov chain is a random process (namely, a process whose development over time is not pre-determined but described by probability distributions) which (i) has a discrete (finite or countable) state space, and which (ii) exhibits the *Markov property* (namely, the future development of the process does not depend on its history but only on its present state). *Continuous-time Markov Chains* (CTMC) allow for state transitions at any time; *Discrete-time Markov Chains* (DTMC) restrict transitions to certain points in time, according to a discrete time scale. Many real-life processes can feasibly be represented by Markov chains, and a comprehensive theory has been developed to examine various properties of the created chains.

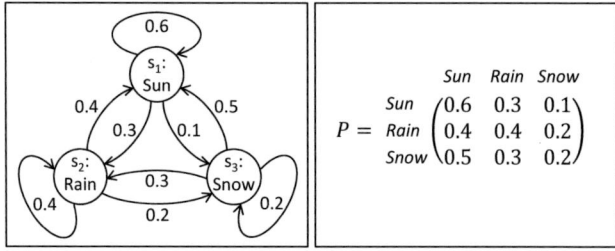

Figure 2.3: DTMC Example

A DTMC can be described through a set of states $S := \{s_1, ..., s_n\}$ and transitions $T := \{t_1, ..., t_m\}$, where each transition t_k connects a source state $Source(t_k) \in S$ and a target state $Target(t_k) \in S$ and is associated with a transition probability value $P(t_k) \in [0, 1]$. Alternatively, the DTMC can be described through its *n-by-n transition matrix P*, with each entry $p_{ij} \in [0, 1]$ $\forall i, j \in \{1, .., n\}$ denoting the transition probability from s_i to s_j. For each row, the sum of its entries equals to one: $\sum_{j=1}^{n} p_{ij} = 1$ $\forall i \in \{1, .., n\}$. As an example, Figure 2.3 shows a DTMC that represents weather conditions, together with its transition matrix. On each day, the weather is in one of the states $S_{weather} := \{s_1 := Sun, s_2 := Rain, s_3 := Snow\}$. The weather may change between days or stay the same. For example, a sunny day is followed by another sunny day with probability $p_{11} = 0.6$, by rain with $p_{12} = 0.3$ or by snow with $p_{13} = 0.1$. The Markov property dictates that tomorrow's weather only depends on today and not on the weather history of previous days. While this is a simplifying assumption compared to reality, it keeps the model analytically tractable. In spite of its simplifying abstractions, the model may still be a feasible representation of the corresponding real-world process with respect to a certain purpose, such as forecasting tomorrow's weather.

A DTMC state $s_i \in S$ is an *absorbing state* if it – once visited – is never left again: $p_{ii} = 1$ and $p_{ij} = 0$ $\forall j \neq i$. An *absorbing DTMC* has at least one absorbing state and a possible path from each state to an absorbing state. Each run through an absorbing DTMC eventually finishes in one of its absorbing states with probability 1, no matter how the DTMC is structured and in which state the process starts. If the DTMC has multiple absorbing states, Markov theory allows for calculating the absorption probabilities for each of them (depending on the initial state in which the process starts). This calculation involves determining two reduced transition matrices Q (considering non-absorbing states only) and R (considering transitions from non-absorbing to absorbing states), calculating the *fundamental matrix* $N = (I - Q)^{-1}$ based on Q and the identity matrix I, as well as multiplying N and R (for further details, see [KB09]).

A CTMC is described through a set of states S and transitions T like a DTMC. However, the transitions t_k of the CTMC are annotated with *transition rates* $R(t_k) \in \mathbb{R}_0^+$ rather than probabilities, and the CTMC is characterized through a *rate matrix R*. A positive rate $r_{ij} > 0$ indicates that transitions from state s_i to s_j occur with frequencies determined by an exponential distribution $Exp(1/r_{ij})$ with parameter $1/r_{ij}$. A zero rate $r_{ij} = 0$ indicates that the corresponding transition never occurs. In contrast to a DTMC specification, each state of a CTMC has an individual variable *sojourn time* according to a continuous time scale. The expected sojourn time of each state can be determined based on all outgoing transitions and transition rates of the state.

DTMCs, CTMCs and related formalisms (such as *semi-Markov processes* [BL08]) are a powerful and widely established means for ASRP approaches to represent software architectures in terms of interconnected components, as well as the transition of control between them during service execution (see Section 2.5). In contrast to other formalisms that focus on a system's inputs, internal state progressions and produced outputs (such as finite state machines [HMU01], state charts [Har87] or timed automata [AD94]), Markov models provide a high-level architecture-oriented representation of system behaviour, naturally capturing uncertain aspects such as system usage and its influence on the service execution through the probabilistic model annotations. Existing Markov theory [Tri02] can readily be applied to evaluate the created models with respect to reliability. The PCM-REL approach developed in this thesis focuses on absorbing DTMCs and explores novel ways to use them for comprehensive reliability modelling and prediction (see Chapter 5).

2.5 Architecture-Based Software Reliability Prediction

This section shortly introduces the field of architecture-based software reliability prediction (ASRP; for surveys, see [Gok07, GPT01, IN08]), to which also PCM-REL belongs. As the general discussion in Section 2.1.2 shows, ASRP approaches aim to overcome the weaknesses of traditional reliability analysis methods regarding component-based software systems. Like reliability block diagrams, fault trees and related analyses, ASRP approaches assume that the overall failure potential of a system can be determined from a set of internal failure potentials associated with individual system components or parts, together with a structural view indicating how the components themselves or their failure potentials are related to each other. However, traditional ways to express system structure and usage relationships between components (such as *OR* or *AND* relationships in fault trees) are too simplistic to cover the potentially complex interrelations of software components. Therefore, ASRP approaches choose more expressive formalisms to represent system structure, based on an architectural view on the system and the control flow of its service execution.

An early publication of Roger Cheung in 1980 [Che80] had much influence on the development of the field and serves as a raw model for many ASRP approaches until today. The approach expresses a system's architecture through an absorbing DTMC whose states represent the individual software components. Transitions represent the transfer of control between components when executing a certain system service operation or task. The transition probabilities allow for expressing the fact that different control flow paths through the architecture may be taken, depending on the system's internal state at the time of service execution, as well as the specific input data given to the service invocation. For reliability evaluation, each component is annotated with an individual independent failure probability, denoting the possibility that a visit to this component during service execution produces a service failure. The DTMC is augmented with two "final" absorbing states, indicating successful service execution and service failure. Without loss of generality, another "initial" state can be added such that service execution always starts in this state. Markov theory allows for calculating the probability of successful service execution as the probability of reaching the success state from the initial state (see Section 2.4). By its construction, the formalism assumes a "terminating application" (namely, a limited service behaviour that always ends up in either of the success and failure states). Being based on the architectural model and component failure probabilities only, the approach can be applied even before the system itself is implemented, thereby anticipating or *predicting* the expected reliability of the implemented system at run-time. However, applying the approach is only possible if the required inputs can feasibly be obtained; sensitivity analyses should be conducted to assess the impact of uncertain input estimations (see Section 6.1).

As an example for a software architecture modelled through an absorbing DTMC, Figure 2.4 shows an architecture with three components *A*, *B*

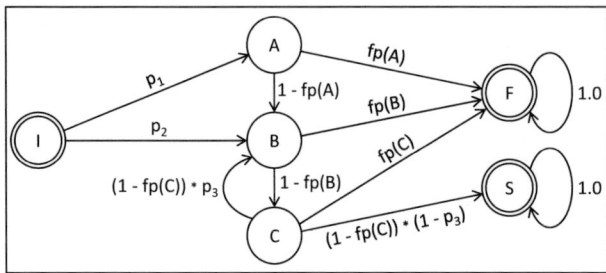

Figure 2.4: Example of an Architectural DTMC Model

and C, augmented by an initial state I and the absorbing success and failure states S and F. The parameters of the model to estimate are the transition probabilities p_1 to p_3, as well as the failure probabilities of the components $fp(A)$ to $fp(C)$. Given these estimations, the model allows for calculating the probability of successful service execution. Moreover, the model indicates the possible control flow paths and their probabilities. For example, service execution may follow the path I-B-C-S with probability $p_2 \times (1 - fp(B)) \times (1 - fp(C))(1 - p_3)$. A cycle exists between states B and C, leading to an infinite overall number of possible paths through the model. By its construction, the model assumes the Markov property with respect to the transfer of control between components. This assumption can lead to paths that are possible in the model but not in reality. For example, the number of performed cycles between components B and C in the figure may be limited to a maximum number of n in reality, while the model allows for an arbitrary number of cycles before moving on to either success or failure. However, the method can still provide sufficiently accurate results, if transition probabilities are chosen such that the additional paths of the model have low occurrence probabilities or mutually even out their reliability impacts. For architectural cycles such as the one between B and C, a well-established method is to choose transition probabilities such that the expected number of performed cycles in the model corresponds to the average number of performed cycles in reality.

Throughout the years, numerous ASRP approaches have been presented, including [BMP09, CG07a, DS95, FGGM10, GL05, GPHG+03, Gra05, KM97, PDAC05, RSP03, RRU05, ST07a, ST06, WPC06, YCA04, ZL10], and others. Beyond absorbing DTMCs, other DTMC and CTMC types, as well as semi-Markov processes, have been used to represent the software architecture and its failure potentials; a comprehensive overview is given by the survey of Goseva-Popstojanova et al. [GPT01]. Further categories of approaches use less related formalisms, but are still counted towards ASRP by the survey. These categories include the *path-based* and the *additive* approaches. Path-based approaches explicitly enumerate the possible control flow paths through the architecture, together with their occurrence probabilities. While these approaches are not affected by the Markov assumption, the potentially high number of possible paths often makes a comprehensive enumeration impossible and instead requires considering the most frequent paths only. Additive approaches calculate a system's failure rate in a straightforward fashion as the sum of the individual component failure rates, thereby imposing the strong assumption that service execution essentially always visits each of the system's components.

Existing ASRP approaches include several differences and extensions compared to the Cheung model, such as the consideration of error propagation [CG07a, FGGM10, MZ08, PDAC05], inclusion of uncertainty analysis [GPK03, YST01] or provision of a design-oriented input modelling language [BMP09, CSC02, GPHG+03, RSP03, RRU05, YCA04]. However, their consideration of reliability-influencing factors is still incomplete, and their capabilities to support software architects during system design are correspondingly limited. They have no or only basic means to take hardware failure potentials into account (see Section 7.1) and to express fault tolerance capabilities of the system under study (Section 7.2). Furthermore, they encode the influence of the system's usage profile implicitly into model parameters such as transition probabilities, thereby strongly reducing the reusability of the architectural specifications (Section 7.3). Hence, the PCM-REL approach presented in this thesis constitutes further progress in the ASRP field. It overcomes the mentioned weaknesses and provides a comprehensive solution supporting the design of IT systems.

2.6 Fault-Tolerant IT Systems

Fault tolerance (FT) has briefly been introduced in Section 2.1.1 as one of the four means to attain dependability and security. The notion of FT includes any capabilities of an IT system to autonomously prevent the occurrence of system service failures in the presence of faults that have already been activated and resulted in errors within the system[5]. Obviously, such capabilities influence the probability of successful service execution. PCM-REL allows for explicit modelling of FT capabilities and takes them into account for reliability prediction. This section introduces the most important concepts related to FT, based on existing overviews and surveys [ALRL04, Kie03, Lyu95, Lyu07, MR07, Ran75].

Existing techniques to achieve fault tolerance have a wide and heterogeneous scope. In order to achieve a categorization, several authors distinguish between *hardware fault tolerance* and *software fault tolerance*, depending on the question if a FT technique mainly targets hardware faults or software faults. Typically, both kinds of faults are different in nature (physical faults in hardware versus design faults in software) and produce different failure behaviour (randomly failing hardware versus systematically failing software, see Section 2.3). However, various interdependencies between both dimensions exist, and several FT techniques combine capabilities for tolerating hardware and software faults [LABK90].

Other proposals for FT categorization refer to *redundancy*. Employing redundancy means provisioning a system with additional resources beyond those that are required as a minimum for proper functioning. Redundancy is the most fundamental concept enabling fault tolerance. Kienzle [Kie03]

---

[5]Existing FT synonyms include *self-repair*, *self-healing* and *resilience* [ALRL04].

distinguishes *functional redundancy*, *data redundancy* and *temporal redundancy* for software FT. Functional redundancy denotes the presence of multiple software designs (namely, different implementations, also referred to as *design diversity*) of the same functionality. Data redundancy refers to the presence of multiple different expressions of the same data (also referred to as *data diversity*), as well as the presence of additional FT-specific data. Temporal redundancy includes all time overheads during service execution induced by FT activities. Other authors [Lyu07, TP00] more roughly distinguish between *single-version software techniques* (denoting the absence of functional redundancy) and *multi-version software techniques* (employing functional redundancy). To include hardware FT into the consideration, one could extend Kienzles categorization by adding *physical redundancy*, namely the replication of identical hardware resources.

A wide variety of *fault tolerance mechanisms* has been proposed that follow a general pattern of activities as outlined by Avižienis et al. [ALRL04]. The two main involved activities are *error detection* and *system recovery*, where the latter includes *error handling* and possibly *fault handling*. Error detection denotes identifying the presence of an error and can be performed on-demand (for example, checking the result of a computation with an acceptance test) or pre-emptively (for example, by regular system health tests, heartbeat or ping/echo signalling). Error handling removes the error from the system and may involve a *rollback* to a prior error-free system state, a *rollforward* that reaches a new state without error, or a *compensation* that masks an existing error using the redundancy contained in the system. The system may conduct error handling on-demand (for example, after the identification of a wrong computational result by an acceptance test) or pre-emptively (for example, by regular restart of software components as a means of *software rejuvenation* [HKKF95]). Fault handling shall prevent existing faults from being activated again and may include fault diagnosis, isolation, component or system reconfiguration and reinitialization. Fault handling may be followed by *fault removal* through *corrective maintenance* (which requires the participation of an external agent and is therefore not included in the notion of FT).

The majority of the proposed software FT mechanisms are either completely pre-emptive in nature (carried out as independent periodic activities), or they focus on the ability of an individual service execution to tolerate activated faults in an on-demand fashion. The latter category includes, amongst others, *Recovery Blocks, Retry Blocks, N-Version Programming* and *N-Copy Programming* [Kie03]. Recovery Blocks include the sequential execution of a primary behaviour and, potentially, further alternative behaviours. The result of each alternate is checked by an acceptance test; upon failure, a rollback to an established checkpoint is performed. The recovery block is left after either one alternate succeeds or the last alternate fails. Recovery Blocks employ functional redundancy (multiple alternates providing equal functionality) and temporal redundancy (the overhead of executing alternative behaviours). Retry Blocks are similar to Recovery Blocks but do not employ functional redundancy. Instead, they execute the same behaviour multiple times with different re-expressions of the input data. N-Version-Programming and N-Copy-Programming are the parallel equivalents to Recovery and Retry Blocks, respectively: they execute all functional or data alternatives concurrently. Instead of conducting costly acceptance tests for explicit error detection, they typically rely on *voting algorithms* to select among the results of the alternatives. Several variations of these mechanisms have been proposed, including their extension towards hardware FT through replication of the underlying hardware resources [LABK90]. Additionally, FT mechanisms have been proposed that explicitly consider the interdependencies of multiple concurrent service executions. These include *Transactions* with FT-specific extensions, *Conversations* and *Atomic Actions* [Kie03].

Traditionally, fault tolerance has been associated with implementation and technological levels of an IT system rather than the architectural level. Hence, it was not in the primary focus of research related to software architecture. Within the specific field of ASRP, still very few approaches explicitly consider FT capabilities (see Section 7.2). However, the structural and behavioural aspects of FT mechanisms clearly have an architectural dimension. FT mechanisms may assign special responsibilities to architectural components or even introduce new components for FT-specific purposes. Muccini et al. [MR07] provide a comprehensive survey of works that deal with the architectural aspects of FT. Examples of FT capabilities explicitly introduced as architectural patterns or styles include *Idealized Fault-Tolerant Components* [GRdL02], *Recovery-Aware Components* (RAC) [YSP09, YSP11] and *Redundant Arrays of Independent Components* (RAIC) [LR02]. Furthermore, Harrison et al. [HA08] examine several traditional architectural patterns and describe how they can be extended with FT capabilities.

PCM-REL acknowledges the fact that fault tolerance is part of an IT system's design and may considerably influence its reliability. The approach offers explicit modelling of FT capabilities in terms of a specific action type that has the ability to recover from failure-on-demand occurrences during service execution. See Section 4.7 for a detailed discussion.

2.7 The Palladio Component Model

This section introduces the Palladio Component Model (PCM) [BKR09], which provides the conceptional and technical foundation for PCM-REL. The description focuses on the PCM as a design-oriented modelling language for component-based software architectures, allowing for distributed model creation by multiple independent developer roles. The discussion of the PCM's meta-model is not exhaustive but reduced to the core concepts that are required for understanding the following thesis chapters. In particular, all performance-specific parts are omitted from the discussion (for a full discussion of the original PCM meta-model, see [RBB+11]). PCM-REL builds upon the presented core concepts and adds new concepts to create an architectural modelling language for IT system reliability (see Section 4).

2.7.1 PCM Developer Roles

Component-based development is – ideally – a distributed process with multiple contributing developer roles which are independent and decoupled from each other. The PCM approach supports this idea by splitting the meta-model into independent parts along the concerns of each role, and by representing reusable real-world artefacts through reusable specifications on the model level. In the envisioned development process, *component developers* create individual software components and store them in a repository. As "units of composition with contractually specified interfaces and explicit context dependencies only" [Szy02], software components are subject to being reused in varying contexts [RPS03]. *System architects* take components from the repository, connect them according to their provided and required interfaces, and define a system boundary with system-provided and system-required service interfaces. *System deployers* know about the available IT infrastructure and allocate a system's software components to the computing nodes of the infrastructure. Finally, *domain experts* contribute knowledge about the expected usage profile of the system.

According to the discussed developer roles and responsibilities, the PCM provides a *repository model* representing the component repository and containing the individual component specifications, a *system model* specifying component instances, connections and the system's boundaries, a *resource environment model* for the IT infrastructure, an *allocation model* mapping software components to computing nodes, and a *usage model* specifying the system's usage profile. All these meta-model parts are introduced in detail in the following subsections.

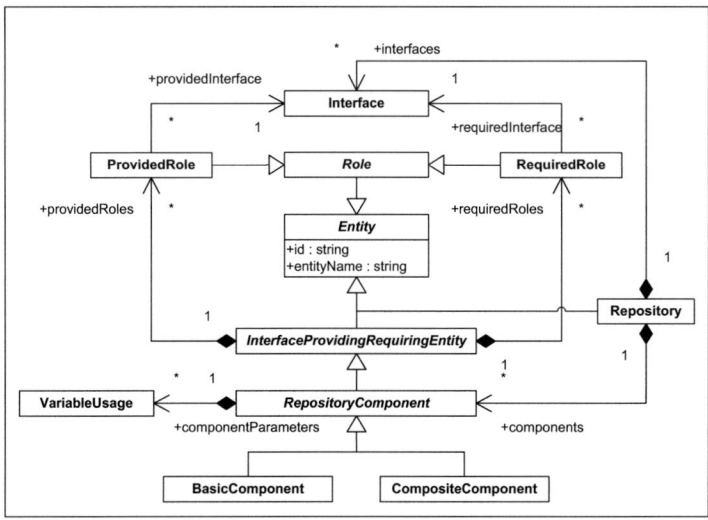

Figure 2.5: PCM Meta-Model Classes for Components, Roles and Interfaces

2.7.2 Repository Model

The PCM repository model contains all specifications for which component developers are responsible, namely component types, interfaces, data types and component behaviour. Figure 2.5 gives a high-level overview of the meta-model classes involved in component definitions. The `Repository` constitutes the top-level entry point to the model and contains a list of `RepositoryComponents` and `Interfaces`. `RepositoryComponents` are `InterfaceProvidingRequiringEntities` – namely, they can provide or require `Interfaces` through the specification of contained `ProvidedRoles` and `RequiredRoles`. This concept allows for reusing interface definitions within multiple component specifications. A component is either a `BasicComponent` (which cannot be further decomposed) or a `CompositeComponent` (see Section 2.7.3 for further explanation of composition concepts). Each component can be parametrized through `VariableUsages` (see Section 2.7.6), expressing variable component con-

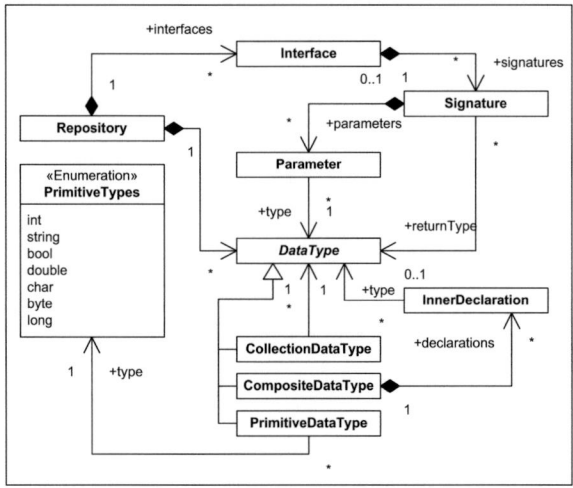

Figure 2.6: PCM Meta-Model Classes for Data Types and Parameters

figurations. Moreover, components, roles and the repository itself are Entities, equipped with a unique id and a name.

Figure 2.6 further details the specification of interfaces and data types. Each Interface contains a list of Signatures, defining input Parameters and a return type of a specific service operation. Both the parameters and the return type refer to DataTypes specified within the repository. While a fully featured type system is out of scope of PCM modelling, the approach does support the specification of PrimitiveDataTypes, CollectionDataTypes and CompositeDataTypes. Primitive types conform to one out of a list of given types including "int", "string", "bool", and others. Collection types represent a set of data items of a specific base type. Composite types contain a list of InnerDeclarations pointing to contained types.

For BasicComponents, each offered service operation (as specified through the provided roles of the component) must be accompanied by a corresponding behavioural specification as shown in Figure 2.7, defin-

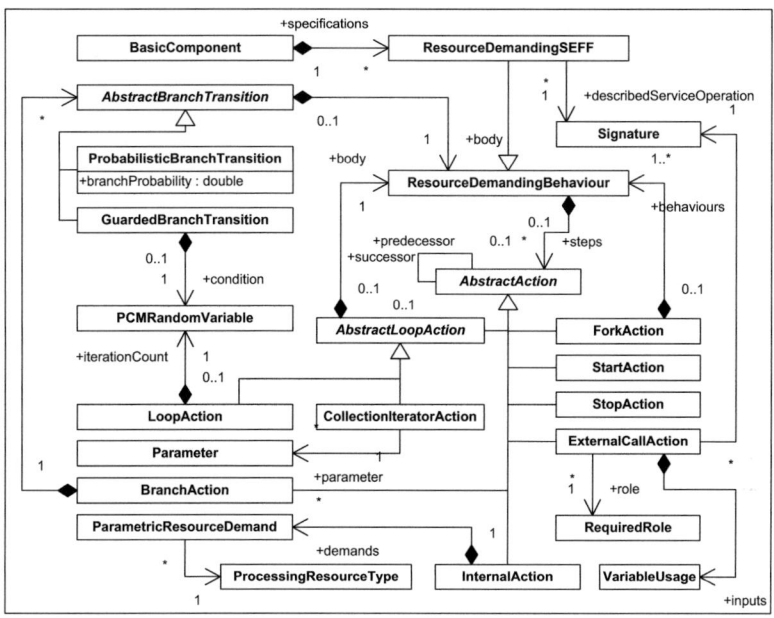

Figure 2.7: PCM Meta-Model Classes for Behavioural Specifications

ing how the component reacts when the service operation is invoked. To this end, the component's execution is represented by a hierarchy of nested `ResourceDemandingBehaviours`, with the topmost behaviour being a `ResourceDemandingSEFF` (where "SEFF" stands for service effect specification). Each behaviour contains a sequence of `AbstractActions`, with each action pointing to its predecessor and its successor. Different action types represent different kinds of execution steps. `AbstractLoopActions` represent a repeated execution of a referenced body behaviour. They are either standard `LoopActions` with a loop iteration count specified through a `PCMRandomVariable` (see Section 2.7.6) or `CollectionIterator-Actions` with an iteration count given by the size of a `Parameter` with a `CollectionDataType`. `BranchActions` represent decisions within the service execution control flow. They contain a set of `AbstractBranch-`

Transitions between which a decision is to be made. Each transition references an own body behaviour. While a ProbabilisticBranchTransition contains a fixed value expressing the probability of being taken, a GuardedBranchTransition evaluates a PCMRandomVariable (see Section 2.7.6) as a condition for being taken. A ForkAction defines a set of concurrently executed forked behaviours. An ExternalCallAction represents an invocation of another service operation provided by a foreign component. To avoid direct wiring between components, the call only references the corresponding RequiredRole of the current component and the Signature of the invoked service operation. Moreover, input parameter properties of the call can be determined through VariableUsages. An InternalAction represents a computational step during service execution. It abstracts from the details of the computation and instead only lists its associated resource consumption through ParametricResourceDemands. A resource demand refers to a certain ProcessingResourceType (e.g. a CPU or hard disk). StartActions and StopActions act as delimiters of action sequences.

Figure 2.8 shows part of a modelled PCM repository instance for the audio hosting example as introduced in Section 1.5. The figure shows definitions of components, interfaces, roles and data types. A BasicComponent "WebFrontend" has RequiredRoles pointing to Interfaces "IUserManagement" and "IAudioManagement" and a ProvidedRole pointing to an Interface "IWebFrontend". "IAudioManagement" is provided by the "AudioManagement" component, which in turn requires multiple other interfaces. The interfaces contain signatures specifying service operations, including input parameter names and data types, as well as a return data type. The example contains PrimitiveDataTypes such as "string" or "int", as well as CompositeDataTypes "UserLoginInfo" and "AudioFile" with inner declarations and a CollectionDataType "AudioFileList" representing a set of audio files. Furthermore, the figure indicates that each

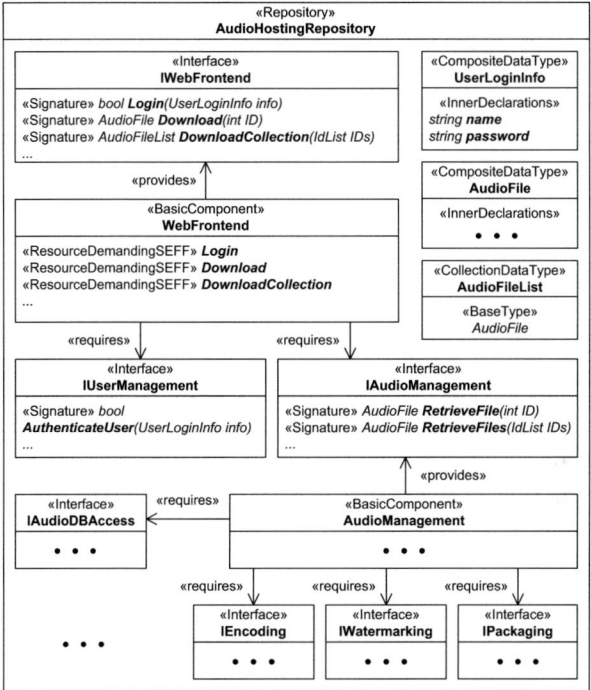

Figure 2.8: Repository Model for the Audio Hosting Example (Excerpt)

component contains a behavioural specification for each provided service operation in terms of a ResourceDemandingSEFF.

Figure 2.9 continues the example by showing two of the Resource-DemandingSEFFs specified for the audio hosting scenario. When the "I-WebFrontend.DownloadCollection" operation of the "WebFrontend" component is invoked, a sequence of 5 actions is executed. After the Start-Action, an InternalAction "ParseWebRequest" represents initial request processing requiring a "CPU" ProcessingResourceType. As a consequence, the "WebFrontend" component must be allocated to a computing node with a modelled CPU resource (see Section 2.7.4). The following ExternalCallAction represents an invocation of the "Retrieve-

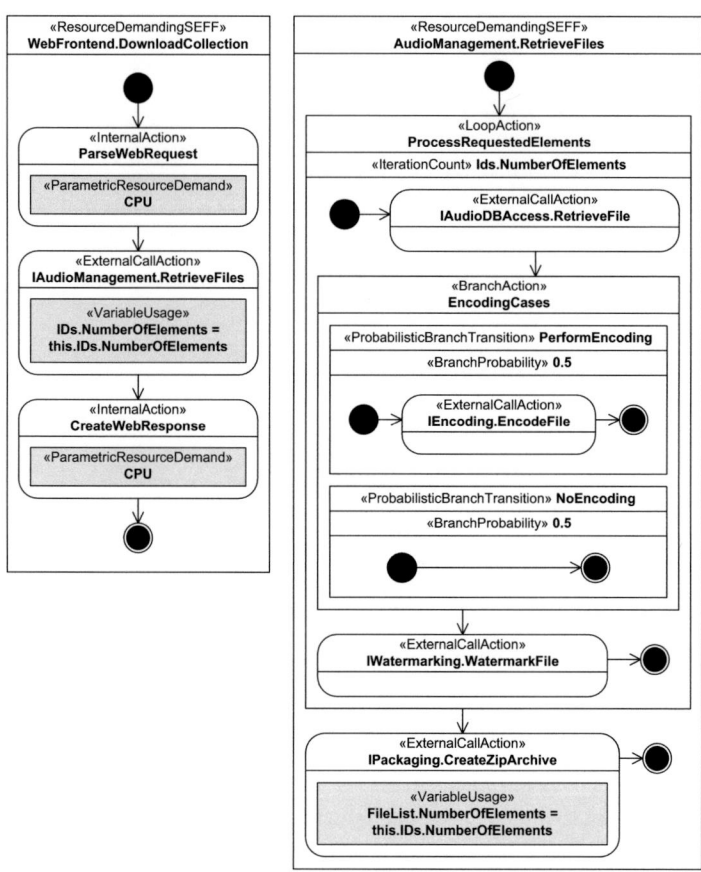

Figure 2.9: Behavioural Specifications for the Audio Hosting Example (Excerpt)

Files" operation of the required "IAudioManagement" interface, specifying a VariableUsage for the "IDs" input parameter of the call (see Section 2.7.6). Another InternalAction "CreateWebResponse" and a StopAction conclude the modelled behaviour.

The second ResourceDemandingSEFF shown in Figure 2.9 depicts the behaviour of the "AudioManagement" component upon invocation of the "IAudioManagement.RetrieveFiles" operation. A LoopAction "Process-RequestedElements" iterates over all IDs given as an input to the call. Its body behaviour includes an invocation to "IAudioDBAccess.RetrieveFile" for retrieving the audio file from the underlying database, as well as further invocations to trigger file encoding and watermarking. File encoding is only to be performed if the requested bitrate for the download is smaller than the original encoding stored in the database. In the PCM model, the encoding decision is represented by a BranchAction "EncodingCases" and two ProbabilisticBranchTransitions "PerformEncoding" and "NoEncoding", each with an estimated branch probability 0.5 of being taken. In the latter case, no encoding is performed and "NoEncoding" contains an empty body behaviour with only a StartAction and a StopAction. After all requested IDs have been processed, the last execution step is another ExternalCallAction triggering the packaging of all collected audio files into a ZIP archive that is offered for download.

2.7.3 System Model

The PCM system model captures the modelling responsibilities of system architects. Figure 2.10 shows the involved meta-model classes. The System is the topmost entry point to the model. It is both an Interface-ProvidingRequiringEntity and a ComposedStructure. The latter provides the ability to instantiate RepositoryComponents through AssemblyContexts and to to connect these instances through AssemblyConnectors. The connectors associate component instances through their

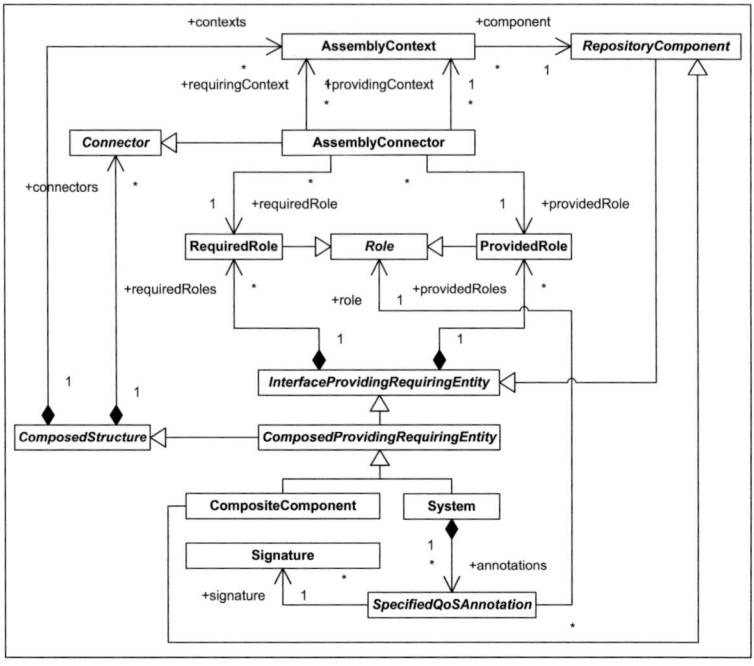

Figure 2.10: PCM System Meta-Model Classes

RequiredRoles and ProvidedRoles (such that a component requiring a certain interface is connected to another component providing this interface). The system itself offers services to users or requires services from other systems through its own required and provided roles. It can also contain SpecifiedQoSAnnotations associating quality properties to provided or required service operations (identified by a referenced Role and Signature). While systems represent the highest level of composition, the corresponding meta-model concepts can also be used to express composition on lower levels through CompositeComponents, which are contained in a PCM Repository along with BasicComponents (see Figure 2.5).

Figure 2.11 depicts a system definition for the audio hosting example. The "AudioHostingSolution" contains 7 AssemblyContexts instantiating

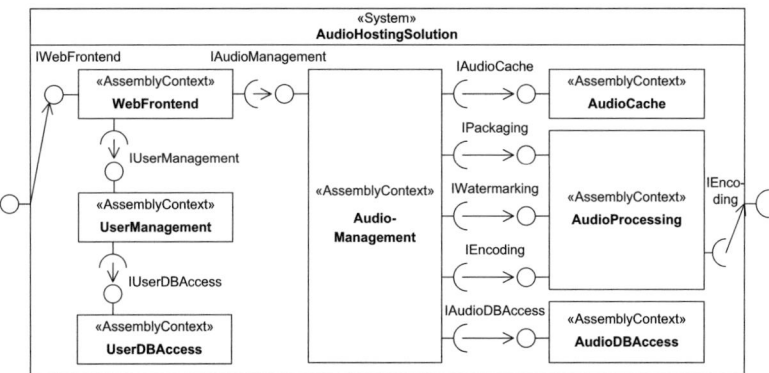

Figure 2.11: System Model for the Audio Hosting Example

component types from the underlying repository model. The system provides the "IWebFrontend" Interface to its users. Calls to this interface are served by the instantiated "WebFrontend" component, which in turn relies on the provided services of "AudioManagement" and "UserManagement". "UserDBAccess" and "AudioDBAccess" allow for storing and retrieving user-related data and audio files. The "AudioProcessing" aggregates encoding, watermarking and packaging functionality, and the "AudioCache" enables fast audio file retrieval without accessing the database itself. The core encoding functionality is not provided by the system itself but by an external encoding engine upon which the system relies. In the model, this is expressed through the system's RequiredRole referencing the "IEncoding" Interface.

2.7.4 Resource Environment and Allocation Models

The perceived quality of IT service execution typically not only depends on the software layer but also on the properties of the underlying IT infrastructure. Therefore, PCM includes modelling constructs for a physical resource environment and the allocation of software components to computing nodes, as shown in Figure 2.12. This information is contributed by sys-

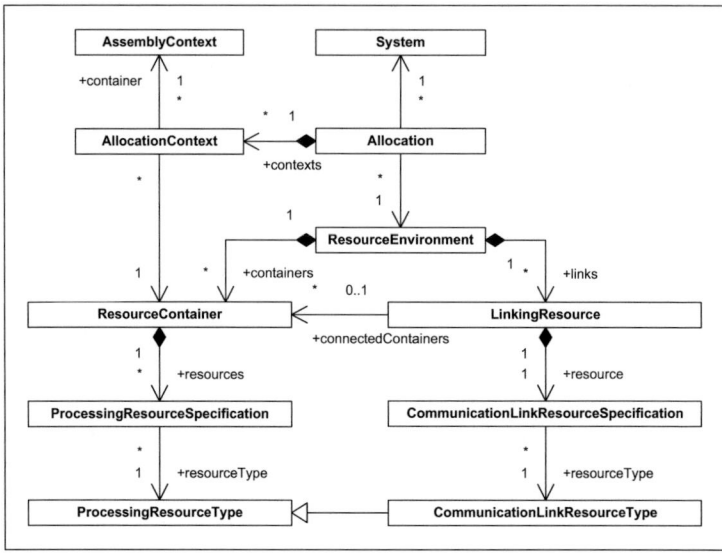

Figure 2.12: PCM Meta-Model Classes for Resource Environments and Allocations

tem deployers, as discussed in Section 2.7.1. The ResourceEnvironment contains a set of ResourceContainers (namely, computing nodes) and LinkingResources (network links). Each ResourceContainer hosts physical resources declared as ProcessingResourceSpecifications of specific ProcessingResourceTypes. A LinkingResource contains a single CommunicationLinkResourceSpecification that references a CommunicationLinkResourceType (such as a LAN communication link). An Allocation maps a System to a ResourceEnvironment and contains AllocationContexts, each of which associates an Assembly-Context (namely, an instantiated component within the system) to a ResourceContainer (namely, a computing node).

A resource environment and allocation specification for the audio hosting solution is shown by Figure 2.13. The software components defined in the repository model (see Figure 2.8) and instantiated in the system model (Figure 2.11) are distributed across two ResourceContainers

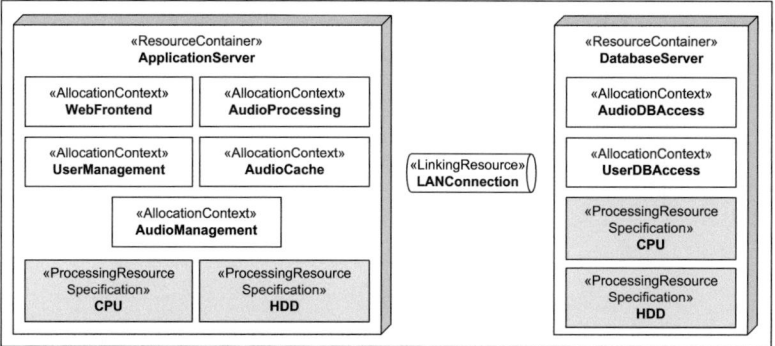

Figure 2.13: Audio Hosting Resource Environment and Allocation

"ApplicationServer" and "DatabaseServer", which are connected through a LinkingResource "LANConnection". The distribution is chosen such that the data storage and the corresponding access functionality is separated from the rest of the application. The modelled connection allows for system-internal service invocations including input and return data to be transmitted between the servers. Each server includes a "CPU" and "HDD" (hard disk drive) ProcessingResourceSpecification allowing for consumption of those resources by service execution.

2.7.5 Usage Model

The PCM offers explicit modelling constructs to express an IT system's usage profile and its influence on service execution. Figure 2.14 depicts the involved meta-model constructs, which are used by domain experts (as discussed in Section 2.7.1). A UsageModel is the topmost entry point for the specification of user behaviour. It consists of a list of UsageScenarios, where each scenario describes a certain use case of the system. The user behaviour itself is captured through ScenarioBehaviours, similarly to the specification of system behaviour through ResourceDemandingBehaviours (see Figure 2.7). Each ScenarioBehaviour contains a sequence

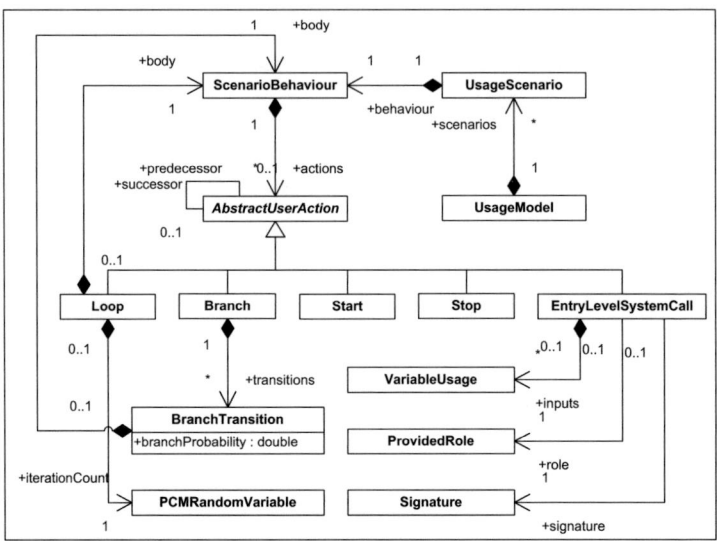

Figure 2.14: PCM Usage Meta-Model Classes

of AbstractUserActions, referencing each other as successors and pre-
decessors. The actions represent repetition (Loop), decision (Branch),
begin and end of behaviour (Start, Stop) and invocations of system
service operations (EntryLevelSystemCall). Loops specify iteration
counts through PCMRandomVariables (see Section 2.7.6); branches contain BranchTransitions with individual branch probabilities. Both loops
and branch transitions reference nested body behaviours. An Entry-
LevelSystemCall references one of the system's ProvidedRoles and
a Signature pointing out a certain service operation; input parameter values can be determined through VariableUsages.

   In the audio hosting example, two separate modes of usage are of interest and modelled through individual ScenarioBehaviours, as shown in
Figure 2.15. A user session with the system may be interactive or may be
a batch request (used for automated management of stored audio contents).
Both modes are highly similar, conducting either an audio upload or down-

Figure 2.15: Specification of User Behaviour in the Audio Hosting Example

load, surrounded by login and logout commands. The Branches "InteractiveUploadDownloadCases" and "BatchUploadDownloadCases" model the decision between up- and download. Downloads are far more frequent than uploads, with corresponding BranchTransition probabilities of 0.9 versus 0.1. The only difference between the interactive and batch modes lies in the download case, which requests a single file in interactive mode (invoking "IWebFrontend.Download") and multiple files in batch mode (invoking "IWebFrontend.DownloadCollection"). The number of requested files in batch mode is given through a VariableUsage (see Section 2.7.6) and set to an estimated average number of 30.

2.7.6 PCM Variables and Parameter Solving

An essential feature of the PCM modelling language is its ability to express parameter properties and their propagation throughout the component-based architecture. While the PCM does not aim at capturing all details of the data flow through the architecture, it enables modelling those properties of service invocation inputs which have an influence on the subsequent control flow and hence on the execution paths taken through the system. Figure 2.16 shows the involved meta-model classes. Through `VariableUsages`, `EntryLevelSystemCalls` and `ExternalCallActions` can specify input parameter properties, and `RepositoryComponents` can specify component parameter properties. These inputs can be used by `Loops` and `LoopActions` to specify iteration counts, by `GuardedBranch-Transitions` to specify branch conditions, and again by `ExternalCall-Actions` to specify parameter properties depending on given input parameters of the current `ResourceDemandingSEFF`. A `VariableUsage` includes a parameter identification through an `AbstractNamedReference` and a characterisation of a parameter property through a `VariableCharacterisation`. The identification may be a `VariableReference` (such as "ID" references the input parameter of the service operation "IWebFrontend.-Download" in Figure 2.8) either on its own or combined with `Namespace-References` (such as "info.name" references an inner declaration of the input parameter "info" of "IWebFrontend.Login"). The characterisation specifies one out of a given set of properties (such as "Value" or "NumberOfElements") and provides the value of this property through a `PCM-RandomVariable`. The `PCMRandomVariable` may be a single number, a probability distribution or a mathematical expression, and it may contain references to any parameter that is available in the current execution context. PCM provides a dedicated *Stochastic Expressions* (StoEx) language for the specification of `PCMRandomVariables` [Koz08].

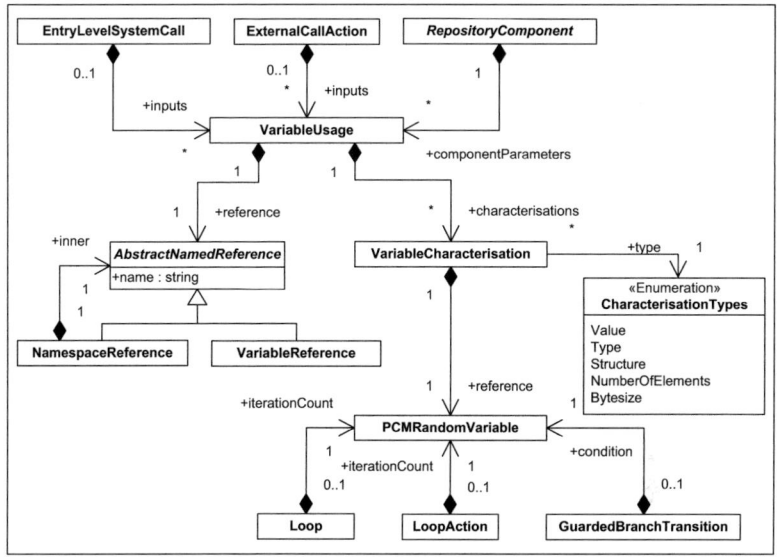

Figure 2.16: PCM Meta-Model Classes for Variable Usages

In the audio hosting example, the EntryLevelSystemCall to "IWeb-Frontend.Download-Collection" (see Figure 2.15) contains a Variable-Usage referencing the input parameter "IDs" of the invoked service operation (see Figure 2.8) and characterising its property "NumberOfElements" with the value "30". According to the system definition (Figure 2.11, the call is served by the "WebFrontend" component and its ResourceDemandingSEFF "DownloadCollection" (Figure 2.9). The ExternalCallAction within this behaviour employs another VariableUsage to propagate the value of the "NumberOfElements" property of "IDs" to the equally named input parameter of "IAudioManagement.RetrieveFiles". The call is served by the "AudioManagement" component with its "RetrieveFiles" ResourceDemandingSEFF. The propagated input parameter property guides the iteration count of the LoopAction "ProcessRequestedElements", and it is further propagated to the "IPackaging.CreateZip-

59

Archive" service operation through another `VariableUsage` of the corresponding `ExternalCallAction`.

Putting all information together, it is evident that the `LoopAction` displayed in Figure 2.9 has 30 iterations, and that the invocation of "IPackaging.CreateZipArchive" includes a list of 30 audio files as an input parameter. This is due to the fact that the system user has invoked "IWebFrontend.DownloadCollection" with 30 requested IDs (Figure 2.15). This resolving of parameter dependencies to concrete values or probability distributions throughout the modelled behavioural specifications is automated by PCM's tool support and a preliminary step to further model transformations and analyses. It is done by the *dependency solver* [Koz08], which transforms an original PCM instance to one without any parameter dependencies. The PCM-REL Markov analysis (see Chapter 5) builds upon the output of the dependency solver.

3 PCM-REL Methodology

While the preceding foundations chapter has introduced a rich set of existing methodology related to IT systems and reliability, the individual discussed aspects are not yet connected and cannot be directly used for integrated IT system reliability prediction. First, basic reliability concepts
are established through the taxonomy of Avižienis et al. [ALRL04] (Section 2.1.1). However, this taxonomy has a broad scope. It covers multiple
dependability attributes, and it does not go into the details of distinguishing
software-level and hardware-level reliability aspects. Second, the Palladio
Component Model (PCM, Section 2.7) provides a comprehensive architectural modelling language capturing software components and their behaviour, hardware resources and their consumption by service execution,
as well as the system's usage profile and its influence on the control and
data flow throughout the architecture. However, the PCM does not include
any reliability-specific considerations. Finally, approaches to architecture-
based software reliability prediction (ASRP, Section 2.5) provide analysis
methods for reliability based on software architecture, but do not consider
relevant architectural factors required for supporting design decisions.

This chapter combines the discussed methodological aspects and fills the
remaining gaps, in order to create a unified methodology as a comprehensive basis for PCM-REL reliability modelling and prediction. Section 3.1
develops a refined view on reliability concepts for integrated IT systems,
followed by a discussion in Section 3.2 how reliability prediction can be
embedded in a system engineering process. Section 3.3 focuses on methodology adoption from PCM, and Section 3.4 concludes with a discussion of
relevant degrees of freedom during reliability modelling.

3.1 Reliability Concepts for Integrated IT Systems

As the discussion of reliability analyses (see Section 2.1.2) shows, hardware-oriented and software-oriented reliability communities each build upon their own failure models and related assumptions. This section develops an integrated view, capturing how service execution – from the user's point of view – is affected by both software-level and hardware-level failure potentials. To this end, the discussion revisits the definition of the term "failure" and examines the interplay of the hardware and software parts of an IT system.

In their taxonomy, Avižienis et al. [ALRL04] define a "service failure" – of a component or system service – as "the transition from correct service to incorrect service", where "correct" means in accordance with the expectation of the service users. The authors further state that an error becomes a failure when it "reaches the external state" of a component or a system, where "external" means "perceivable at the service interface". This definition does not necessarily imply that a failure is actually perceived by a user of the system or component service. The failure may be completely unrecognised if no invocations of the service occur. On the other hand, a failure may also be perceived multiple times, if the transition to incorrect service is permanent and multiple service invocations occur. On the other hand, Cheung [Che80] states in his foundational ASRP publication: "A failure is said to occur if, given the input values and specifications of the computations to be performed by the program, the output values are either incorrect or indefinitely delayed". Hence, Cheung focuses on the user-perceived effect of a transition to incorrect service, rather than the transition itself. Many subsequent publications in the software and hardware reliability fields use the term "failure" (and related terms such as "failure rate" or "failure-free operation") without clarifying these inconsistencies, which reduces the understandability and clarity of the presentation. This problem becomes particularly apparent if failure potentials of both the software and hardware dimensions shall be considered in an integrated way. Therefore, the following discussions in this thesis distinguish between a *service failure* and a *failure-on-demand* (FOD). The former denotes a transition from normal service to any type of degraded service; the latter is the user-perceived effect of the transition in terms of an unwanted service invocation result. An unwanted result is any phenomenon that deviates from the expected course of service execution, including delivery of wrong outputs, untimely delivery of outputs, or infinitely delayed processing.

A second prerequisite for the integrated consideration of the software and hardware dimensions is an explicit identification of the specifics of both of them, as well as the relations between them. Avižienis et al. introduce a *system* as an "entity that interacts with other entities, i.e. other systems, including hardware, software, humans, and the physical world with its natural phenomena". Furthermore, they see a system as being "composed of a set of components bound together in order to interact, where each component is another system, etc. The recursion stops when a component is considered to be atomic". Hence, while providing a unified and compositional view on all imaginable types of components, the authors do not go into the specifics of software components as opposed to hardware components. On the other hand, Cheung and many subsequent ASRP publications focus purely on software components (see Section 7.1), thereby reducing the perspective to the software part of an IT system only. A more comprehensive picture is given by PCM (see Section 2.7), which models an IT system as a set of instantiated basic and composite software components, executed in a physical resource environment. The environment includes a set of resource containers representing computing nodes, as well as linking resources representing network connections. Each resource container includes a set of modelled hardware resources, and each software component is allocated to one of the containers. During service execution, each visited software component consumes hardware resources on its allocated container, depending on its modelled software behaviour. The PCM semantics provide a differentiated IT system perspective and hence a solid foundation for integrated reliability modelling.

Based on the refined terminology and the distinction of software and hardware specifics, Figures 3.1 and 3.2 illustrate how system users are affected by failure potentials on both levels. For clarity of presentation, the discussion initially focuses on a basic configuration with a single software component and a single supporting hardware resource only. First, Figure 3.1 depicts *software-induced* FOD occurrences, caused by existing faults in the software component's implementation. The left-hand side of the figure shows the software component initially providing normal service, and a first service invocation being successfully completed. Then, the component exhibits a service failure, changing over to degraded service. The failure may be triggered by another service invocation, or it may be a consequence of autonomously conducted actions of the component. If the failure is triggered by an invocation, this invocation results in a FOD. In the example, the resulting state of degraded service persists, and subsequent service invocations result in further FODs. Generally, states of degraded service may be temporary, or they may require a re-initialization or restart of the component. Service invocations to degraded components may always result in FODs, or they may just have a higher probability of resulting in FODs. The right-hand side of the figure shows the component again providing normal service, and a first successful service invocation. A second invocation results in a FOD, but it does not have any consequences on further service execution, as indicated by a third – again successful – invocation. Typical examples for such situations are calculation errors that produce wrong outputs but do not impact any of the component's internal state. Technically, the component can be considered as experiencing a service failure with a zero-time duration.

Figure 3.2 shows an extended scenario comprising both a software component and a hardware resource, with each of them initially providing normal service. Correspondingly, a first service invocation is successfully

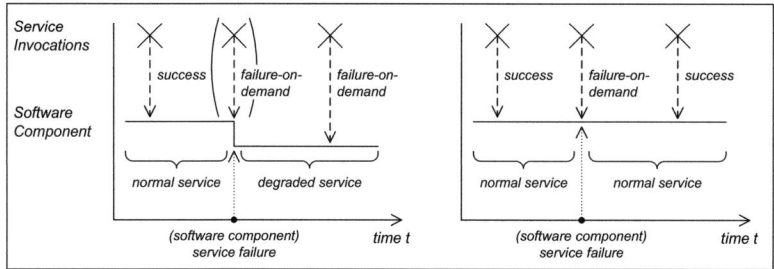

Figure 3.1: Software-induced Failures-on-Demand

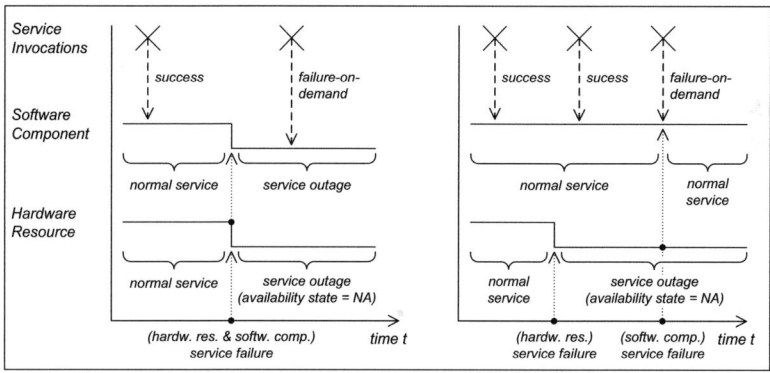

Figure 3.2: Hardware-induced Failures-on-Demand

completed. Then, the hardware resource exhibits a service failure and changes to a state of degraded service. Following the well-established hardware failure model as presented in Section 2.2, the service degradation corresponds to a *service outage*, with the resource being in availability state *NA*. In the example, the execution of the software component depends entirely on the availability of the resource; hence, the resource failure instantly causes a corresponding software component service failure. Such a situation can occur if a central hardware resource of a computing node, such as a CPU, is strictly required for the operation of the node. Any further service invocations to the component result in *hardware-induced* FODs until the underlying hardware resource is repaired or exchanged by a new one. The right-hand side of the figure depicts both the component and the resource providing normal service again, as well as a first successful service invocation. Here, the execution of the component does not strictly depend on the resource, and an occurring resource service failure does not have an immediate impact on the component. Examples include data storage devices that may become unavailable while the overall computing node keeps operating. Service invocations during the service outage of the resource may fail or may be successful, depending on the question if access to the resource is required by the specific service operation. If so, the invocation results in a hardware-induced FOD, and the component can be considered as experiencing a service failure with a zero-time duration. Alternatively, the component may be able to mask the resource failure and, in spite of the resource being unavailable, provide service as expected (not shown in the figure).

A further extended scenario of an IT system with multiple software components and hardware resources can be based on the discussion of a "fundamental chain of dependability and security threats" introduced by Avižienis et al. in their survey. In short, the authors state that if a system component C_1 receives service from another system component C_2, a service failure of C_2 constitutes a fault for C_1 and can eventually result in a service failure of C_1. Applying this principle to FOD occurrences and software components, a service invocation to a software component S_1 can result in a FOD if the service execution of S_1 includes a service invocation of another component S_2, and if this invocation results in a FOD (alternatively, S_1 may mask the FOD of S_2 and still provide service as expected). In this sense, FOD occurrences can be "propagated" along a hierarchy of service invocations. Furthermore, each software component can require one or multiple hardware resources for its service execution, and each service failure of a required resource can cause FOD occurrences on the software level.

Considering all discussed scenarios, both software components and hardware resources may exhibit service failures. For software components, service failures may not have any impact on further execution, or they may lead to temporary or permanent service degradations or outages. Service failures of hardware resources lead to service outages, making the resources unavailable until repair or replacement. Service invocations can result in FODs as a consequence of both software-level and hardware-level service failures. FOD occurrences can be propagated along a service invocation hierarchy involving multiple software components, until they reach the system border and are perceived as a FOD by a system user. Reliability modelling as done by PCM-REL builds upon this integrated view of IT system reliability (see Section 4.1).

3.2 A Reliability-Aware System Engineering Process

While many ASRP publications claim that their presented approaches support architectural decisions during system design stages, they typically do not discuss how reliability predictions can be embedded in and used throughout a system engineering process. Yet, such a discussion is important to give evidence that software architects can actually benefit from applying the approaches. Therefore, this section outlines how a system engineering process can be enriched by continuous IT system reliability prediction as provided by PCM-REL.

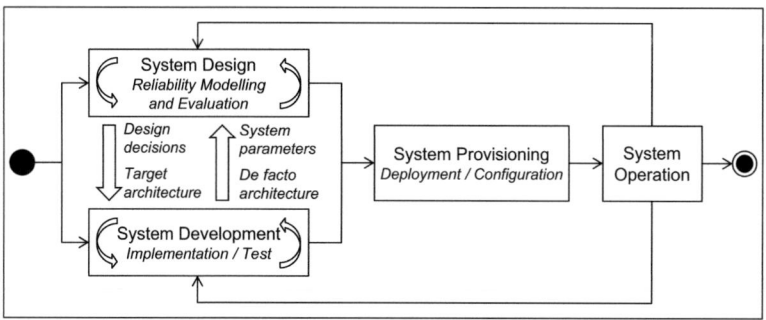

Figure 3.3: System Engineering Process

Figure 3.3 gives an overview of the envisioned process. As the figure shows, the creation of the final product involves two major activities, namely *system design* and *system development*. Without restricting the scenario to any single process type or definition, the figure only assumes that both activities run in parallel (with the main focus shifting over time from design to development), inform each other, and are iterative each for itself. Design, which includes reliability modelling and evaluation activities, informs development with design decisions and the definition of a target architecture. Development includes implementation and test as its main activities and delivers (potentially re-engineered) information about the existing or *de facto* architecture, as well as estimations or measurements for a variety of *system parameters*. The parameters refer to usage properties of the system, included failure potentials, as well as system-internal behaviour and state properties. Information about software and hardware failure potentials can be derived using methods such as the ones described in Sections 2.2 and 2.3.

Within a single system design iteration, the provided inputs are used for reliability modelling, creating a set of architectural candidates for the system under study. Multiple candidates are created to reflect possible design alternatives or to vary system parameter values, accounting for existing uncertainties during their estimation. Reliability evaluation analyses all created candidates to determine their expected reliabilities. Based on the obtained prediction results, design alternatives can be ranked, supporting the required design decisions and providing a recommended target architecture. If the results are not significant enough to allow for decision-making, the scope of considered design alternatives can be increased by creating and evaluating new candidates. If the results violate given reliability requirements, new candidates can be created with the specific goal to improve reliability compared to the previously considered candidates. Reliability-improving measures include decreasing individual failure potentials (for example, employing intensively tested software components or high-availability hardware resources) and introducing fault tolerance mechanisms throughout the architecture. Other architectural changes such as adjusted component configurations or changed allocations of components to computing nodes may have reliability-improving effects as well. The process of creating and evaluating architectural candidates continues until satisfactory results are available and stable recommendations can be derived. Being based on PCM, the PCM-REL approach proposed in this thesis offers a design-oriented modelling language, strong capabilities for reusing model artefacts and comprehensive tool support, thereby enabling efficient handling of system design iterations.

As the number of performed design and development iterations increases, the amount of available information grows. The target architecture becomes more stable, complete and detailed. At the same time, the information delivered by development becomes more reliable and exact. This fruitful exchange is only possible if reliability modelling and prediction accompanies the development as a continuous design activity. If reliability is only considered late in development, it may not be feasible or possible any more to apply necessary but fundamental changes to the architecture. Once the implementation is finalized, the system can be provisioned (i.e. deployed and configured) and brought into operation. Being operating in the field, the system may still undergo revisions for fault elimination and evolution. These revisions again involve design and development activities. At this stage, existing reliability measurements and experiences regarding system usage and behaviour in the field may constitute a valuable additional input to reliability modelling and prediction.

Apart from reliability considerations, other quality attributes such as performance, safety and security also influence design decisions, and trade-offs between the attributes may arise. Furthermore, reliability-improving measures are typically associated with monetary costs and have to be assessed against these costs. While trade-off analyses and economical considerations are not in the focus of the thesis itself, the proposed engineering process can be augmented to take these aspects into account. To this end, an extended system design iteration creates not only reliability-specific models of architectural candidates, but also other representations suited for evaluating further quality attributes and associated costs. In the case of PCM-REL (which is based on the existing PCM modelling and evaluation capabilities), it is even possible to create one common model and evaluate this model with respect to reliability, performance [BKR09] and costs [Koz11]. Furthermore, automated optimization can be conducted to cope with a high number of possible candidates within a large design space, and existing trade-off relations are presented to software architects as a basis for decision-making [Koz11]. Hence, reliability prediction as done by PCM-REL is well suited to be embedded in an overall engineering process considering reliability and other system quality attributes.

3.3 Adoption of PCM Methodology by PCM-REL

This section explicitly discusses methodological aspects of the original PCM approach [BKR09] that have been developed from a performance point of view but are also relevant and reused in the context of this thesis. The discussion shows why these aspects are relevant with respect to reliability, and how PCM-REL benefits from their adoption. The discussed aspects include (a) the explicit modelling of the different factors influencing service quality, (b) the separation of modelling concerns along the lines of multiple developer roles, (c) the representation of component behaviour through a high-level service effect specification, and (d) the concept of parameter dependencies and their solving.

Regarding the quality influence factors (a), PCM distinguishes between four major influences on the quality of a component service, namely its *implementation*, *usage*, quality of *required services*, and quality of the physical *execution environment*. These four factors are also essential when reasoning about reliability. The implementation of a component service defines its behaviour, which may result in a FOD upon service execution, caused by software faults contained in the implementation. The service usage governs the execution paths taken through the component's implementation and influences the progression of the component's software state. The failure potential of required services affects the service under study, as it depends on the results of the external service invocations. Finally, unavailable hardware resources may prevent a successful service execution (as discussed in Section 3.1), which makes the execution environment a further influencing factor to the component's service reliability. By explicitly taking all these factors into account, the developed PCM-REL approach allows for a differentiated view upon service reliability and its influencing factors, enabling well-informed design decisions for the system under study.

The separation of modelling concerns (b) provided by PCM as discussed in Section 2.7.1 is an essential ingredient to supporting a truly distributed software development process. It is a feature not discussed by existing ASRP approaches (see Section 7.4); hence, their application is essentially limited to scenarios where a single role possesses or collects all required information for creating the entire architectural model. In contrast, the developed PCM-REL approach adheres to the separation of concerns. All developed meta-model extensions are included in such a way that each developer role contributes only the information that is available from its own specific perspective (see Chapter 4).

The PCM behavioural specifications (c) (or `ResourceDemandingSEFFs` as described in Section 2.7.2) represent high-level component behaviour, including control flow decisions, external service invocations and the consumption of hardware resources. They abstract from component-internal computations and state dependencies. Compared to existing ASRP approaches building upon the Cheung model (Section 2.5), these behavioural specifications allow for more accurate modelling of possible control flow paths and are not affected by the Markov assumption regarding inter-component control transfer. PCM-REL reuses the capabilities for its behavioural specifications and extends them with reliability-specific constructs and annotations, thereby also providing highly flexible modelling capabilities for failure potentials included in the control flow (see Section 4).

Parameter dependencies (d) are vital to the PCM (see Section 2.7.6). They are a prerequisite to the separation of modelling concerns between component developers and domain experts. Furthermore, their automatic solving [Koz08] releases software architects from the burden to explicitly specify the usage profile of each component within an architecture, and instead automatically deduces all component usage profiles from a given system-level usage profile. The thesis takes full advantage of this concept and integrates the dependency solver into the prediction workflow as presented in Section 5.1, in order to perform the Markov analysis based on a PCM-REL instance with solved parameter dependencies.

3.4 Degrees of Freedom for Reliability Modelling

This section discusses further requirements for reliability prediction in terms of relevant modelling degrees of freedom. Even though a context for reliability prediction is given through the envisioned reliability-aware system engineering process (see Section 3.2), concrete use cases may vary significantly in their characteristics. The system under study may vary in its size and complexity, and the knowledge about the system may be detailed or coarse. Existing ASRP publications rarely discuss this issue. In order to adapt to the specifics of each use case, relevant degrees of freedom include (a) the modelling granularity, (b) the modelled system fragment, (c) the distinction of FOD types, and (d) the flexible modelling of points of failure. The PCM-REL approach developed in this thesis offers all of these degrees of freedom.

Regarding the modelling granularity (a), reliability modelling should offer a hierarchical view on a software component architecture, with components being compositions of other components. Thus, a system can first be modelled very coarse-grained, as an assembly of top-level components. This model can stepwise be refined by adding the inner structure of higher-level components being composed of lower-level components. Typically, this process also leads to a refinement of the involved interfaces and behavioural specifications. Modellers are free to choose the level of detail when modelling the system under study. This level of detail may also vary for different parts of the architecture, or for different stages of a surrounding system engineering process. While a higher level of detail rises the modelling effort and requires more system knowledge, it also generally yields a higher quality (accurateness and significance) of the results. Through the concept of `CompositeComponents` (see Section 2.7.2), PCM-REL supports hierarchical software architecture modelling – a feature used by both case studies reported in the thesis (see Chapter 6).

A further degree of freedom refers to the modelled system fragment (b). To keep modelling efforts within feasible bounds, modellers should be able to determine *system cuts* that are most relevant to the reliability analysis, and limit the modelling scope to these cuts. A *vertical cut* takes advantage of the fact that under a certain system usage, only certain parts of the system (such as a subset of application-level components and their services) are active and can contribute to the system's failure potential. Limiting the model to those parts reduces its reusability with respect to usage profile changes, but also reduces the modelling effort. A *horizontal cut* refrains from explicit modelling of supporting software layers (such as middleware or operating systems). However, these layers are still active and have to be taken into account in an implicit way (e.g. by integrating the failure potential of the operating system into application-level FOD probabilities). Such implicit modelling reduces effort, but also the reusability with respect to changes in supporting software layers.

Another desirable degree of freedom is the specification of custom FOD types (c). While most ASRP approaches only consider a generic "failure"

73

situation capturing any deviation from service as expected (see Section 7.4), failure situations may actually be categorized according to various dimensions (some of which are discussed in Section 2.1.1). Modellers should be free to determine a use case specific set of relevant FOD types. A more differentiated distinction of FOD types requires more detailed knowledge about the system under study (such as individual FOD occurrence probabilities), but also yields more differentiated prediction results (such as user-perceived FOD probabilities per FOD type). PCM-REL allows for specifying custom FOD types for each system under study (see Section 4.2).

Finally, modellers should be free to flexibly specify a relevant set of *potential points of failure* (PPOF) (d) throughout the architectural model. While the Cheung model (Section 2.5) and related approaches assume a strict 1 : 1 relationship between software components and PPOFs by annotating each component with a "per-visit" failure probability, modellers may want to specify failure potentials of different components with different granularities. A more fine-grained PPOF modelling requires more detailed knowledge about the system's failure potentials but tends to yield more accurate predictions. The modelling of component behaviour with PCM-REL allows for specifying a variable number of PPOFs visited during a component's service execution (see Section 4.1).

4 Modelling IT Systems with PCM-REL

This chapter discusses how to create reliability-tailored abstractions of IT systems using PCM-REL. The discussion focusses on the aspects that are specific to system reliability, and hence on the distinguishing modelling features of PCM-REL compared to PCM. Section 4.1 defines the concrete meaning of system reliability in the context of the approach and gives an overview over the involved modelling concepts. The following sections from 4.2 to 4.7 discuss those concepts in detail. They introduce the corresponding meta-model constructs, along with an explanation of their semantics, design rationales and examples. The examples generally refer to the audio hosting service as introduced in Section 1.5, and show how the model of the service as presented throughout Section 2.7 can be extended to account for all relevant reliability-specific aspects. Section 4.8 concludes the chapter with a short presentation of the implemented tool support.

4.1 Overview

Summarizing the central theme of the thesis, the proposed approach predicts the reliability of IT systems based on their component-based software architectures, represented through fully specified PCM-REL instances, as the probability of successful service execution. More concretely, the main output of the approach is the probability of a successful run through a given usage scenario, as part of a PCM-REL usage model (see Section 2.7.5). A usage scenario run is successful if each system service invocation during the run finishes without any system-level failure-on-demand (FOD). There may be FODs within the system during service execution, but they must be handled before they reach the system border. If the usage model contains multiple usage scenarios, reliability prediction is conducted independently for each scenario.

In the following, the concept of a successful run through a usage scenario is further illustrated by taking a closer look at the specifications of user and system behaviour in PCM, and by describing how these specifications – together with the PCM-REL-specific modelling extensions – form the basis of the reliability evaluation. The behavioural specifications comprise the ScenarioBehaviours of the usage model and the ResourceDemandingSEFFs of the repository model (Sections 2.7.5 and 2.7.2). The given assembly of BasciComponents to CompositeComponents and to the System allows for the aggregation of the behavioural specifications to an overall *behavioural view* that integrates the user behaviour (i.e. the user actions in the involved ScenarioBehaviours) and the system behaviour (i.e. the system actions in the involved Resource-DemandingBehaviours). This view constitutes a tree of nested action sequences. The topmost action sequence begins with the Start of the ScenarioBehaviour referenced by the considered UsageScenario and ends with its Stop. Loops and Branches of system users contain one or several nested action sequences. An EntryLevelSystemCall points to a ResourceDemandingSEFF (i.e. the behavioural specification that belongs to the corresponding Signature within the executing BasicComponent) as its nested action sequence. Within the system, LoopActions, Branch-Actions, ForkActions, RecoveryBlockActions (see Section 4.7) and ExternalCallActions contain nested action sequences.

As an example, Figure 4.1 depicts parts of the behavioural view of the audio hosting service, based on the behavioural specifications shown in Figures 2.9 and 2.15. The figure integrates the user behaviour in batch mode with the relevant system behaviour, showing not all individual actions but only the set of nested action sequences. The "BatchRequest-Behaviour" constitutes the topmost sequence. It includes two Entry-

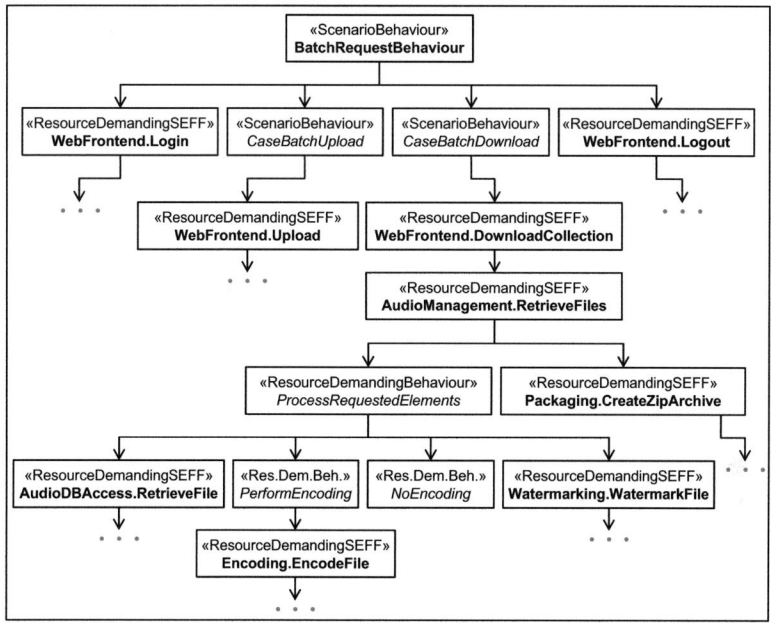

Figure 4.1: Behavioural View Example (Excerpt)

`LevelSystemCalls` and a `Branch` with two `BranchTransitions` (see
Figure 2.15). Hence, it has a total of four nested sequences, namely the
`ResourceDemandingSEFFs` "WebFrontend.Login" and "WebFrontend.-
Logout" and the body behaviours of the "CaseBatchUpload" and "Case-
BatchDownload" `BranchTransitions`. Each of these sequences has other
nested sequences in turn. For example, the "CaseBatchDownload" behaviour includes an `EntryLevelSystemCall` referencing the "IWebFront-
end.DownloadCollection" service operation and a corresponding nested
`ResourceDemandingSEFF` "WebFrontend.DownloadCollection". In the
example, further action sequences are included in the view by `External-
CallActions` (such as the call to "IAudioManagement.RetrieveFiles"), as
well as body behaviours of `LoopActions` (such as the "ProcessRequestedElements" loop) and `ProbabilisticBranchTransitions` (such as the

transitions of the "EncodingCases" branch). The tree reaches its leaves when an action sequence contains no further nested sequences (such as the body behaviour of the "NoEncoding" transition). Notice that any action sequence specified in the architectural model may occur at multiple places in the tree, if the usage scenario execution includes invocations of the same component service operations at different points in the control flow. For example, if the batch mode scenario included multiple invocations of the "EncodeFile" service operation of the "Encoding" component, the behavioural view would contain multiple occurrences of the corresponding action sequence (as well as all nested sequences)[1].

Each run through a usage scenario proceeds along the action sequences of its corresponding behavioural view, beginning with the Start of the topmost ScenarioBehaviour and ending with its Stop. Within each action sequence, actions are visited according to their specified order. Nested action sequences are processed according to the specified PCM behavioural semantics (see Section 2.7.2). For example, the invoked ResourceDemandingSEFF of an ExternalCallAction is completely executed before the control flow moves on to the successor action of the call. The body behaviour of a LoopAction is executed multiple times, according to the specification of loop iteration counts. In case of a BranchAction, exactly one of the given body behaviours is executed. The nested behaviours of a ForkAction are all executed in parallel. Overall, the behavioural view specifies a set of possible sequences of system service invocations and a set of possible execution paths for each such invocation. The occurrence probabilities of all invocation sequences and execution paths are implicitly given through probabilistic annotations to control flow constructs (such as loop iteration counts and branch transition probabilities). Each usage

---

[1]Multiple occurrences of an action sequence representing a certain component service operation (namely, a certain ResourceDemandingSEFF) are not unified in the behavioural view, because each invocation of the service operation may have different characterisations of input parameter properties, leading to different behaviours during service execution.

Category	Action Type	Failure Cause	Quantification of Failure Potential
Potential Point-of-Failure (PPOF)	InternalAction	system-internal software faults	FOD probabilities
		unavailable system-internal hardware resources	MTTF / MTTR values
	ExternalCallAction	system-external service failures	FOD probabilities
		system-internal network communication faults	FOD probabilities
		unavailable system-internal hardware resources	MTTF / MTTR values
Point-of-Recovery (POR)	RecoveryBlockAction	*(recovers from all failure types)*	

Table 4.1: PCM-REL Points of Failure and Recovery

scenario run selects one invocation sequence and one execution path per invocation, according to the given occurrence probabilities.

Along the execution paths of a service invocation, certain types of actions may exhibit *local FOD occurrences* (i.e. their execution may not finish successfully or lead to unexpected behaviour and unwanted results). The term "local" indicates that the FOD is initially internal to the executing software component and not instantly perceived at the component's border. Instances of these action types constitute the *potential points of failure* (PPOF) of the service execution. Table 4.1 summarizes PPOFs and corresponding failure causes (which will be discussed in greater detail in the following sections). As the table shows, service execution may fail either at InternalActions or at ExternalCallActions. Other action types have their purpose in determining the control and data flow, but do not represent PPOFs. InternalActions (as introduced in Section 2.7.2) represent the computations along the execution path and may fail due to software faults in the implementation (Section 4.3) or due to unavailable required hardware resources (Section 4.4). ExternalCallActions involve inter-component communication. If they invoke service operations provided by components on other ResourceContainers within the system (Section 4.5), they may exhibit FODs due to network transmission failures or due to unavailable resources required for the operation of the target containers (Section 4.4).

79

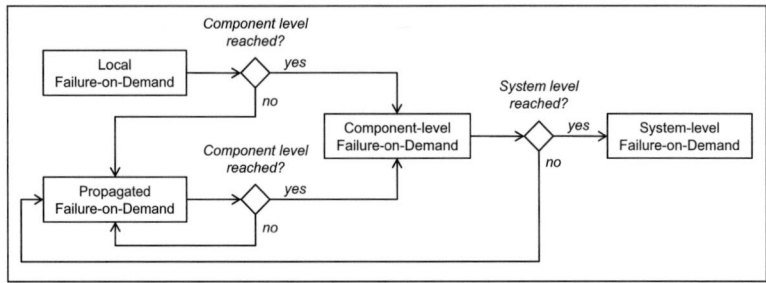

Figure 4.2: PCM-REL Failure-on-Demand Propagation

If they represent invocations of system-external services, they may exhibit FODs due to failures of these (Section 4.6).

Based on the considerations of Section 3.1, PCM-REL defines a standard "propagation" of FOD occurrences. In contrast to many existing ASRP approaches (Section 7.4), failure potentials are not associated with visits to software components but with individual actions that represent PPOFs within the behavioural view. Correspondingly, FOD occurrences are propagated along nested action sequences rather than component service invocations only. Figure 4.2 illustrates this principle. A local FOD occurrence at an action representing a PPOF leads to an FOD of the surrounding action sequence in the behavioural view, which is in turn a *propagated FOD occurrence* of the action pointing to this sequence (such as a `BranchAction` pointing to the action sequence of a contained `ProbabilisticBranch-Transition`). The FOD propagates upwards the hierarchy of nested action sequences, until it reaches the component-level `ResourceDemandingSEFF` and becomes a *component-level FOD occurrence*. After that, the failure propagates to the calling component and further upwards, until it finally reaches the system border as a *system-level FOD occurrence*. The only way to interrupt this propagation chain is a `RecoveryBlockAction` situated within the hierarchy that handles the FOD occurrence and prevents it from further propagation, thereby representing a *point of recovery* (POR, see Table 4.1 and Section 4.7). In the audio hosting example, a local FOD occurrence at the `InternalAction` "ParseWebRequest" (see Figure 2.9) leads to an FOD of the surrounding `ResourceDemandingSEFF` and thus to a component-level FOD of the "WebFrontend" component, which in turn constitutes a system-level FOD occurring at the `EntryLevelSystemCall` to "IWebFrontend.DownloadCollection" within the batch mode usage scenario (assuming the behavioural view as shown in Figure 4.1). In conclusion, each FOD occurrence along the service execution path is either handled within the hierarchy of nested action sequences or leads to a system-level FOD and thus ultimately to a failed usage scenario run.

As Table 4.1 shows, the failure potentials of individual PPOFs are given as an input to the approach in terms of software and network FOD probabilities, as well as MTTF and MTTR values for hardware resources. Based on this information, the reliability evaluation (Chapter 5) determines the probabilities of system-level FOD occurrences, and ultimately the envisioned success probability of a usage scenario run. The following sections discuss all reliability-specific modelling constructs in detail.

4.2 Failure-on-Demand Types

In the conception of PCM-REL, any FOD occurring during service execution is of a certain *FOD type*. The notion of FOD types allows for a differentiated reliability evaluation calculating the occurrence probability of each FOD type rather than the overall FOD occurrence probability only (see Section 5.1.1). Moreover, when specifying `RecoveryBlockActions` as PORs in the control flow, it is important to determine the exact types of FODs that can be handled by these (see Section 4.7). The differentiation of multiple FOD types is one of the distinguishing features of PCM-REL compared to many other ASRP approaches that only consider a single type of failure (see Section 7.4).

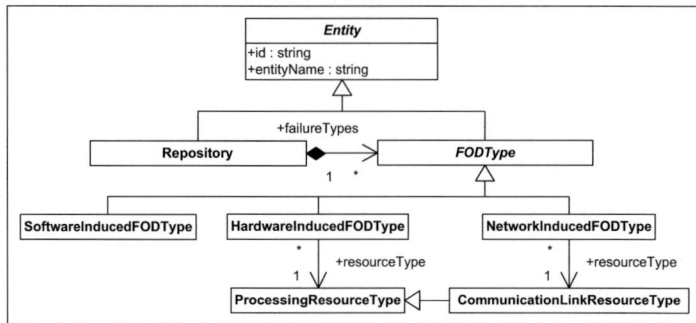

Figure 4.3: Meta-Model for Failure-on-Demand Type Specifications

The PCM-REL meta-model explicitly captures FOD types through corresponding meta-model classes, as shown in Figure 4.3. On the highest level, an abstract class FODType inherits from the common Entity class, thereby gaining an *entityName* and an *id*. FODTypes are specified within and belong to a PCM-REL Repository. Like data types, they constitute a common ground that is shared by all component developers contributing to the Repository. PPOFs and PORs within behavioural specifications can only refer to FODTypes that have been specified in the Repository.

The first level of differentiation below the general FODType is given through the SoftwareInducedFODType, the HardwareInducedFODType and the NetworkInducedFODType. These classes correspond to the main failure dimensions in IT systems, and they are used to describe FOD occurrences caused by software-level, hardware-level and network-level failure potentials, respectively. The distinction of dimensions assures that each PPOF can only be associated with appropriate failure causes as shown in Table 4.1. Moreover, prediction results show which dimension contributes to the overall failure potential of the system to what extend, thereby delivering valuable additional information to system designers.

Within each of the three categories, concrete FOD types are specified through instantiating the meta-model classes. For SoftwareInducedFOD-

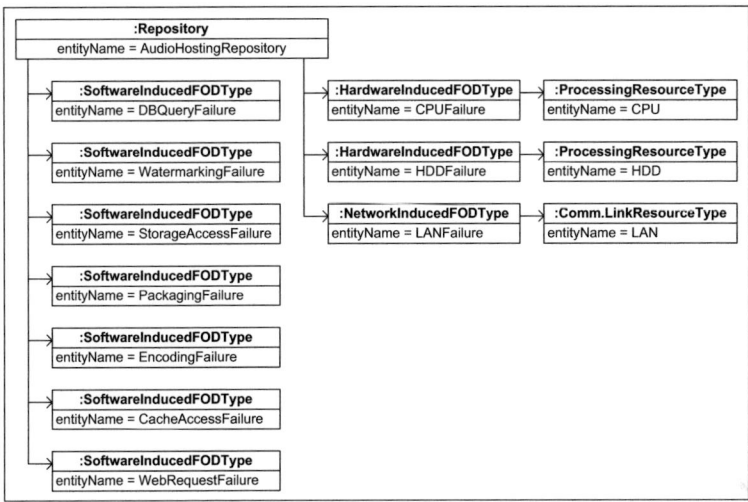

Figure 4.4: Failure-on-Demand Type Specifications in the Audio Hosting Example

Types, system designers are free to decide about the level of modelling granularity (see Section 3.4). They may use the FOD type instantiation to create sub categories as they wish. Examples for possible sub categories include the failure-causing software layer (e.g. application-level, middleware, operating system), the failing task (e.g. wrong computation result, synchronisation error) and the consequence of failure (e.g. minor, critical, catastrophic). Alternatively, instantiated failure types may be specific to the system under study (such as an audio file encryption failure in the audio hosting example). HardwareInducedFODTypes are restricted to the ProcessingResourceTypes that have been defined in the model; each HardwareInducedFODType describes a FOD occurrence caused by an unavailable hardware resource of the corresponding type. Similarly, a NetworkInducedFODType is used to describe network transmission failures due to unreliable LinkingResources of the associated CommunicationLinkResourceType.

Figure 4.4 shows the specified FOD types for the audio hosting example. The model distinguishes several SoftwareInducedFODTypes according to the main tasks during the upload and download of audio files, namely the processing of user requests through the web interface ("WebRequestFailure"), the audio processing ("EncodingFailure", "WatermarkingFailure", "PackagingFailure"), as well as the data storage and retrieval ("DBQueryFailure", "StorageAccessFailure", "CacheAccessFailure"). Moreover, the Repository contains two HardwareInducedFODTypes "CPUFailure" and "HDDFailure", according to the CPU and HDD resources contained in the audio hosting ResourceEnvironment (see Section 2.7.4). Finally, a NetworkInducedFODType "LANFailure" represents communication failures of the modelled "LANConnection".

4.3 Software Failure Potentials

This section describes how software-level failure potentials are specified within a PCM-REL architectural model. These failure potentials stem from faults that are included in the implementation of the software components involved in service execution. A fault may be a bug introduced by a programming error, the realization of a flawed requirements specification, or a natural limitation of a computational procedure (such as a virus detection algorithm with an imperfect success rate). As software failures are subject to multiple types of uncertainty (see Section 2.3), the thesis follows the path of the Cheung model (Section 2.5) and many other subsequent ASRP approaches by using probabilistic abstractions in terms of independent "per-visit" failure probabilities to specify software failure potentials. For clarity of presentation, the thesis denotes these as failure-on-demand (FOD) probabilities (see Section 3.1).

While the Cheung model associates each software component in the architecture with one FOD probability, this method may be too inflexible in practice. The specification of potential points of failure (PPOF) during service execution is associated with computational tasks rather than component borders. Some components carry out many individual tasks; other components provide only thin wrappers for existing functionality. Therefore, the thesis allows for a flexible specification of PPOFs by assigning FOD probabilities to individual InternalActions, which represent any data processing or other computational steps during service execution (see Section 2.7.2).

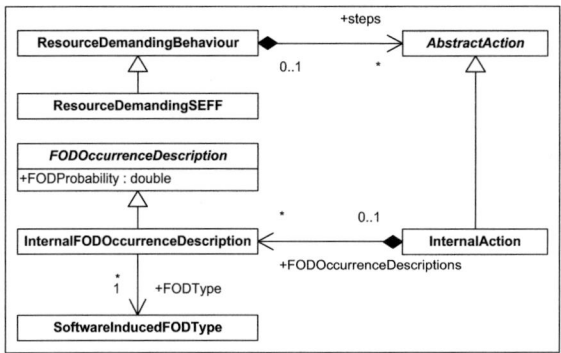

Figure 4.5: Meta-Model for Software Failure Potentials

Figure 4.5 shows the PCM-REL meta-model constructs involved in the specification of software failure potentials. Component developers specify such potentials through InternalFODOccurrenceDescriptions, which inherit from the abstract base class FODOccurrenceDescription. These descriptions are associated with InternalActions, which thereby become PPOFs within the action sequence of a ResourceDemandingBehaviour, or in particular, a ResourceDemandingSEFF. Each Internal-FODOccurrenceDescription includes a FODProbability between 0.0 and 1.0 and references a SoftwareInducedFODType, specifying that a software-induced FOD of the given type may occur with the given probability upon the execution of the associated InternalAction. If an InternalAction contains multiple InternalFODOccurrenceDescriptions, then each description must reference another SoftwareInducedFODType. The InternalAction either executes successfully or results in one of the specified SoftwareInducedFODTypes. The cumulated FOD probability of all InternalFODOccurrenceDescriptions of an InternalAction represents its overall software failure potential and must not exceed 1.0. If the InternalAction does not contain any InternalFODOccurrence-Descriptions, it may only fail due to unavailable required hardware resources (see Section 4.4).

The association of software FOD probabilities with InternalActions allows for specifying a component service operation as a sequence of executed PPOFs. The sequence is structured through control flow constructs such as BranchActions and LoopActions, with branch transition probabilities and loop iteration counts specified depending on properties of service invocation input parameters and component configuration parameters. The individual InternalActions are atomic entities within the behavioural specification; no details about the represented code are revealed, and no context information is considered when evaluating the associated FOD probabilities. Modellers are free to adjust the granularity of the behavioural specification such that independent estimates for all InternalFODOccurrenceDescriptions of each InternalAction can feasibly be obtained. Alternatively, if the model shall distinguish PPOFs at fine granularity but only coarse-grained estimates are available, individual PPOFs can be aggregated to groups, and estimations can be done for the groups rather than the individual PPOFs. In all cases, existing uncertainties with respect to input estimations can be tackled by sensitivity analyses (as done for the audio hosting service in Section 6.4.2). The estimates themselves can be determined through methods such as the ones discussed in Section 2.3. In the thesis, the Astaro ASG case study (Section 6.5) includes the estimation of software FOD probabilities for an industrial IT system based on existing qualitative and statistical failure data.

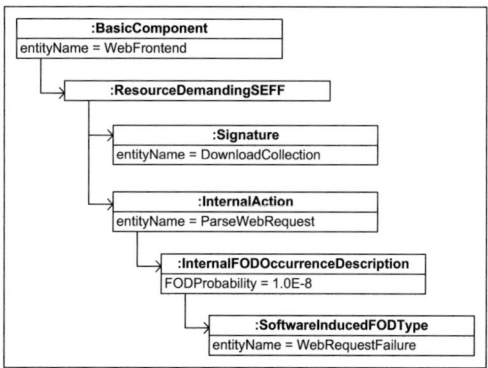

Figure 4.6: A Software Failure Potential in the Audio Hosting Example

To illustrate the specification of software failure potentials, Figure 4.6 shows how the "DownloadCollection" service operation in the audio hosting example (see Figure 2.9) is enriched by a corresponding annotation. The BasicComponent "WebFrontend" references a ResourceDemandingSEFF that describes the behaviour of the component when "Download-Collection" is invoked. Within the action sequence of the ResourceDemandingSEFF, there is an InternalAction "ParseWebRequest" which represents the initial processing of user requests. To express that this processing may lead to a FOD occurrence of type "WebRequestFailure" (see Figure 4.4), an InternalFODOccurrenceDescription is added to the InternalAction that references this FOD type. A FOD probability of 10^{-8} indicates that a visit to "ParseWebRequest" during service execution is expected to result in a "WebRequestFailure" in one out of 10^{-8} cases on average. Overall, the audio hosting model contains 19 system-internal software failure potentials, each associated with an individual InternalAction and mapped to the SoftwareInducedFODTypes as shown in Figure 4.4. The corresponding FOD probabilities are set to 10^{-8} (for InternalFODOccurrenceDescriptions referring to "WebRequestFailures") or 10^{-6} (for other FOD types). In the example, illustrative

FOD probabilities are chosen as a basis for demonstrating the capabilities of PCM-REL in the audio hosting case study (see Section 6.4).

4.4 Hardware Failure Potentials

One contribution of PCM-REL is that it does not only consider FOD occurrences due to software faults, but also due to unavailable hardware resources. Both sources of failure add to the overall risk of a system-level FOD occurrence, as discussed in Section 3.1. Related approaches that do not consider hardware unavailability effects either produce over-optimistic prediction results (assuming perfect hardware) or implicitly encode the impact of unavailable hardware resources into software-level FOD probabilities, thus strongly reducing the reusability of software component specifications. PCM-REL includes the specification of hardware resources as part of its resource environment model (see Section 2.7.4) and allows for associating an independent failure potential with each hardware resource. A corresponding specification of hardware usage during service execution allows for determining the likeliness that hardware unavailability actually leads to user-perceived FOD occurrences.

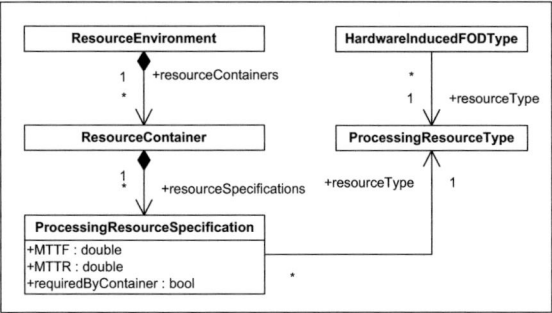

Figure 4.7: Meta-Model for Hardware Failure Potentials

Figure 4.7 depicts the part of the PCM-REL meta-model that allows for the specification of hardware resources and their failure potentials. System deployers specify the `ResourceEnvironment` including a set of `ResourceContainers`. A `ResourceContainer` represents a computing node and contains several hardware resources, whose characteristics are captured through `ProcessingResourceSpecifications`. Each `ProcessingResourceSpecification` references a `ProcessingResourceType` and includes an MTTF and MTTR value. Hence, PCM-REL follows the well-established failure model as presented in Section 2.2 for each individual hardware resource. The MTTF and MTTR values are specified in abstract *time units*, which implicitly translate to concrete time units (such as seconds, hours or days) in the context of a concrete PCM instance. Generally, the values must be positive. As an exception to this rule, system deployers may set both the MTTF and MTTR values of a certain resource to zero, in order to express that this resource never fails. The referenced `ProcessingResourceType` can be selected from a list of predefined types. Currently, PCM-REL supports "CPU" and "HDD" (hard disk drive) as the two main types of hardware resources. Alternatively, modellers can define custom `ProcessingResourceTypes` for a specific PCM-REL instance. A further boolean attribute `requiredByContainer` of the `ProcessingResourceSpecification` expresses how the operation of the surrounding `ResourceContainer` depends on the resource, according to the possible cases discussed in Section 3.1. If *requiredByContainer =* *true*, the resource is central to the container, and the container cannot operate while the resource is unavailable. A value *requiredByContainer =* *false* indicates that the overall container keeps operating even if the resource is unavailable.

Beyond capturing the hardware failure potentials themselves, the semantics of PCM-REL must clearly specify the impact of hardware unavailability on the control and data flow during service execution. Figure 4.8 shows the involved meta-model classes. The impact of hardware

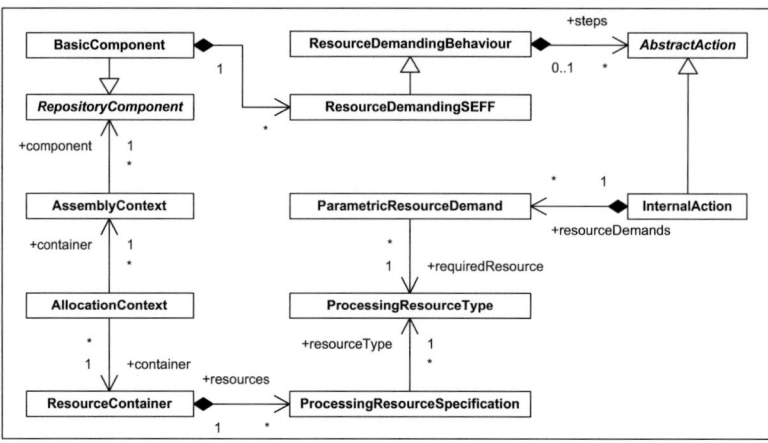

Figure 4.8: Meta-Model for Impacts of Hardware Failure Potentials on Service Execution

failure potentials depends on the question if a hardware resource is required for the operation of the surrounding `ResourceContainer` as specified through the `requiredByContainer` attribute of the corresponding `ProcessingResourceSpecification`. If this attribute is set to *true*, any `BasicComponent` instantiated in the system through an `AssemblyContext` and allocated to the container through an `AllocationContext` is only operational when the resource is available. Hence, the unavailability of the resource leads to a hardware-induced FOD occurrence of the corresponding `HardwareInducedFODType` for any `ExternalCallAction` invoking a service operation of the non-operational component. If the resource is not strictly required for the operation of the container, an FOD occurs only if the resource is specifically requested by an `InternalAction` while being unavailable. To this end, `InternalActions` may specify a list of `ProcessingResourceTypes` which they require for their execution, each embedded into a corresponding `ParametricResourceDemand`. The connection of the abstract `ProcessingResurceType` to a concrete `ProcessingResourceSpecification` is given through the allocation of the executing `BasicComponent` to the `ResourceContainer`. The un-availability of a resource requested by an `InternalAction` leads to a hardware-induced FOD of the corresponding `HardwareInducedFODType`. Hence, `InternalActions` may fail either due to software faults (as discussed in Section 4.3) or due to unavailable hardware resources. If an `InternalAction` requires multiple unavailable resources, it fails with a `HardwareInducedFODType` that corresponds to one of the unavailable resources.

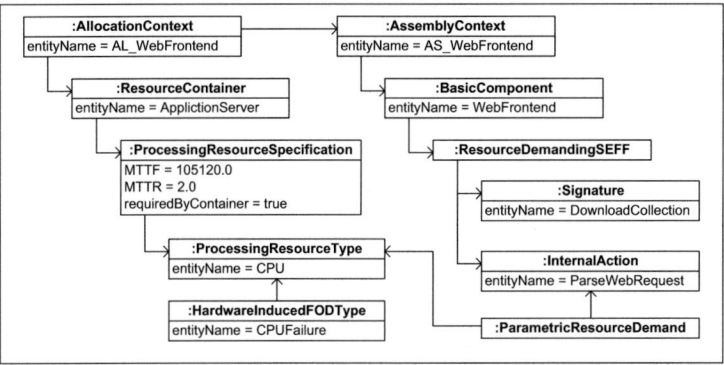

Figure 4.9: A Hardware Failure Potential in the Audio Hosting Example

In the audio hosting example, the "WebFrontend" `BasicComponent` is instantiated through the "AS_WebFrontend" `AssemblyContext` and allocated through the "AL_WebFrontend" `AllocationContext` to the "ApplicationServer" `ResourceContainer` (see Figure 2.13). As Figure 4.9 shows, the container includes a `ProcessingResourceSpecification` for the "CPU" `ProcessingResourceType`. The CPU is required by the container and has a MTTF of 105 120 hours or 12 years and a MTTR of 2 hours. Overall, both the "ApplicationServer" and the "DatabaseServer" have a CPU and a HDD with MTTF values of 12 years (for the CPUs) and 4 years (for the HDDs). Each server strictly requires its CPU to operate but can tolerate the HDD (which holds user data only) being unavailable. As the figure shows, the unavailability of the "ApplicationServer" CPU leads to a "CPUFailure" whenever the "WebFrontend.DownloadCollection" service operation is invoked because the "WebFrontend" is allocated to the "ApplicationServer". In the example, the operation would fail even if the CPU was not strictly required by the container, because it includes the InternalAction "ParseRequest", which is always executed as part of the operation (see Figure 2.9), and which explicitly requires the "CPU" ProcessingResourceType through its included ParametricResourceDemand. Considering both Figures 4.6 and 4.9, there are three possible outcomes of the execution of "ParseRequest": the execution either succeeds, or it fails with a SoftwareInducedFODType ("WebRequestFailure"), or with a HardwareInducedFODType ("CPUFailure").

4.5 Network Failure Potentials

Beyond software and hardware failure potentials, PCM-REL also considers the possibility of network transmission failures, which may have significant impact on the system's reliability, depending on the degree of distribution of the application, as well as the amount of required remote communication. PCM-REL does not aim to provide a comprehensive network simulation, nor does it consider the specifics of network devices and protocols. Instead, the approach considers the overall probabilities that communication messages sent over network links get lost or corrupted, thereby preventing service execution from being successful.

Figure 4.10 shows the involved meta-model constructs. LinkingResources represent network links over which service invocation and return messages travel between the software components of the system. Each LinkingResource contains a CommunicationLinkResourceSpecification with a FODProbability attribute. The FODProbability is a value between 0.0 and 1.0 and represents the probability that a message sent over this link is corrupted or lost, which may happen due to a number of

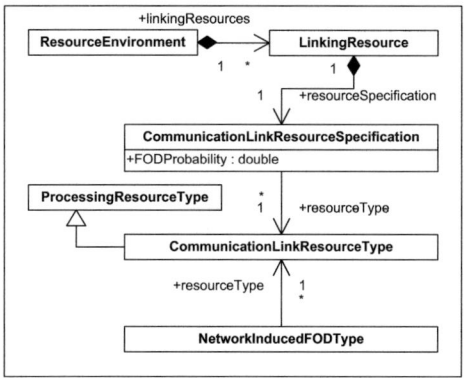

Figure 4.10: Meta-Model for Network Failure Potentials

reasons including communication overload, transmission protocol errors, physical interference of transmission lines, or unavailability of transmission devices. The specified FODProbability is evaluated independently for each message transport. The CommunicationLinkResourceSpecification references a CommunicationLinkResourceType. By default, PCM-REL supports one CommunicationLinkResourceType "LAN". In the PCM-REL behavioural specification, ExternalCallActions represent invocations of other component services. A network-induced FOD occurs if an ExternalCallAction refers to a component that is allocated to a remote ResourceContainer, and if either the invocation message or the return message is not correctly transported over the corresponding LinkingResource. Hence, ExternalCallActions are the PPOFs with respect to network failure potentials.

To illustrate the specification of network failures potentials, Figure 4.11 shows an ExternalCallAction "RetrieveFileCall" that is part of the "RetrieveFiles" service operation of the "AudioManagement" component. "RetrieveFileCall" refers to the "RetrieveFile" operation provided by the "AudioDBAccess" component. Both components are allocated on different ResourceContainers "ApplicationServer" and "DatabaseServer", as in-

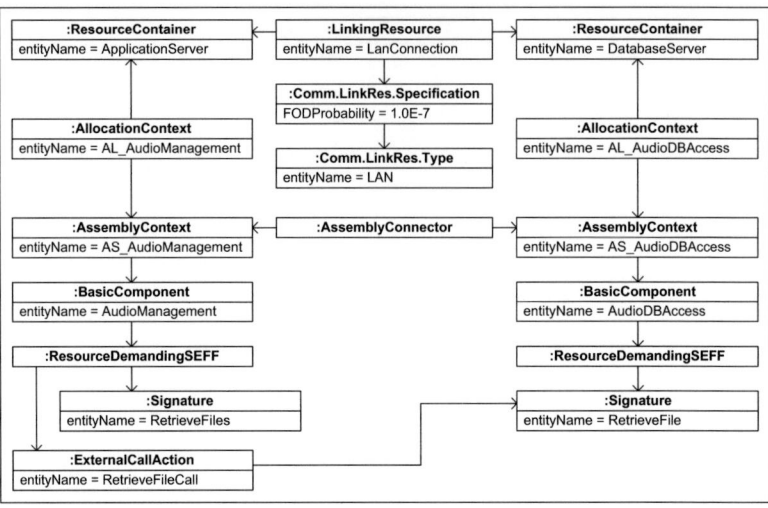

Figure 4.11: Network Reliability Specifications in the Audio Hosting Example

dicated by the corresponding AssemblyContexts and AllocationContexts. The two ResourceContainers are connected through a LinkingResource "LANConnection", which includes a CommunicationLinkResourceSpecification with a failure probability of 10^{-7} and a reference to the CommunicationLinkResourceType "LAN". Overall, the specification indicates that the message transports over "LanConnection" required for the invocation of (and return from) "AudioDBAccess.RetrieveFile" through "RetrieveFileCall" may fail with a probability of 10^{-7}, leading to a network-induced FOD occurrence at "RetrieveFileCall".

4.6 System-External Failure Potentials

Although an IT system can be completely represented through a PCM-REL instance, the approach also takes into account interdependencies between multiple systems. Such interdependencies are increasingly common in the sense that systems act as users of other systems and invoke their services. However, integrating all systems into a common architectural model may not be feasible due to several reasons. First, the complexity of the overall system landscape may be very high. Second, the individual systems may be provided by different parties, with each party having architectural knowledge only of their own system (in particular, service-oriented architectures may span across multiple providers and organizational boundaries). Therefore, PCM-REL principally focusses on individual systems and their architectures, but includes the possibility of *system-external calls*, invoking services that have to be provided by other systems at run-time.

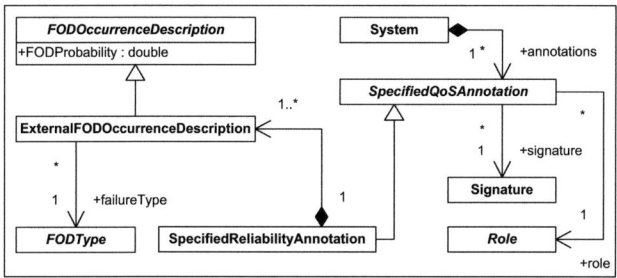

Figure 4.12: Meta-Model for System-External Failure Potentials

The system's reliability is influenced by the reliability of its system-external services, as a FOD occurrence resulting from an external invocation can lead to a FOD of the target service invoked by the system users. A system-external service invocation is represented by an `ExternalCallAction` that does not refer to a service operation provided by another component in the system, but instead references a `RequiredRole` of the modelled `System` (see Section 2.7.3). As Figure 4.12 shows, the `System` references a set of `SpecifiedQoSAnnotations`. Each `SpecifiedQoSAnnotation` refers to an external service operation through a system-required `Role` and a `Signature`. The `SpecifiedReliabilityAnnotation` inherits from `SpecifiedQoSAnnotation` and adds a list of `ExternalFODOccur-`

renceDescriptions, expressing the possibility that certain FODTypes
may occur with given FODProbabilies when the external service operation is invoked. The list of ExternalFODOccurrenceDescriptions
must adhere to the same rules as the InternalFODOccurrenceDescriptions specified for an InternalAction (see Section 4.3): Each description must reference another FOD type, and the cumulated FOD probability
of all descriptions must not exceed 1.0. In contrast to InternalActions,
system-external calls may exhibit all FOD types including Hardware-
InducedFODTypes and NetworkInducedFODTypes, because a FOD of
an external service invocation may have arbitrary reasons. If an external
service operation does not have a corresponding SpecifiedReliabilityAnnotation, the reliability prediction assumes that invocations of this
service operation always succeed.

It is the task of system architects to determine SpecifiedReliabili-
tyAnnotations for the external services of their systems. As these external services may be under the control of third party service providers, there
may be no direct possibilities to change their FOD probabilities, or to estimate the probabilities based on internal knowledge of the providing system
architecture. Rather, the FOD probabilities may be contractually specified
between the providers, or they may be collected from historical data of the
target service provider using the external service.

The System definition of the audio hosting example contains one RequiredRole for using external audio encoding engines rather than built-
in functionality (see Figure 2.11). Figure 4.13 shows how the System is
annotated to account for the involved failure potential. To this end, the
System containes a SpecifiedReliabilityAnnotation that references
its RequiredRole, as well as the "EncodeFile" Signature. Additionally, the annotation specifies an ExternalFODOccurrenceDescription
denoting that any invocation of the external service operation "IEncod-
ing.EncodeFile" may lead to a software-induced FOD occurrence of type
"EncodingFailure" with a probability of 10^{-6}. The specified failure po-

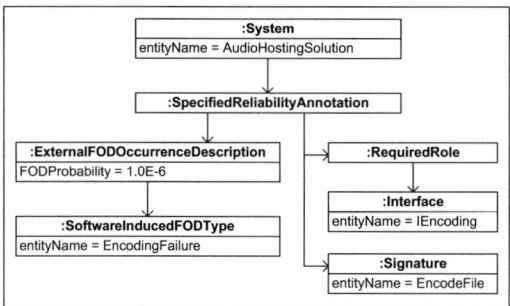

Figure 4.13: System-External Failure Potentials in the Audio Hosting Example

tential is taken into consideration by the reliability evaluation whenever an ExternalCallAction during service execution performs an invocation of the system-external service operation.

4.7 Failure Recovery

All modelling constructs for reliability discussed so far deal with the specification of the various failure potentials and PPOFs of an IT system (see Section 4.1). Thereby, the general assumption is that any FOD occurrence eventually "propagates" to the system border and constitutes a system-level FOD occurrence (as shown in Figure 4.2). In practice, however, IT systems exhibit capabilities for *fault tolerance* (FT). In PCM-REL terminology, FT is the ability to recover from FOD occurrences so that they do not propagate to the system border. Ideally, the user perceives the system as operating failure-free despite local FODs occurring during service execution. As discussed in Section 2.6, a wide variety of FT mechanisms exist that introduce different types of redundancy in the system under study. FT mechanisms may be tailored towards tolerating all kinds of FOD occurrences, including software-induced, hardware-induced and network-induced FODs.

Existing ASRP approaches typically do not provide explicit modelling constructs to consider FT mechanisms (see Section 7.2). Depending on the

97

system under study, an implicit consideration of FT capabilities may be possible through adaptation of certain model annotations such as software FOD probabilities. For example, the FOD probability of the InternalAction "ParseWebRequest" in Figure 4.6 could be changed from 10^{-8} to 0 under the assumption that "ParseWebRequest" has internal FT mechanisms in place to recover from FOD occurrences of type "WebRequestFailure". However, architecture-level FT mechanisms cannot be represented in this implicit way. Rather, they need an explicit representation in the architecture. This is especially true if recovery activities change the high-level control and data flow throughout the architecture, or if components have capabilities to recover from FOD occurrences that have been propagated to them from other components. In such cases, the system's behaviour in the presence of FOD occurrences can only be accurately represented through model constructs that explicitly reflect the activities related to failure recovery.

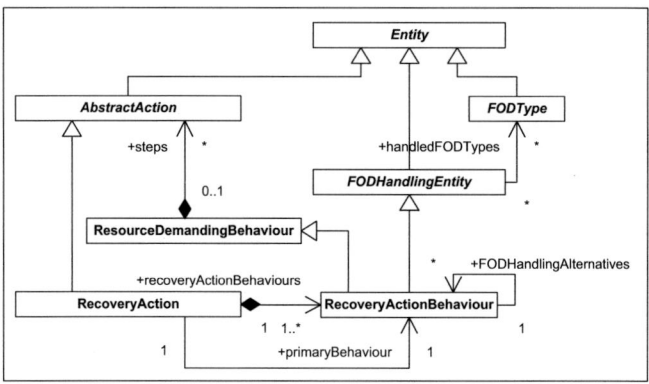

Figure 4.14: Meta-Model for Failure Recovery Specifications

PCM-REL accounts for the need for explicit FT modelling through the RecoveryAction, which is a general construct for recovery from FOD occurrences during service execution. The semantics of this construct include three fundamental aspects of the recovery process, namely (i) stopping the FOD occurrence from its further propagation (according to Figure 4.2), (ii) handling the failure situation through the execution of one or multiple alternative behaviours, and (iii) returning back to normal service execution. Thus, RecoveryActions constitute the points of recovery (POR) in the control and data flow (as listed in Table 4.1). Figure 4.14 shows the involved meta-model constructs. The RecoveryAction inherits from the AbstractAction and includes a list of one or multiple RecoveryActionBehaviours. Being a ResourceDemandingBehaviour, each RecoveryActionBehaviour represents an action sequence within the overall behavioural view as introduced in Section 4.1. Moreover, each behaviour constitutes a FODHandlingEntity, defining a set of handled FODTypes. Within a RecoveryAction, each RecoveryAction-Behaviour may reference other behaviours through the "FODHandlingAlternatives" property. Exactly one of the behaviours is pointed out by the RecoveryAction as its "primaryBehaviour".

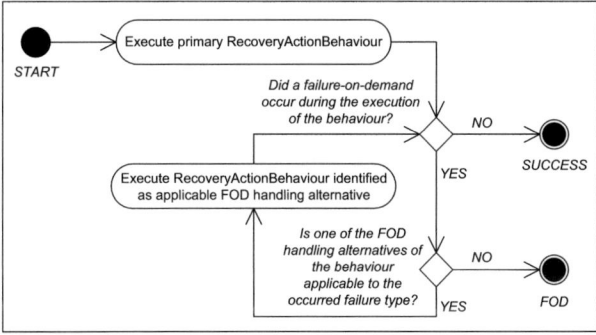

Figure 4.15: Execution Flow through Recovery Actions

Figure 4.15 illustrates the general flow of execution through a Recovery-Action. Upon entering the action, the control flow proceeds to the primary behaviour and executes it. If a FOD occurs, the control flow searches through the "FODHandlingAlternatives" of the primary behaviour. If one of the alternatives is specified to handle the occurred FODType, the execution proceeds with this alternative. If not, the RecoveryAction fails by the occurred FODType. If the primary behaviour executes failure-free, the RecoveryAction is deemed successful and the control flow proceeds to its successor action. As the figure indicates, RecoveryActions may specify multiple stages of recovery so that FOD occurrences during recovery procedures may be handled in turn by other recovery procedures. The RecoveryActionBehaviours within a RecoveryAction constitute a tree with each behaviour referencing a list of successor behaviours by its "FODHandlingAlternatives" property. To ensure a consistent tree structure, none of the behaviours may reference itself as a successor, and no behaviour may be a successor of multiple other behaviours. Furthermore, all successors of a certain behaviour must differ in the FODTypes that they handle. Hence, upon a FOD occurring during the execution of a RecoveryActionBehaviour, its list of "FODHandlingAlternatives" contains at most one applicable successor, which – if existent – will be executed next. The process of moving through the tree of RecoveryActionBehaviours continues until either one behaviour completes failure-free or no more applicable successors exist. In the first case, the RecoveryAction is successful; in the second case, it fails by its last FOD occurrence.

Figures 4.16, 4.17 and 4.18 illustrate typical examples of modelling FT capabilities through RecoveryActions (the audio hosting example does not contains any modelled RecoveryActions by default, but further design alternatives including FT capabilities are introduced in Section 6.4.1). First, Figure 4.16 shows how a *recovery block* (as introduced in Section 2.6) can be represented in the model. The RecoveryActionBehaviours "Main" and "Alternative_i" ($1 \leq i \leq n$) of the RecoveryAction denote the primary behaviour and the alternative behaviours of the recovery block. Each "Alternative_i" handles the same "fodType" to which the whole recovery block is designated, and it references a single successor "Alternative_i+1". The recovery block is left upon either the first successful execution of an "Alternative_i" or a FOD of the last "Alternative_n". Upon any FOD occurrence other than "fodType", the execution directly

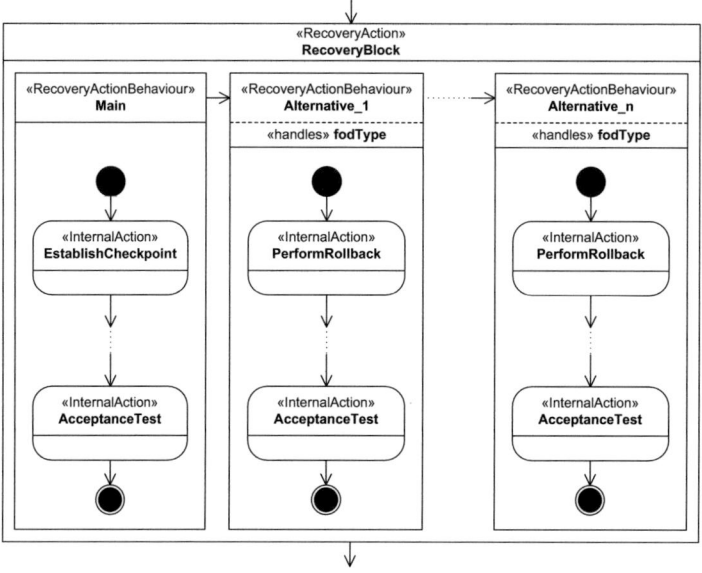

Figure 4.16: Recovery Block Example

leaves the recovery block as it is only designated to handle "fodType" oc-currences. As shown in the figure, modellers can add typical activities of a recovery block such as establishing checkpoints, acceptance testing and roll-backs as `InternalActions` to the model. This may help to un-derstand the modelled recovery block pattern. Furthermore, the activities can be annotated with resource demands and failure probabilities to reflect additional failure potentials during recovery or performance impacts intro-duced by the recovery block (when used in combination with performance prediction for trade-off analyses, see Section 3.1).

Fig. 4.17 shows an example of multiple stages of recovery, where each stage handles a specific FOD type that occurs at the previous stage. In the example, three `RecoveryActionBehaviours` represent a fault-tolerant data retrieval process. The first behaviour accesses a primary data source for data retrieval. Corruption of the data may lead to a software-induced

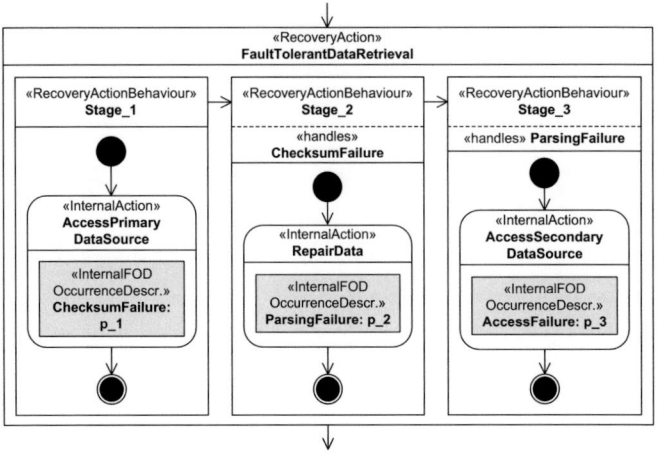

Figure 4.17: Multi-Stage Recovery Example

FOD type "ChecksumFailure" (with probability p_1), upon which a second behaviour tries to repair the retrieved data. The repair requires parsing the data contents and may lead to a "ParsingFailure" (with probability p_2), which is in turn handled by the third behaviour through switching to a secondary data source. If the data cannot be successfully retrieved from the secondary source, no further alternative is available and the whole retrieval process fails. While in the example, the action sequences of each behaviour consist of a single InternalAction, they could also be more complex, comprising ExternalCallActions, BranchActions, LoopActions and other action types as presented in Section 2.7.2.

The third example shown in Fig. 4.18 models a case in which multiple different types of recovery are available depending on the type of FOD occurrence. The example again represents a data retrieval process (the figure omits the action sequences within the behaviours for brevity). The primary behaviour accesses a remote data source to retrieve the data. Multiple FOD types may occur in this scenario, and each one requires a specific handling. First, a network connection problem may prevent successful data

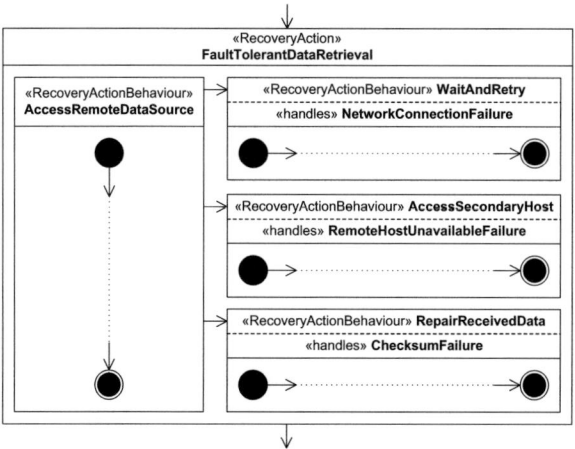

Figure 4.18: Multi-Type Recovery Example

transport; a handling alternative behaviour performs a wait-and-retry strategy to obtain the data. Second, the remote host itself may be unavailable; a corresponding alternative handles this case by switching to a secondary host. Finally, data corruption may be indicated by a "ChecksumFailure" and is handled by a data-repairing alternative. A second FOD occurrence within any of the alternative behaviours leads to a FOD of the whole retrieval process.

While each of the discussed examples illustrates certain possibilities of modelling FT capabilities through RecoveryActions, they can be freely adapted to reflect individual FT mechanisms of an IT system under study. An adaptation can be achieved by combining the demonstrated possibilities (for example, combining multiple recovery types and stages), but also by integrating RecoveryActions with other PCM-REL behavioural constructs. In the context of PMC-REL modelling, RecoveryActions allow for a highly flexible and expressive modelling of FT capabilities, considering the following aspects:

Interplay of software and hardware layers: PCM-REL considers the various interdependencies that may exist between software components and hardware resources when evaluating FT capabilities. A software FT mechanism may be designed to tolerate hardware faults (for example, the RecoveryActionBehaviours in Figure 4.16 may send requests to different replicated servers, and each alternative may test one of the replicas for its availability). Even a "pure" software FT mechanism is affected by the unavailability of the underlying resources. PCM-REL accurately models the boundaries of this impact through the well-defined PPOFs within the control flow (see Section 4.1). For example, if exactly one out of the different recovery stages in Figure 4.17 required a certain hardware resource, only this recovery stage would be affected by the unavailability of the resource.

System usage: The system's usage profile influences the execution and effect of an FT mechanism in various ways. The usage modelling and input parameter propagation of PCM-REL allows for considering the usage dependencies of FT execution, namely the number of executions of a RecoveryAction during a usage scenario run, the control and data flow within each RecoveryActionBehaviour, as well as the success and FOD probabilities of each included invocation of other component service operations.

Limited FT coverage: Considering the *coverage* of an FT mechanism, namely the fraction of failure situations handled by the mechanism, is an important ingredient to realistic FT modelling, as virtually no FT mechanism can handle all potential kinds of FOD occurrences [DT89]. PCM-REL expresses limited FT coverage through the differentiation of multiple FODTypes (see Section 4.2) and a specification of the types that each RecoveryActionBehaviour handles. In the presence of a FOD occurrence, a RecoveryAction cannot be successfully completed if it does not contain a RecoveryActionBehaviour that handles the corresponding FODType.

Imperfect recovery and multiple recovery stages: Any activity that a system performs to recover from a FOD occurrence is itself subject to failure. PCM-REL allows for considering imperfect recovery and its influence on the FT effectiveness. For example, the checkpoint establishing, acceptance testing and roll-back activities in Figure 4.16 can be annotated with InternalFODOccurrenceDescriptions to express their included failure potentials. Furthermore, FOD occurrences during recovery may again be handled by further recovery stages or levels [VPMM05], as illustrated by Figure 4.17.

Multiple recovery types: In many practical cases, a FT mechanism offers multiple recovery procedures, and a concrete procedure is selected based on the characteristics of a concrete failure situation to be handled. This is due to the fact that different failure situations may require completely different strategies for recovery. PCM-REL allows for explicit modelling of the different recovery procedures and their selection based on the occurred FODType, as illustrated by Figure 4.18.

Failure correlation: The effectiveness of a FT mechanism may be severely affected by failure correlation between its different recovery alternatives [AKL90, EL85, LM89, PSMK03]. For example, different versions of a software algorithm tend to fail for the same inputs, even if they are created by different developer teams. PCM-REL allows for a consideration of failure correlation between multiple RecoveryActionBehaviours, as in each behaviour the history of already executed behaviours and occurred FODs is known. For instance, when specifying each "p_i" in Figure 4.17, one can take into account the fact that recovery stages 1 to $i-1$ have already failed[2]. Moreover, multiple RecoveryActionBehaviours that depend on the same hardware resources (either directly or indirectly via ex-

---

[2]Notice that the capabilities of PCM-REL to account for failure correlation are limited due to its included state abstractions. For example, it is not possible to consider stochastic dependencies due to failure correlation between two external service invocations within a RecoveryAction.

ternal component service invocations) are all equally affected by resource unavailability and thus automatically correlated.

Interplay of multiple FT mechanisms: While the great majority of existing work evaluating FT reliability and availability impacts targets individual FT mechanisms and structures (see Section 7.2.2), PCM-REL allows for an integrated consideration of multiple FT mechanisms employed within a component-based software architecture. If multiple components in the architecture exhibit different FT capabilities, they can mutually influence each other's effectiveness in positive or negative ways. For example, a component may propagate internal FOD occurrences through a specific *failure mode* (modelled as a custom FODType in PCM-REL) to its callers. FT capabilities of the callers are only effective if they are prepared to handle the received failure mode. If multiple components are designed to work together, their FT capabilities can complement each other, or multiple components can join a co-operative effort to handle a certain failure situation. Such joint FT capabilities can be expressed in PCM-REL through multiple RecoveryActions in different components and through custom FODTypes propagated between the components.

4.8 Implementation

This section briefly describes the implemented tool environment for reliability modelling with PCM-REL. The implementation is based on the existing *PCM Workbench* [FZI12] for PCM architectural modelling and analysis. The Workbench is an Eclipse Rich Client Platform application (RCP, see [Ecl12b]); Figure 4.19 shows a screenshot of the environment. The PCM meta-model, as well as the PCM-REL extensions, have been created using the Eclipse Modeling Framework (EMF, see [Ecl12a]). Thanks to this technological base, the user can create PCM-REL instances through tree-structured model editors, with each of the PCM's sub models (see Section 2.7) being represented by a specific EMF editor. Moreover, graph-

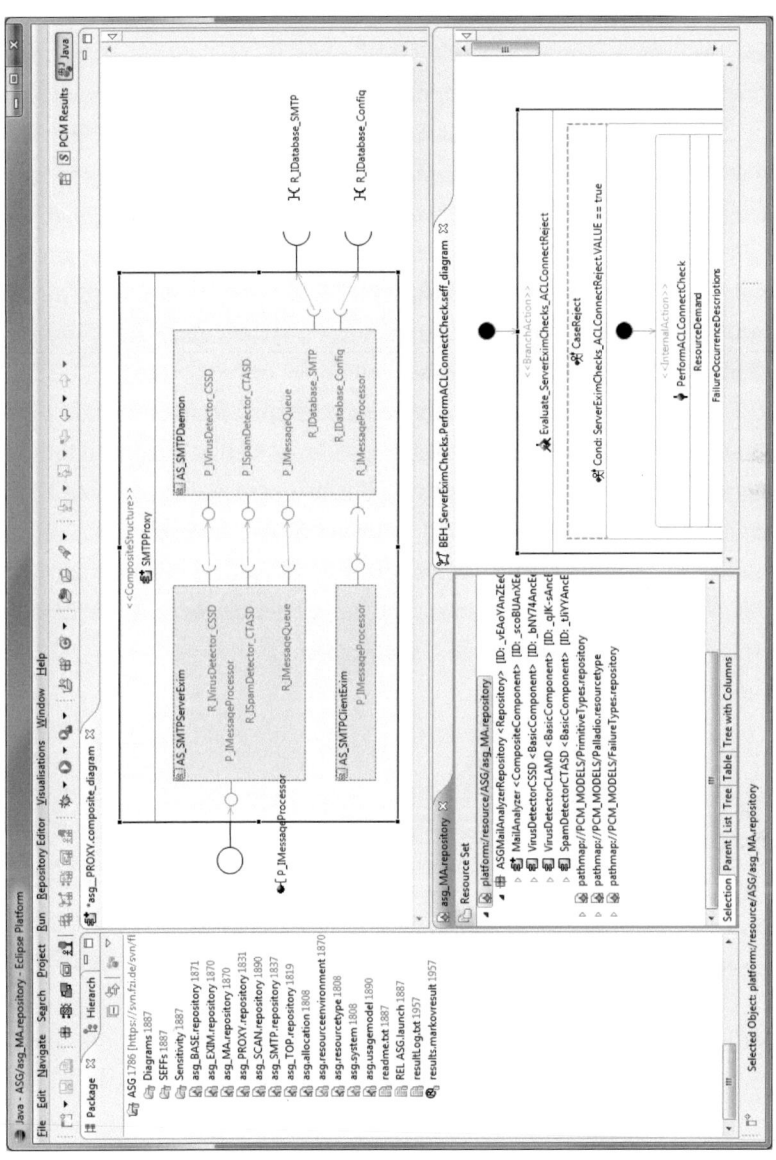

Figure 4.19: PCM-REL Modelling Environment

ical editors for various model parts have been realized using the Eclipse Graphical Modeling Framework (GMF, see [Ecl12c]), allowing for comfortable model creation and editing. The figure shows different views on a PCM-REL instance and its parts, including a listing of model files and directories (left-hand side), a graphical system model editor (upper part), a tree-structured repository model editor (lower middle part) and a graphical editor for ResourceDemandingSEFFs (lower right part). The separation of the PCM-REL instance in multiple model files allows for reusing model parts for multiple architectural variations of a system under study (for example, multiple PCM-REL System definitions can reuse the same PCM-REL Repository definition). Advanced modelling features include automated consistency checks for created models, as well as integrated browsing of model contents across individual model parts in the provided EMF editors. In conclusion, the PCM Workbench with integrated PCM-REL extensions provides a comprehensive graphical tool environment for reliability modelling of IT systems. For further details about the reliability evaluation of the created models, see Section 5.5.

5 PCM-REL Reliability Evaluation

Once a complete PCM-REL instance has been created specifying the component-based architecture of a system under study and its included failure potentials (see Section 4), PCM-REL provides the capabilities for automated evaluation of the model and delivers the prediction of the system's reliability as a result. The main outcome of the evaluation is the probability of a successful (in other words, failure-free) progression through a specified PCM-REL usage scenario. In analogy to related work, PCM-REL uses discrete-time Markov chains (DTMCs) in order to represent the system under study and to predict its reliability. DTMCs have been introduced in Section 2.4 and are a well-established means for architecture-based software reliability prediction (ASRP). However, while other approaches use DMTCs to represent software components and the transfer of control between them (see Section 2.5), PCM-REL additionally reflects the user behaviour, the intra-component (high-level) control flow, the state of the system's hardware resources and multiple failure modes through DTMCs. This representation allows for a much more differentiated analysis, but it may also lead to significantly larger DTMC models. To assure the feasibility of DTMC creation and evaluation, PCM-REL takes three measures. First, system engineers don't need to go through the laborious and error-prone process of manually creating DTMCs according to a given set of rules. Instead, the DTMCs are automatically derived through a model-to-model transformation from the design-oriented PCM-REL meta-model, which is called *Markov transformation* in the following. Second, the approach realizes the transformation through a time- and space-efficient transformation algorithm. This algorithm exploits specific structural properties of a given PCM-REL instance and produces a very compact DTMC as its result. Third, the approach offers configuration options which speed up the evaluation on the cost of prediction accuracy or granularity of results, allowing for a flexible adaptation to the requirements of a specific application scenario and the complexity of the underlying PCM-REL instance. In conclusion, PCM-REL provides a fine-grained reliability evaluation that is fully automated and employs an efficient algorithm to realize the underlying Markov transformation in a flexibly configurable manner.

This chapter discusses the process of predicting a system's reliability through evaluation of a PCM-REL instance. First, Section 5.1 gives an overview of the process and discusses methodological aspects. Sections 5.2 and 5.3 then present the two major building blocks of the Markov transformation, namely the evaluation of system hardware states and system behaviour. Section 5.4 investigates the complexity of the evaluation procedures, before Section 5.5 briefly introduces the corresponding implementation.

5.1 PCM-REL Evaluation Overview

This section provides an overview of the concepts and methodology of the reliability evaluation as done by PCM-REL. The evaluation uses DTMCs to represent IT systems and their failure potentials. Hence, it is called *Markov analysis* in the following. Although basic semantics and solution methods of DTMCs are well established (see Section 2.4), the representation of an IT system architecture and its failure potentials through a DTMC, as well as an efficient handling of this DTMC, are highly context-specific problems, and the PCM-REL Markov analysis provides unique solutions to these problems.

The discussion starts with an overview of the Markov analysis steps, results and configuration options in Section 5.1.1, followed by an introduction to the employed DTMC meta-model and structural properties of cre-

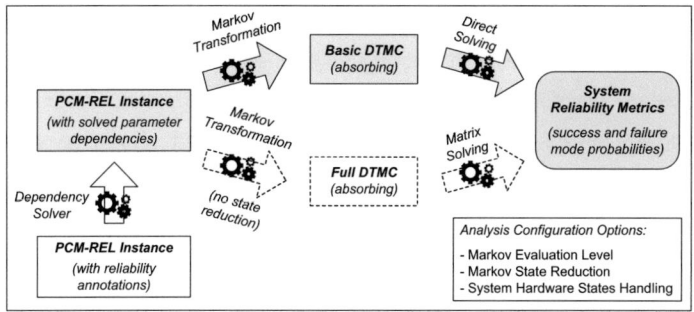

Figure 5.1: PCM-REL Markov Analysis Overview

ated DTMCs in Section 5.1.2. Finally, Section 5.1.3 outlines the Markov
transformation algorithm and specifies its basic operations.

5.1.1 PCM-REL Markov Analysis

Figure 5.1 gives an overview of the PCM-REL Markov analysis and its
most important configuration options. This analysis is carried out for reliability evaluation during system design iterations (see Section 3.2). It builds
upon the work of the dependency solver, which resolves all parameter dependencies contained in the model to concrete values or probability distributions (see Section 2.7.6). At the core of the analysis is the Markov transformation, generating an absorbing DTMC from a PCM-REL instance. The
transformation uses a proprietary DTMC meta-model as its target, which
accounts for the specific PCM-REL context (see Section 5.1.2). Afterwards, a solving procedure determines the system's reliability metrics from
the DTMC. The figure shows two alternative ways to conduct the analysis.
In the default case (shown in grey), the Markov transformation includes
inherent *state reduction operations* (see Section 5.1.3). A state reduction
decreases the number of states in the DTMC without changing the results
of the analysis. The transformation finally produces a *basic DTMC*, namely
a DTMC with a basic structure (see Figure 5.3b). The basic DTMC allows

for *direct solving* without the need for further calculation – the results of the analysis are equal to the transition probabilities of the DTMC. As an alternative, the Markov transformation can be performed without any state reductions. In this case, it produces a *full* (and potentially large) DTMC, which can be tackled through *matrix solving* as discussed in Section 2.4 (calculating the absorption probabilities of the DTMC). This second alternative is far less efficient than the first one, but it can be used to learn about the structure of the resulting DTMC for debugging purposes and for comparison with other DTMC-based reliability prediction approaches. The PCM-REL user decides between the two alternatives through a configuration option named "Markov State Reduction".

Regarding the analysis results, PCM-REL predicts the probability of a successful run through a specified usage scenario, as denoted in Section 4.1. More concretely, the analysis results comprise the occurrence probabilities of all possible outcomes of the random experiment constituted by a usage scenario run. The two main outcomes of the random experiment are *Success* – namely, completion of the scenario run without any system-level failure-on-demand (FOD) occurrence – and *Failure* (meaning that at least one system-level FOD occurs). The analysis further differentiates the *Failure* outcome into multiple *failure modes* (meaning possible categories or types of failure) and evaluates the occurrence probability of each failure mode. The set of considered failure modes follows from the FODTypes that have been specified for the PCM-REL instance (see Section 4.2), as well as a user-selected *evaluation level* (as indicated through the configuration option "Markov Evaluation Level" in Figure 5.1), which balances the time needed for the analysis and the granularity of its results.

Table 5.1 shows the available evaluation levels. At the fastest and most basic level 0 (or *Single*), the analysis only considers a single failure mode. This level is suited for cases in which only the probability of success versus the general probability of failure-on-demand is of interest. Level 1 (or *Category*) distinguishes between FOD occurrences induced by software,

Evaluation Level	Distinguished Failure Modes	Markov Analysis
0 (Single)	• FOD	Simplified (no failure recovery)
1 (Category)	• Software-induced FOD • Hardware-induced FOD • Network-induced FOD	Simplified (no failure recovery)
2 (Type)	• Software-induced FOD *per* SoftwareInducedFODType • Hardware-induced FOD *per* ProcessingResourceType • Network-induced FOD *per* CommunicationLinkResourceType	Full

3 (PointOf-Failure)	• Internal software-induced FOD
	    per SoftwareInducedFODType *per* InternalAction
	• Internal hardware-induced FOD
	    per ProcessingResourceType *per* ResourceContainer
	• Internal network-induced FOD
	    per CommunicationLinkResourceType *per* LinkingResource
	• External software-induced FOD
	    per SoftwareInducedFODType *per* Role *per* Signature
	• External hardware-induced FOD
	    per ProcessingResourceType *per* Role *per* Signature
	• External network-induced FOD
	    per CommunicationLinkResourceType *per* Role *per* Signature
		Full

Table 5.1: Markov Evaluation Levels

hardware and network, thereby indicating the individual failure potential of each of these dimensions. Level 2 (or *Type*) further distinguishes the individual user-defined SoftwareInducedFODTypes, as well as the failure-inducing ProcessingResourceTypes as well as CommunicationLink-ResourceTypes. Finally, level 3 (or *PointOfFailure*) provides the most detailed analysis, differentiating all failing InternalActions, failure-causing ResourceContainers and LinkingResources, as well as the individual Roles and Signatures that cause system-external service failures. As a general distinction, levels 0 and 1 use a predefined set of failure modes, while levels 2 and 3 use an instance-specific set of failure modes.

The different granularities of the evaluation levels influence the relationship between FODTypes and failure modes. At level 2, each FODType of a PCM-REL instance corresponds to one distinguished failure mode in the Markov analysis. At levels 0 and 1, multiple FODTypes are aggregated to one failure mode. In contrast, each FODType may be related to multiple failure modes at level 3, if the PCM-REL instance contains multiple potential points of failure (PPOF) where this FODType can occur. As a consequence, RecoveryBlockActions (see Section 4.7) are fully evaluated at levels 2 and 3 only. At the other levels 0 and 1, the distinguished failure modes are too coarse-grained to determine if a RecoveryBlockAlternativeBehaviour handles a certain FOD occurrence (see Section 5.3.8). Hence, levels 0 and 1 do not consider failure recovery and introduce inaccuracies for PCM-REL instances that include RecoveryBlockActions.

Given a PCM-REL instance with a set of specified usage scenarios $U :=$ $\{U_1, \ldots, U_m\}$ and a selected evaluation level, the Markov analysis determines the corresponding set of failure modes $F := \{F_1, \ldots, F_n\}$ and predicts the occurrence probabilities of each possible outcome per scenario, as shown in Table 5.2. Each scenario is evaluated independently, and the probabilities of all possible outcomes per scenario sum up to 1. As a further illustration, Table 5.3 depicts all distinguished outcomes for the batch mode usage scenario of the audio hosting example (see Section 1.5) under all possible evaluation levels. As for all PCM-REL instances, the analysis predicts the overall success and failure probabilities at level 0 and distinguishes the main FOD dimensions at level 1. At level 2, all specified FODTypes (see Figure 4.4) are individually considered, leading to 7 software-induced and 2 hardware-induced failure modes, as well as 1 network-induced failure mode. Finally, level 3 distinguishes 13 InternalActions where individual software-induced FODs may occur, 4 specified hardware resources which may become unavailable (see Figure 2.13), 1 specified network link and 1 system-external service operation which may result in an "EncodingFailure".

Another element shown in Figure 5.1 is the "System Hardware States Handling" configuration option, which refers to different evaluation variants for the hardware failure potential of the system under study. Section 5.2 discusses these variants in detail.

PCM-REL UsageScenario	Markov Analysis Results					Σ
U_1	P(Success$|U_1$)	P(F$_1|U_1$)	P(F$_2|U_1$)	...	P(F$_n|U_1$)	1.0
U_2	P(Success$|U_2$)	P(F$_1|U_2$)	P(F$_2|U_2$)	...	P(F$_n|U_2$)	1.0
...	...					...
U_m	P(Success$|U_m$)	P(F$_1|U_m$)	P(F$_2|U_m$)	...	P(F$_n|U_m$)	1.0

Table 5.2: Markov Analysis Results

Evaluation Level	Markov Analysis Results ("batch mode" Usage Scenario)
0 (Single)	• [1] P(Success) • [1] P(Failure)
1 (Category)	• [1] P(Success) • [1] P(Software-induced FOD), • [1] P(Hardware-induced FOD) • [1] P(Network-induced FOD)
2 (Type)	• [1] P(Success) • [7] P(WebRequestFailure), P(CacheAccessFailure), P(DBQueryFailure), ... • [2] P(CPUFailure), P(HDDFailure) • [1] P(LANFailure)
3 (PointOf- Failure)	• [1] P(Success) • [13] P(ParseWebRequest-WebRequestFailure), P(CreateWebResponse-WebRequestFailure), ... • [4] P(ApplicationServer-CPUFailure), P(DatabaseServer-CPUFailure), ... • [1] P(LANConnection-LANFailure) • [1] P(IEncoding-Encode-EncodingFailure)

Table 5.3: Distinguished Analysis Results for the Audio Hosting Example

5.1.2 Markov Chain Structure

Figure 5.2 shows the DTMC meta-model used by PCM-REL as the target of the Markov transformation. This meta-model follows a standard DTMC definition as presented in Section 2.4), but it adds a few additional concepts required by PCM-REL. A MarkovChain contains a set of States and Transitions. All three classes inherit a name attribute from Entity. Each transition is directed and connects exactly two states, determined by its fromState and toState attributes, with a given transition probability. Each state has a StateType, which allows certain states to be marked as "Initial", "Success" or "Failure". Additionally, states can contain further information in terms of Labels, each with a key and value attribute. The labels are used to distinguish the individual failure modes

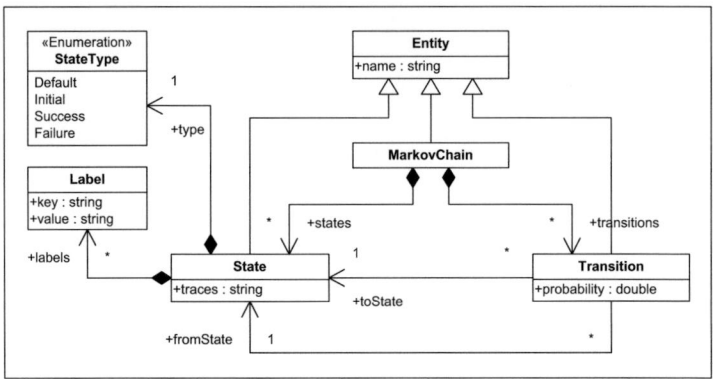

Figure 5.2: DTMC Meta-Model

that are considered by the Markov analysis. Additionally, states can contain `traces`. This feature is used by the Markov transformation to equip each created state with a unique identification, enabling comparisons between multiple created DTMCs. Additional constraints limit the set of valid `MarkovChain` instances: The probabilities of all outgoing transitions of a state must sum up to 1. Each `MarkovChain` has exactly one initial and one success state. The initial state has no incoming transitions. The success and failure states each have exactly one outgoing transition leading back to the same state. Hence, these states are absorbing. They are the only absorbing states of the `MarkovChain`. The DTMC states and transitions are used to represent different aspects of the system under study such as its hardware states, its usage and its behaviour; a detailed discussion is given by Sections 5.2 and 5.3.

All DTMCs generated by the Markov transformation, during intermediate steps or as a final result, exhibit specific structural properties as shown in Figure 5.3. In the general case, a created DTMC corresponds to a *generic structure* (Figure 5.3a). This structure includes an initial state I, a success state S, a set of failure states $\{F_1, \dots, F_n\}$ and an inner region with additional states and transitions. The generic structure constitutes an *absorbing*

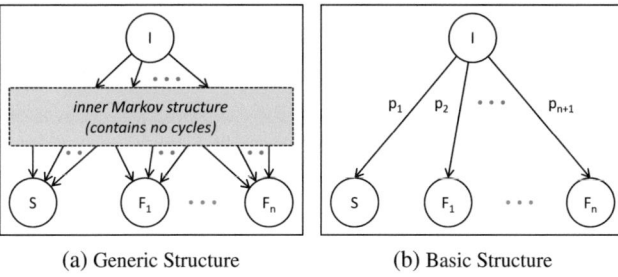

(a) Generic Structure   (b) Basic Structure

Figure 5.3: Markov Chain Structure

DTMC (see Section 2.4) with S and all F_i as its absorbing states (the self-transitions of the absorbing states with probability 1 are omitted from the figure). Moreover, the structure is free of cycles – starting from I, each state can be visited at most once. The Markov transformation creates the DTMCs in a way such that the wanted success and failure mode probabilities are equal to the probabilities of reaching S and F_i starting from I.

Through the application of state reduction operations (Section 5.1.3), each generic DTMC structure can be converted to a *basic structure* (Figure 5.3b). The basic structure (which is itself a special case of the generic structure) contains no inner states and transitions; the only transitions are the ones leading from I to S and all F_i. Hence, the success and failure mode probabilities are equal to the transition probabilities $\{p_1, \ldots, p_{n+1}\}$.

5.1.3 Markov Transformation Algorithm

One factor determining the feasibility of reliability prediction with PCM-REL is the efficiency of the Markov transformation as the central part of the Markov analysis (see Section 5.1.1). To this end, the thesis does not define a pure mapping from the PCM-REL meta-model to the DTMC meta-model, but it describes a time- and space-efficient algorithm that realizes the transformation. The description is given as a set of pseudo-code procedures throughout Sections 5.2 and 5.3, together with corresponding DTMC illustrations. As a foundation, this section specifies basic operations that are repeatedly executed throughout the transformation, and it introduces the general pattern followed by the transformation algorithm. Section 5.4 completes the discussion by examining the transformation's computational complexity.

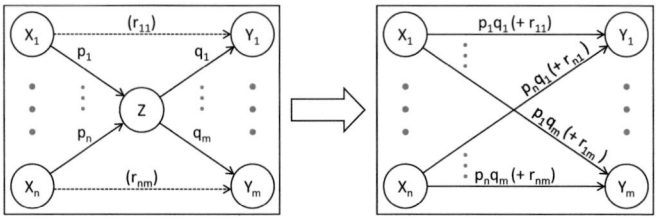

Figure 5.4: Markov State Reduction

```
1   // DTMC:   considered DTMC
2   // Z:      inner state of considered DTMC
3
4   reduce (DTMC, Z){
5     X := getSetOfPredecessorStates (DTMC, Z);
6     Y := getSetOfSuccessorStates (DTMC, Z);
7     n := getNumberOfElements (X);
8     m := getNumberOfElements (Y);
9     for (i = 1; i <= n; i++) {
10      for (j = 1; j <= m; j++) {
11        p_i := getTransitionProbability (DTMC, X(i), Z);
12        q_j := getTransitionProbability (DTMC, Z, Y(j));
13        if (transitionExists (DTMC, X(i), Y(j)) {
14          r_ij := getTransitionProbability (DTMC, X(i), Y(j));
15          setTransitionProbability (DTMC, X(i), Y(j),
16            p_i * q_j + r_ij );
17        } else {
18          createTransition (DTMC, X(i), Y(j), p_i * q_j);
19        }
20        deleteTransition (DTMC, X(i), Z);
21        deleteTransition (DTMC, Z, Y(j));
22      }
23    }
24    deleteNode (DTMC, Z);
25  }
```

Listing 5.1: State Reduction Procedure

The repeatedly performed basic operations of the transformation algorithm are *state reduction*, *state substitution* and *state resolution*. Figure 5.4 shows the state reduction, which may be conducted on each inner state of a generic DTMC structure as shown in Figure 5.3a. The state Z that shall be removed has n incoming transitions from a set of states $X := \{X_1, \ldots, X_n\}$ with probabilities $\{p_1, \ldots, p_n\}$ and m outgoing transitions to a set of states $Y := \{Y_1, \ldots, Y_m\}$ with probabilities $\{q_1, \ldots, q_m\}$. As the DTMC contains no cycles, the sets X and Y are disjoint, and there are no backward transitions from a state in Y to a state in X. However, there may be direct transitions from X to Y (as suggested in the figure). Moreover, the initial, success and failure states may be contained in the two sets. The state reduction removes Z from the chain without changing the probabilities of reaching the success and failure states from the initial state. To this end, Z and its incoming and outgoing transitions are replaced by direct transitions from X to Y according to the procedure shown in Listing 5.1. After the reduction, the overall DTMC still conforms to the generic structure.

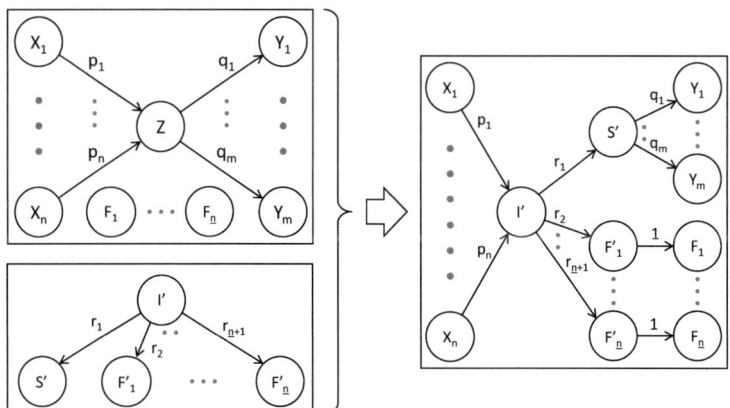

Figure 5.5: Markov State Substitution

Figure 5.5 illustrates the state substitution, which is done for an inner state Z of a generic DTMC. In analogy with the presentation in Figure 5.4, the

119

sets X and Y denote the states with incoming and outgoing transitions to and from Z. Additionally, the figure shows the failure states of the DTMC (although not depicted in the figure, the set of failure states can overlap with Y). The substitution replaces Z with an existing intermediate DTMC that conforms to the basic structure (see Figure 5.3b), according to the procedure depicted in Listing 5.2. The intermediate DTMC provides a refined view on a certain activity or step that was formerly aggregated by Z. The incoming transitions of Z now lead to the intermediate initial state I'. From the intermediate success state S', further states are reachable as they were from Z. However, the failure potential of the intermediate DTMC is directly propagated to a failure of the surrounding DTMC. Hence, a transition with probability 1 is added from each intermediate failure state F'_k to its outer counterpart F_k. The state substitution adds to the overall failure potential and thus changes the success and failure probabilities of the surrounding DTMC, but it does not break its generic structure. The newly introduced states I', S' and F'_k become part of the inner structure of the surrounding DTMC.

The state resolution operation is a combination of the substitution and reduction operations. Given a generic DTMC structure with an inner state Z to replace and an intermediate basic DTMC, the resolution first substitutes Z with the intermediate DTMC as shown in Figure 5.5 and then reduces all intermediate states, namely the initial state I', the success state S' and the failure states F'_k. As a result, the state Z and all intermediate states are completely removed from the surrounding DTMC, which still conforms to its generic structure. Listing 5.3 shows the corresponding procedure.

With the basic transformation operations in place, the transformation algorithm can be described as following a hierarchical DTMC creation pattern, which is outlined by Figure 5.6. As the figure shows, DTMC creation takes place at multiple levels within a hierarchy. At the top level, the transformation considers the possible hardware states of the system. All other levels are devoted to the evaluation of user and system behaviour. The

```
1   // DTMC:        considered DTMC
2   // Z:           inner state of considered DTMC
3   // DTMC_inter:  intermediate DTMC
4
5   substitute(DTMC, Z, DTMC_inter){
6     X := getSetOfPredecessorStates(DTMC, Z);
7     Y := getSetOfSuccessorStates(DTMC, Z);
8     n := getNumberOfElements(X);
9     m := getNumberOfElements(Y);
10    F := getSetOfFailureStates(DTMC);
11    n_f := getNumberOfElements(F);
12    I_inter := getInitialState(DTMC_inter);
13    S_inter := getSuccessState(DTMC_inter);
14    F_inter := getSetOfFailureStates(DTMC_inter);
15    for (i = 1; i <= n; i++) {
16      p_i := getTransitionProbability(DTMC, X(i), Z);
17      createTransition(DTMC, X(i), I_inter, p_i);
18      deleteTransition(DTMC, X(i), Z);
19    }
20    for (j = 1; j <= m; j++) {
21      q_j := getTransitionProbability(DTMC, Z, Y(j));
22      createTransition(DTMC, S_inter, Y(j), q_j);
23      deleteTransition(DTMC, Z, Y(j));
24    }
25    for (k = 1; k <= n_f; k++) {
26      createTransition(DTMC, F_inter(k), F(k), 1);
27    }
28    deleteNode(DTMC, Z);
29  }
```

Listing 5.2: State Substitution Procedure

```
1   // DTMC:        considered DTMC
2   // Z:           inner state of considered DTMC
3   // DTMC_inter:  intermediate DTMC
4
5   resolve(DTMC, Z, DTMC_inter){
6     I_inter := getInitialState(DTMC_inter);
7     S_inter := getSuccessState(DTMC_inter);
8     F_inter := getSetOfFailureStates(DTMC_inter);
9     n := getNumberOfElements(F_inter);
10    substitute(DTMC, Z, DTMC_inter);
11    reduce(DTMC, I_inter);
12    reduce(DTMC, S_inter);
13    for (k = 1; k <= n; k++) {
14      reduce(DTMC, F_inter(k));
15    }
16  }
```

Listing 5.3: State Resolution Procedure

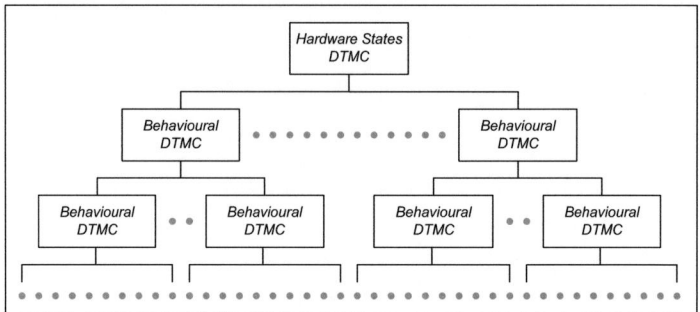

Figure 5.6: Hierarchical DTMC Creation Pattern

DTMC creation procedures at all levels are similar in that they include two generic steps:

1. *DTMC Initialization*: At level l, an initial generic $DTMC_l$ is created that reflects a certain aspect of the original PCM-REL instance. $DTMC_l$ contains a set of inner states $S := \{S_1, \ldots, S_n\}$ that aggregate other aspects and need to be resolved.

2. *Repeated State Resolution*: For each S_i, the transformation creates a corresponding lower-level $DTMC_{l+1}(i)$, converts it to its basic structure and resolves S_i with $DTMC_{l+1}(i)$. After all S_i have been resolved, $DTMC_l$ conforms to the basic structure.

At the lowest level of the DTMC creation hierarchy, DTMCs are initialized directly with a basic structure (which means that $S = \emptyset$). Hence, there is no need for further state resolution. The overall result of the transformation is the top-level DTMC, converted to its basic structure. The alternative transformation with Markov state reductions switched off (as introduced in Section 5.1.1) is equal to the one described here, apart from the fact that only state substitutions are done instead of state resolutions. With this alternative, the transformation results in a top-level DTMC that explicitly incorporates all lower-level DTMCs and reflects the whole original PCM-REL instance at once.

The following Sections 5.2 and 5.3 discuss the transformation algorithm in detail. The description refers to a transformation with state reduction switched on. However, the alternative transformation can be directly deduced from this description by replacing all state resolution operations in the provided listings with state substitutions.

5.2 Hardware States Evaluation

A major distinguishing feature of PCM-REL compared to related approaches is the explicit consideration of hardware failure potentials and their impact on the system's reliability (see Section 4.4). In PCM-REL, these failure potentials are associated with individual hardware resources such as CPUs and hard disks, and they are annotated to these resources in terms of MTTF and MTTR values. An unavailable hardware resource in an IT system causes hardware-induced FOD occurrences whenever the service execution tries to access the resource (see Section 3.1). By the principles of FOD propagation, a system-level FOD occurrence may be the ultimate consequence of the unsuccessful resource request (see Section 4.1). Hence, unavailable hardware resources impact the system's reliability and are considered as a possible source of failure by PCM-REL's Markov analysis.

In the following, the consideration of a system's hardware failure potential by the Markov transformation is discussed in detail. To this end, Section 5.2.1 introduces system hardware states as combinations of individual resource availability states. The following Sections 5.2.2 to 5.2.4 discuss different alternatives of how the Markov transformation can account for the different possible hardware states of a system under study.

5.2.1 System Hardware States

The consideration of hardware failure potentials constitutes a challenge for the PCM-REL Markov analysis. On the one hand, the approach generally expresses failure potentials through failure probabilities, thereby abstracting from the system's state and its progression over time. On the other hand, the typical hardware failure model introduced in Section 2.2 is a stateful one. At each point in system execution time $t > 0$, each hardware resource r in the system is in one out of two *resource availability states OK* and *NA* (not available). The probability of a request to r at time t being successful depends on the whole state progression history of r since the system's start at $t_0 = 0$ and is a function of the initial state of r at t_0 and its TTF and TTR distributions. To derive a more generic expression of r's failure potential, the Markov transformation condenses the specified MTTF and MTTR values of r to its steady-state availability (as introduced below), and it uses this value as the probability that r is available when requested at an arbitrary point in time. While this strategy may seem to be a strong simplification in the light of the potentially complex TTF and TTR distributions of r, it helps to keep the complexity of the analysis within feasible bounds. Furthermore, it releases the modeller from the burden of specifying complete TTF and TTR distributions for each hardware resource.

The following describes how the Markov transformation expresses the possible hardware states of the system and calculates their occurrence probabilities. Let $R := \{r_1, \ldots, r_n\}$ denote the set of resources in the system, and let $S(t) := \{s_1(t), \ldots, s_m(t)\}$ denote all possible *system hardware states* at time $t > 0$, where each $s_j(t) \in S(t)$ is a unique combination of possible states of all n resources at time t:

$$s_j(t) := (s_j(r_1, t), \ldots, s_j(r_n, t)) \in \{OK, NA\}^n$$
$$\forall t > 0, \quad j \in \{1, \ldots, m\} \tag{5.1}$$

Furthermore, let $MTTF_i$ and $MTTR_i$ be the given reliability annotations of resource r_i. The *steady-state availability* $Av(r_i)$ of resource r_i is calculated as follows:

$$Av(r_i) := \frac{MTTF_i}{MTTF_i + MTTR_i} \quad \forall i \in \{1, \ldots, n\} \tag{5.2}$$

In compliance with the hardware failure model presented in Section 2.2, $Av(r_i)$ denotes the expected fraction of time in which r_i is in the state OK. PCM-REL interprets $Av(r_i)$ as the probability that resource r_i, requested *at an arbitrary point in time* during system execution, is available and can serve the request:

$$P(s(r_i,t) = OK) = Av(r_i), \quad P(s(r_i,t) = NA) = 1 - Av(r_i)$$
$$\forall t > 0, \quad i \in \{1,\ldots,n\} \tag{5.3}$$

where $s(r_i,t)$ denotes the state of resource r_i at time t. From the state probabilities of the individual resources, the probability of each system hardware state can be deduced:

$$P(s_j(t)) = \prod_{i=1}^{n} P(s(r_i,t) = s_j(r_i,t)) \quad \forall t > 0, \quad j \in \{1,\ldots,m\} \tag{5.4}$$

This calculation assumes that the state distributions of the individual resources are independent, which means that resources fail and are repaired independently. Because of the time-independent evaluation of resource state probabilities, $P(s_j(t))$ constitutes a constant value $P(s_j) := P(s_j(t))$, regardless of the time t.

5.2.2 Standard Evaluation

The Markov transformation offers multiple alternatives to account for the possible hardware states of the system under study, as suggested by the configuration option "System Hardware States Handling" in Figure 5.1. In the standard case, the hardware states consideration is situated at the highest level of the DTMC creation hierarchy (see Figure 5.6). The transformation initializes a top-level $DTMC_{top}(U_i)$ for each PCM-REL usage scenario U_i as shown in Figure 5.7, which conforms to the generic structure (Figure 5.3a). Starting from the initial state $I(U_i)$, transitions lead to a set of states $\{E(U_i,s_1),\ldots,E(U_i,s_m)\}$, where each $E(U_i,s_j)$ represents

125

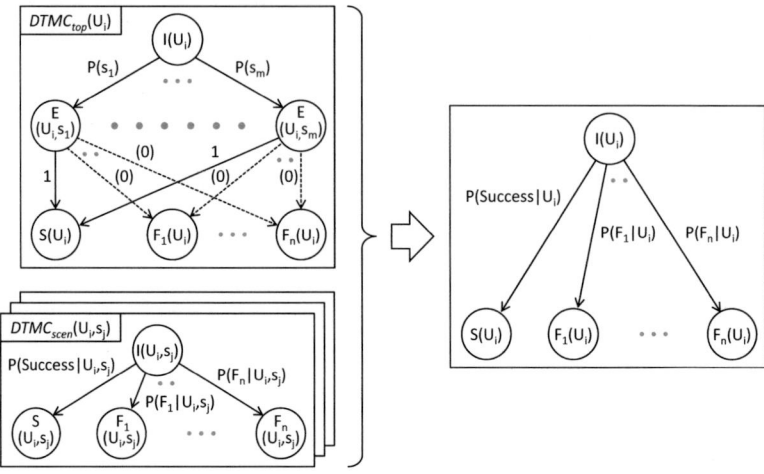

Figure 5.7: Standard Evaluation of System Hardware States

```
1   // U_i:  considered  usage  scenario
2   // R:     set  of  hardware  resources
3   // F:     set  of  considered  failure  modes
4   // returns:  top-level  DTMC  with  basic  structure
5   //              for  the  considered  usage  scenario
6
7   evaluateScenario(U_i, R, F){
8      S := determineSetOfHardwareStates(R);
9      P := determineSetOfHardwareStateProbabilities(R);
10     DTMC_top_i := initTopLevelDTMC(U_i, S, P, F);
11     m := S.getNumberOfElements();
12     for (j = 1; j <= m; j++) {
13        DTMC_scen_ij := evaluateScenarioExecution(U_i, F, S(j));
14        E_ij := getScenarioExecutionState(DTMC_top_i, S(j));
15        resolve(DTMC_top_i, E_ij, DTMC_scen_ij);
16     }
17     return DTMC_top_i;
18  }
```

Listing 5.4: System Hardware States Evaluation Procedure (Standard) the scenario execution under the precondition of the system hardware state being equal to s_j. The transition probabilities are the occurrence probabilities $P(s_j)$ of each hardware state. From each $E(U_i, s_j)$, a transition to the success state $S(U_i)$ is initialized with probability 1. Transitions to the failure states are initially set to probability 0. During the transformation, an intermediate $DTMC_{scen}(U_i, s_j)$ is created for the scenario execution under each hardware state s_j (as described in Section 5.3), and each $E(U_i, s_j)$ is resolved accordingly. The resulting DTMC conforms to the basic structure, directly showing the success and failure mode probabilities of scenario U_i (Figure 5.7). Hence, direct solving as discussed in Section 5.1.1 can be applied to retrieve the wanted Markov analysis results (Table 5.2). Listing 5.4 depicts the corresponding procedure.

Numerically, the overall success probability $P(Success|U_i)$ of scenario U_i can be derived from the success probabilities $P(Success|U_i, s_j)$ of U_i under the precondition of the hardware state s_j:

$$P(Success|U_i) = \sum_{j=1}^{m} (P(Success|U_i, s_j) \times P(s_j)) \qquad (5.5)$$

Similarly, the probabilities of each failure mode F_k resulting from the execution of U_i are:

$$P(F_k|U_i) = \sum_{j=1}^{m} (P(F_k|U_i, s_j) \times P(s_j)) \qquad (5.6)$$

The described standard evaluation of system hardware states has two fundamental consequences. First, the evaluation assumes that the hardware resources do not change their availability states during the scenario execution; each resource keeps the state it has when the execution begins. Being in line with the time-independent evaluation of state occurrence probabilities (see Section 5.2.1), this assumption allows for abstracting from the duration of the scenario execution itself or individual actions within the execution, as well as the concrete TTF and TTR distributions of the involved hardware resources. The assumption is feasible based on the observation that typical TTF and TTR values are significantly longer than a single scenario execution. The former are in the range of years (for TTF) or hours and days (for TTR), the latter mostly in the range of seconds or minutes. Hence, most scenario executions will not experience a changing system hardware state.

As a second consequence, the evaluation needs to explicitly consider each possible system hardware state and evaluate the scenario execution under this state. Hence, the evaluation exhibits exponential complexity with respect to the number of hardware resources in the system – for n hardware resources, there are $m = 2^n$ system hardware states to consider, as each resource can take one out of two possible availability states OK and NA. As this issue constitutes the most severe limitation to the scalability of the approach, PCM-REL takes several measures to tackle it. First, the approach provides an efficient evaluation of the scenario execution under each individual state (Section 5.3). Second, the user-selected evaluation levels allow for speeding up the analysis if the required level of detail of the analysis results is low (Section 5.1.1). Third, the transformation offers two further alternatives for the consideration of system hardware states (Sections 5.2.3 and 5.2.4). Each of these alternatives is significantly more efficient than the standard evaluation, on the cost of prediction accuracy.

5.2.3 Single-State Evaluation

The *single-state evaluation* constitutes an alternative way to consider a system's hardware failure potential, compared to the standard evaluation (see Section 5.2.2). Without distinguishing different system hardware states at the top-level, the transformation creates a $DTMC_{top}(U_i)$ with only one generic Markov state $E(U_i)$ representing the execution of the scenario U_i. Correspondingly, a single intermediate $DTMC_{scen}(U_i)$ repre-

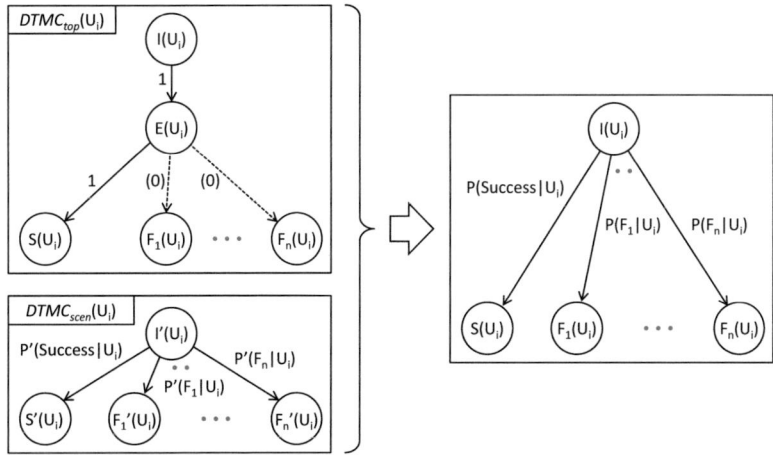

Figure 5.8: Single-State Evaluation of System Hardware States

```
1   // U_i:  considered usage scenario
2   // F:    set of considered failure modes
3   // returns: top−level DTMC with basic structure
4   //          for the considered usage scenario
5
6   evaluateScenario(U_i, F){
7      DTMC_top_i := initSingleStateTopLevelDTMC(U_i, F);
8      DTMC_scen := evaluateScenarioExecution(U_i, F);
9      E_i := getScenarioExecutionState(DTMC_top_i);
10     resolve(DTMC_top_i, E_i, DTMC_scen);
11     return DTMC_top_i;
12  }
```

Listing 5.5: System Hardware States Evaluation Procedure (Single-State)

sents the scenario execution. The consideration of hardware failure potentials is effectively delayed to the processing of the InternalActions that request the hardware resources (see Section 5.3.7), as well as the ExternalCallActions and EntryLevelSystemCalls pointing to potentially non-operational ResourceContainers (Section 5.3.6). Listing 5.5 shows the adapted procedure.

With respect to the numerical solution, no summation across individual hardware states as shown in equations 5.5 and 5.6 is necessary. Instead, the results follow directly from the intermediate $DTMC_{scen}(U_i)$:

$$P(Success|U_i) = P'(Success|U_i) \qquad (5.7)$$

$$P(F_k|U_i) = P'(F_k|U_i) \qquad (5.8)$$

The single-state evaluation is highly efficient because the scenario execution is evaluated only once, rather than repeatedly for all possible system hardware states. Although the effort for evaluating pointer and computation actions slightly increases compared to the standard evaluation (see Sections 5.3.6 and 5.3.7), this additional overhead is small compared to the savings at the top-level DTMC. On the other hand, the single-state evaluation may exhibit poor prediction accuracy. Although it does not assume fixed resource availability states during the scenario execution (as assumed by the standard evaluation), it introduces a significantly harder assumption by ignoring the stochastic dependencies between subsequent accesses to the same resource. Each access to a resource r is evaluated independently from earlier accesses to r within the same scenario execution. To further illustrate the consequences of this assumption by an example, let P be a PCM-REL instance and U a specified usage scenario of P. Let r be a hardware resource that is requested exactly $n \geq 1$ times during the execution of U. Let F_k be the failure mode expressing a FOD occurrence due to r being unavailable. Furthermore, let the unavailability of r be the only potential source of failure (meaning that the execution of U is either successful or results in failure mode F_k), and let there be no recovery actions specified in P (Section 5.3.8). Denoting the probabilities of FOD occurrences according to the standard and single-state evaluation by $P_{standard}(F_k|U)$ and $P_{single}(F_k|U)$, the following relationship holds:

$$P_{standard}(F_k|U) = 1 - Av(r) \leq 1 - Av(r)^n = P_{single}(F_k|U) \qquad (5.9)$$

In the standard evaluation variant, the decision about the availability of r is made once, at the beginning of the execution. The probability of r being available (which is equal to $Av(r)$ according to Equation 5.3) directly decides about success or failure of the execution. In contrast, the single-state evaluation decides about the availability of r independently for each request. Accordingly, there are n chances for r to be unavailable, leading to a higher overall failure mode probability. Based on the observation that the standard evaluation of system hardware states is fairly accurate (as shown for the audio hosting case study, see Section 6.4), the single-state evaluation exhibits a potentially high over-estimation of the system's hardware failure potential. This is also true if P includes other sources of failure and recovery actions, which makes the calculation significantly more complex. Hence, the applicability of the single-state evaluation remains limited to cases with few resource requests during service execution only, or to cases where the hardware failure potential turns out to be very low, without significant influence on architectural decisions.

5.2.4 Approximated Evaluation

In addition to the single-state evaluation (Section 5.2.3), the Markov transformation provides another means to fight the exponential complexity of the standard evaluation (Section 5.2.2), namely the *approximated evaluation*. This evaluation method generally provides a very good trade-off between analysis effort and prediction accuracy. The analysis effort is at most as high as that of the standard evaluation. The PCM-REL user can specify stop conditions to freely configure the analysis towards being faster or more accurate. Using these stop conditions, the user can force the approximated evaluation to deliver a result arbitrarily close to that of the standard evaluation. Due to these characteristics, the approximated evaluation is generally the preferred choice if the number of modelled hardware resources in a PCM-REL instance is too high to perform a standard evaluation.

The approximated evaluation takes advantage of two general aspects of the Markov transformation. First, the standard evaluation procedure of system hardware states as shown in Listing 5.4 is incremental through its `for` loop. An increasing amount of information is available with each executed increment, even though the procedure is not yet finished. Second, a normal hardware resource r can be assumed to be available with high probability: $0 \ll Av(r) \approx 1$. The following discusses the details of the approximation.

In its initial form, the $DTMC_{top}(U_i)$ created for the standard evaluation (Figure 5.7) has a success probability of 1. With each increment j of Listing 5.4, the failure potential of hardware state $s_j(t)$ is added to $DTMC_{top}(U_i)$, thereby reducing its resulting success probability. After $x \in \{1,\ldots,m\}$ increments, the failure potential of states $s_1(t)$ to $s_x(t)$ has been subtracted from the original success probability 1, weighted by their occurrence probabilities $P(s_j)$. The result is an upper bound of the overall $P(Success|U_i)$:

$$
\begin{aligned}
P(Success|U_i) \leq B_x &:= 1 - \sum_{j=1}^{x} (\sum_{k=1}^{n} P(F_k|U_i,s_j) \times P(s_j)) \\
&= \sum_{j=1}^{m} P(s_j) - \sum_{j=1}^{x} ((1 - P(Success|U_i,s_j)) \times P(s_j)) \\
&= \sum_{j=1}^{x} (P(Success|U_i,s_j) \times P(s_j)) + 1 - \sum_{j=1}^{x} P(s_j)
\end{aligned}
$$

$$(5.10)$$

On the other hand, $P(Success|U_i)$ is at least as high as the success probabilities of $s_1(t)$ to $s_x(t)$, again weighted by their occurrence probabilities (see also Equation 5.5):

$$
P(Success|U_i) \geq A_x := \sum_{j=1}^{x} (P(Success|U_i,s_j) \times P(s_j)) \qquad (5.11)
$$

Together, both equations yield $P(Success|U_i) \in [A_x, B_x] \;\; \forall x \in \{1, \ldots, m\}$ with A_x and B_x being calculated from the well-known $P(s_j)$ and the already evaluated $P(Success|U_i, s_1)$ to $P(Success|U_i, s_x)$. Hence, $P(Success|U_i)$ can be approximated through $[A_x, B_x]$ after x increments with a maximal inaccuracy I_x depending only on the state occurrence probabilities $P(s_j)$ and decreasing with each calculated increment:

$$I_x := B_x - A_x = 1 - \sum_{j=1}^{x} P(s_j) \tag{5.12}$$

The failure probabilities $P(F_k|U_i)$ can be approximated in the same way:

$$P(F_k|U_i) \leq \sum_{j=1}^{x} (P(F_k|U_i, s_j) \times P(s_j)) + 1 - \sum_{j=1}^{x} P(s_j) \tag{5.13}$$

$$P(F_k|U_i) \geq \sum_{j=1}^{x} (P(F_k|U_i, s_j) \times P(s_j)) \tag{5.14}$$

With these results, it is not necessary to calculate all increments of Listing 5.4. Instead, stop criteria such as a minimal required accuracy, a maximal evaluation time or a maximal number of increments can be defined. Then, the Markov evaluation approximates $P(Success|U_i)$ and $P(F_k|U_i)$ accordingly.

The proposed approximation strategy is only effective if the order of system hardware states $s_j(t)$ to evaluate is well-chosen, so that the remaining inaccuracy I_x is reduced as fast as possible. Ideally, the states should be sorted according to their occurrence probabilities $P(s_j)$, and the state with the highest occurrence probability should be evaluated first. However, this sorting would already imply evaluating $P(s_j)$ for all $m = 2^n$ states, and the sorting algorithm would have exponential complexity $\mathcal{O}(m \log m) = \mathcal{O}(n \cdot 2^n)$ with respect to the number n of resources in the system. Instead, the Markov transformation follows a heuristic that generally evaluates probable states first, based on the known availabilities $Av(r_i)$ of the individual resources. To this end, a *dominant availability state* $D(r_i)$ is defined for each resource r_i as follows:

$$D(r_i) := \begin{cases} OK & if \ Av(r_i) \geq 0.5 \\ NA & if \ Av(r_i) < 0.5 \end{cases} \tag{5.15}$$

Let $p(i,t) := P(s(r_i,t) = D(r_i))$ be the probability that r_i is in its dominant availability state at time t. Because of the timeless availability evaluation (see Section 5.2.1), $p(i,t)$ is constant over time and can be abbreviated as $p(i) := p(i,t)$. From the definition of $D(r_i)$, it follows that $p(i) \in [0.5, 1] \ \forall i \in \{1, \ldots, n\}$. In most practical cases, we have $D(r_i) = OK$ and $0.5 \ll p(i) \approx 1$. Next, let $Num := R \times \{OK, NA\} \to \{0, 1\}$ be a function that maps resources and availability states to numerical values:

$$Num(r_i, s) := \begin{cases} 0 & if \ s = D(r_i) \\ 1 & if \ s \neq D(r_i) \end{cases} \tag{5.16}$$

Then, the set of system hardware states $S(t)$ can be partitioned into a set of $n+1$ classes $C_k(t)$ as follows:

$$C_k(t) := \left\{ s_j(t) \in S(t) \,\middle|\, \sum_{i=1}^{n} Num(r_i, s_j(r_i, t)) = k \right\} \ \forall k \in \{0, \ldots, n\} \tag{5.17}$$

Thus, each class $C_k(t)$ comprises all system hardware states with k resources being *not* in their dominant state. The classes are disjoint, and their union results in $S(t)$. The number of elements in $C_k(t)$ corresponds to the binomial coefficient for selecting k out of n elements:

$$|C_k(t)| = \binom{n}{k} = \frac{n!}{k!(n-k)!} \tag{5.18}$$

With these definitions, the *heuristic to evaluate probable system hardware states first* can be formulated as follows:

1. Sort the set R of resources according to their dominant state probabilities, namely $\forall r_{i_1}, r_{i_2} \in \{r_1, \ldots, r_n\} : i_1 > i_2 \Rightarrow p(i_1) \geq p(i_2)$.

2. Evaluate each class $C_k(t)$ separately, starting from $C_0(t)$ up to $C_n(t)$. Within each class, prioritize the evaluation of resources with low indices being not in their dominant states. In particular, the first evaluated system hardware state of class $C_k(t)$ is the one with resources r_1 to r_k being not in their dominant availability states; the last evaluation refers to r_{n-k+1} to r_n being not in their dominant availability states.

If $D(r_i) = OK$ for all resources r_i, the heuristic can be reformulated as follows: First, sort all resources r_i according to their availabilities $Av(r_i)$. Then, evaluate the classes from $C_0(t)$ up to $C_n(t)$; in each class, let the resources with the lowest availabilities fail first. Intuitively, this heuristic evaluates probable system hardware states first because states in higher classes are generally less likely to occur than states in lower classes, and because resources with low availabilities are more likely to be unavailable. Moreover, the heuristic avoids the exponential complexity for the sorting of the $m = 2^n$ states – it only sorts n resources with complexity $\mathscr{O}(n \log n)$.

The following example further illustrates how the discussed heuristic can improve the efficiency of the evaluation. Let $Av(r_i) = p \geq 0.5 \ \forall r_i \in R$. Then, each system hardware state $s_j(t)$ of each class $C_k(t)$ has an occurrence probability of $P(s_j) = (1-p)^k p^{n-k}$ (see Equation 5.4). Furthermore, let $f_{n,p} : \{0, \ldots, m\} \to [0, 1]$ be the function indicating the maximal remaining inaccuracy of the approximation after x evaluation increments, depending on the number of resources n and their common availability p:

$$f_{n,p}(x) := \begin{cases} 1 & if \ x = 0 \\ I_x & if \ x > 0 \end{cases} \qquad (5.19)$$

135

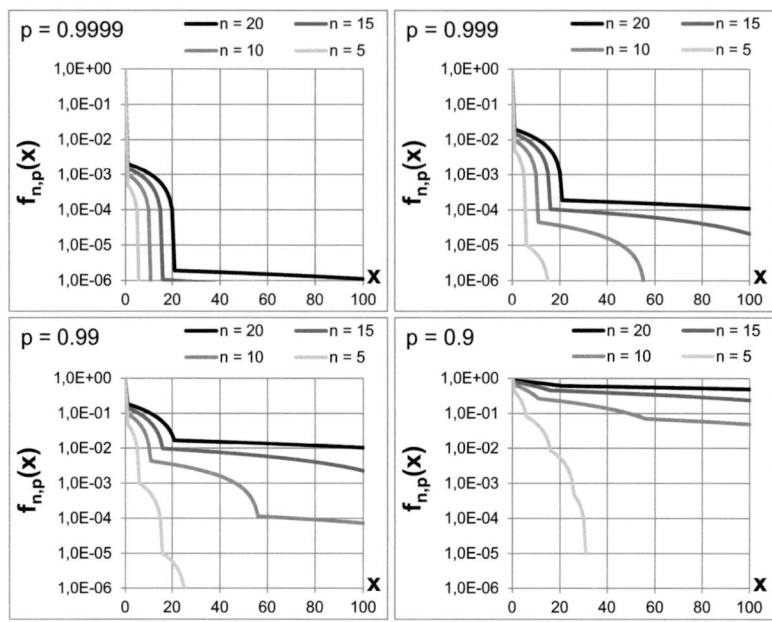

Figure 5.9: Relationship Between Evaluation Increments and Inaccuracy

Figure 5.9 shows the values from $f_{n,p}(0)$ to $f_{n,p}(100)$ for varying n and p. The function values are shown on a logarithmic scale from 1 to 10^{-6}. The function progresses in segments, and each segment marks the full evaluation of a certain class $C_k(t)$. For example, for $n = 10$, the first classes $C_0(t)$ to $C_2(t)$ have 1, 10 and 45 elements. Hence, segment boundaries occur at $x = 1$, $x = 11$ and $x = 56$. Within each segment, the function progresses linearly (due to the logarithmic scale, the figure shows curve segments instead of linear segments). For resources with high availability $p = 0.9999$, the approximation reaches a very low inaccuracy of 10^{-6} within the first 100 increments for systems with up to 20 modelled hardware resources. For $p = 0.999$, an inaccuracy of 10^{-4} or lower is reached, depending on n. For low or very low availabilities $p = 0.99$ and $p = 0.9$, the remaining inaccuracy may require more than 100 evaluation increments, at least for systems with more than 5 (or 10) modelled resources. In the theoretical worst case $p = 0.5$, all states $s_j(t) \in S(t)$ have the same occurrence probability $P(s_j) = 1/m$, and the application of the heuristic has no benefit.

```
1   // U_i:       considered usage scenario
2   // R:         set of hardware resources
3   // F:         set of considered failure modes
4   // C:         set of stop conditions
5   // returns:   evaluation result for the considered
6   //            usage scenario
7
8   evaluateScenario(U_i, R, F, C){
9     result := initEvaluationResult(F);
10    iterator := createHardwareStateIterator(R);
11    while ((hasMoreHardwareStates(iterator) == true) &&
12    (isStopConditionReached(C, iterator, result) == false)) {
13      S := getNextHardwareState(iterator);
14      P := getHardwareStateProbability(S);
15      DTMC_scen_ij := evaluateScenarioExecution(U_i, F, S);
16      updateEvaluationResult(result, DTMC_scen_ij, P);
17    }
18    return result;
19  }
```

Listing 5.6: System Hardware States Evaluation Procedure (Approximated)

Listing 5.6 shows the procedure to evaluate a usage scenario through the approximation method. With this method, the resulting success and failure mode probabilities are approximation intervals rather than single values. Hence, the return value of the procedure cannot be a single basic Markov chain. Instead, the procedure returns a data structure `EvaluationResult`, which contains the cumulated occurrence probability of all evaluated system hardware states $P(s_1) + \cdots + P(s_x)$, as well as the lower bounds for success and failure, calculated as shown in Equations 5.11 and 5.14. With these data, it is possible to also determine the upper bounds (Equations 5.10 and 5.13) and the remaining maximal inaccuracy (Equation 5.12). The logic to select states for evaluation according to the described heuristic is encoded into the call `getNextHardwareState`, which relies on a `HardwareStateIterator` data structure capturing information about the states visited so far. Additionally, a set of stop conditions (such as a satisfying upper bound for the inaccuracy) is given as an input to the procedure, and the call `isStopConditionReached` performs a corresponding test after each increment. As with the standard evaluation procedure (Listing 5.4), each increment requires creating and evaluating an intermediate $DTMC_{scen}(U_i, s_j)$. However, this DTMC is not used to resolve another Markov state, but as an input for the `updateEvaluationResult` call. The call includes a straightforward calculation adding the occurrence probability of the currently evaluated hardware state, as well as its success and failure probabilities, to the existing cumulated values of the `EvaluationResult`. In general, this procedure substantially improves the scalability of the approach compared to the standard evaluation (Section 5.2.2).

5.3 Compact Behavioural Evaluation

This section discusses how the Markov transformation accounts for the failure potential that arises from the execution of a specified PCM-REL usage scenario. The provided analysis is very comprehensive considering system-internal as well as system-external failure potentials related to software, hardware or network that may lead to FOD occurrences during the scenario execution. The DTMCs generated by the transformation reflect the inter-component and intra-component control and data flow including its potential points of failure (PPOF) and points of recovery (POR, see Table 4.1). Such a level of detail comes at a cost – the resulting DTMCs are potentially large, and the transformation procedures to generate them may be very time-consuming. Moreover, it may be necessary to repeat the behavioural evaluation multiple times during the transformation, if the consideration of system hardware states follows the standard evaluation method (Section 5.2.2) or the approximated evaluation method (Section 5.2.4). Therefore, a special focus lies on a *compact* behavioural evaluation, realized through a time- and space-efficient transformation algorithm.

In the following, Sections 5.3.1 and 5.3.2 introduce the general pattern of the behavioural evaluation being aligned to the action sequences of the considered PCM-REL usage scenario and the contained action types. Afterwards, Sections 5.3.3 to 5.3.8 discuss the evaluation of the different action types, along with the measures taken for compactness and the accompanying assumptions.

5.3.1 Action Sequences

The behavioural evaluation of a PCM-REL usage scenario execution is triggered as part of the top-level DTMC creation procedure through the `evaluateScenarioExecution` call in Listings 5.4, 5.5 or 5.6 (depending on the evaluation of system hardware states). The evaluation is itself hierarchical and comprises the second and all further DTMC creation levels as shown in Figure 5.6. It proceeds along the action sequences of the behavioural view that unfolds from the specified usage scenario (see Section 4.1). The evaluation is carried out in a time- and space-efficient way. Time efficiency is achieved because *each action sequence in the behavioural view is evaluated exactly once* (more precisely, each action sequence occurrence is evaluated exactly once – there may be multiple occurrences of a specified action sequence in the behavioural view). Where a repeated evaluation of any part of the behavioural view would be necessary in order to reflect different possible preconditions or execution iterations, the Markov transformation makes corresponding assumptions to avoid the repeated evaluation. Space efficiency is achieved through the hierarchical DTMC creation as discussed in Section 5.1.3, which includes *Markov state reduction operations on the fly*. Thanks to these operations, the DTMCs are never hold in memory as a whole. Instead, created DTMCs at each level are reduced to their most basic form before being incorporated into the next-higher level DTMCs.

The Markov transformation algorithm traverses the behavioural view by processing all of its action sequences $AS = \{AS_1, \ldots, AS_n\}$ hierarchically, such that the evaluation of each sequence includes evaluating all nested sequences. Referring to the behavioural view depicted in Figure 4.1, evaluating the topmost "BatchRequestBehaviour" includes the evaluation of the "WebFrontend.Login" ResourceDemandingSEFF (and all its nested sequences), followed by the "CaseBatchUpload" and "CaseBatchDownload" ScenarioBehaviours, as well as the "WebFrontend.Logout" Resource-DemandingSEFF. Evaluating "CaseBatchDownload" includes "WebFrontend.DownloadCollection", which in turn includes "AudioManagement.-RetrieveFiles", and so on. Each visited action sequence belongs either to a specified ScenarioBehaviour specifying user actions or a Resource-DemandingBehaviour (with the ResourceDemandingSEFF as its special case) specifying system actions in the PCM-REL instance.

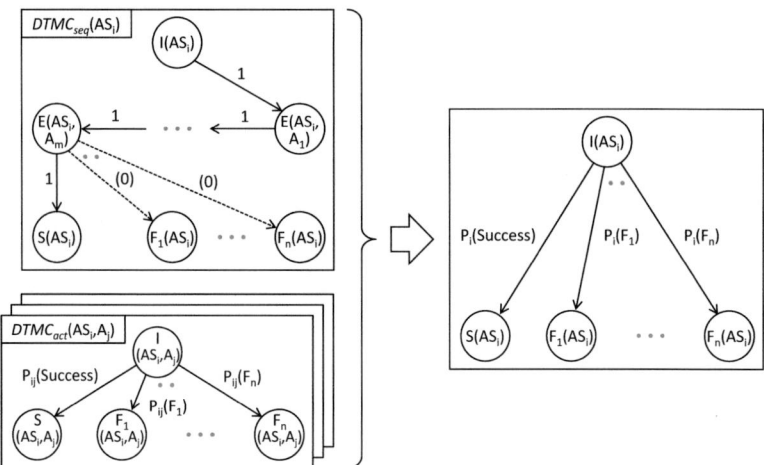

Figure 5.10: Evaluation of Action Sequences

To evaluate an action sequence AS_i with m actions, the Markov transformation creates an intermediate $DTMC_{seq}(AS_i)$ as shown in Figure 5.10,

```
1   // AS_i:      considered action sequence
2   // F:         set of considered failure modes
3   // s:         considered hardware state (optional parameter,
4   //            not used for single-state evaluation)
5   // returns:   basic DTMC for the considered action sequence
6
7   evaluateActionSequence(AS_i, F, s){
8     DTMC_seq_i := initActionSequenceDTMC(AS_i, F);
9     m := getNumberOfActions(AS_i);
10    for (j = 1; j <= m; j++) {
11      A_j := getAction(AS_i, j);
12      E_ij := getActionExecutionState(DTMC_seq_i, A_j);
13      DTMC_act_ij := evaluateAction(A_j, F, s);
14      resolve(DTMC_seq_i, E_ij, DTMC_act_ij);
15    }
16    return DTMC_seq_i;
17  }
```

Listing 5.7: Action Sequence Evaluation Procedure

```
1   // U_i:       considered usage scenario
2   // F:         set of considered failure modes
3   // s:         considered hardware state (optional parameter,
4   //            not used for single-state evaluation)
5   // returns:   basic DTMC for the execution of the
6   //            considered usage scenario
7
8   evaluateScenarioExecution(U_i, F, s){
9     AS_top := getTopmostActionSequence(U_i);
10    DTMC_seq_top := evaluateActionSequence(AS_top, F, s);
11    return DTMC_seq_top;
12  }
```

Listing 5.8: Scenario Execution Evaluation Procedure

where each action of the sequence (specified through a subclass of AbstractAction in the PCM-REL instance) is represented by a corresponding state $E(AS_i, A_j)$. Transitions starting from the initial $I(AS_i)$ across the $E(AS_i, A_j)$ with probabilities 1 express the sequential control flow through the actions of the behaviour; the last transition leads from $E(AS_i, A_m)$ to $S(AS_i)$. For each action, the transformation creates a $DTMC_{act}(AS_i, A_j)$ and resolves the state $E(AS_i, A_j)$ accordingly, eventually transforming the $DTMC_{seq}(AS_i)$ to its basic structure. Listing 5.7 shows the action sequence evaluation procedure.

For the topmost action sequence (which is the "BatchRequestBehaviour" in the example of Figure 4.1), the result can be used to resolve the corresponding scenario execution state in the top-level $DTMC_{top}(U_i)$ (see Figures 5.7 and 5.8). Listing 5.8 depicts the relevant scenario evaluation procedure.

Numerically, the success and failure mode probabilities of each action sequence can be determined as:

$$P_i(Success) = \prod_{j=1}^{m} P_{ij}(Success) \tag{5.20}$$

$$P_i(F_k) = \sum_{l=1}^{m} (\prod_{j=1}^{l-1} P_{ij}(Success) \times P_{il}(F_k)) \tag{5.21}$$

Equation 5.20 expresses the assumption that the whole action sequence AS_i is only successful if each action A_j is successfully executed. Equation 5.21 evaluates the probability $P_i(F_k)$ of failure mode F_k as the probability of F_k occurring in action A_l after successful execution of the first $l-1$ actions, for $l \in \{1,\ldots,m\}$.

The evaluation of an action sequence AS_i as conducted by the Markov transformation assumes that the first failing action A_j of AS_i determines the failure mode F_k of the whole sequence. There is no chance that a success or a second FOD occurring at a later action 'overwrites' F_k. Neither can multiple unhandled FOD occurrences add up to an 'aggregated' failure mode as the result of the sequence. Effectively, the transformation ignores cases where two or more unhandled FODs occur within a single action sequence. An explicit consideration of such cases would require extra effort in terms of modelling as well as analysis. Modellers would need to specify the influence of FOD occurrences on the subsequent control and data flow (which may be arbitrary in theory), and the Markov transformation would need to evaluate individual actions (together with their associated subsequences) multiple times, to account for different preconditions in terms of already occurred FODs. Taken to the extreme, the transformation would need $(n+1)^{j-1}$ evaluations of action A_j in order to account for all possible execution histories of actions A_1 to A_{j-1} in the sequence, each with $n+1$ possible outcomes. Hence, the evaluation of each sequence would have exponential complexity with respect to the number of required evaluations of the contained actions.

In contrast, the above-described assumption enables a compact evaluation of an action sequence AS_i, where each contained action A_j is evaluated exactly once. The inaccuracy introduced by this assumption is generally low, provided that FOD occurrences are rare events and occur independently from each other. As an example, consider an action sequence AS_i with three actions A_1, A_2 and A_3 which may fail independently, each with one specific FOD type F_1, F_2 and F_3 and non-zero FOD probability. In the example, a FOD occurrence during the execution of any individual action does not prevent the subsequent actions from being executed. Hence, the probabilities of success and failure are:

$$P_i(Success) = P_{i1}(Success) \times P_{i2}(Success) \times P_{i3}(Success) \qquad (5.22)$$

$$P_i(F_k) = P_{ik}(F_k) > 0 \quad \forall k \in \{1,2,3\} \qquad (5.23)$$

As multiple FODs of different types F_k may occur during the execution of the sequence, the individual outcomes of AS_i are not mutually exclusive:

$$P_i(Success) + \sum_{k=1}^{3} P_i(F_k) > 1 \qquad (5.24)$$

Table 5.4 shows how the PCM-REL Markov analysis evaluates AS_i. PCM-REL distinguishes only four out of the eight possible execution results. In all cases, the approach considers the first occurred FOD type as being the overall failure mode of AS_i. For PCM-REL, all possible outcomes are mutually exclusive. Regarding prediction accuracy, the approach correctly evaluates $P_i(Success)$ and $P_i(F_1)$, but introduces a numerical error when evaluating $P_i(F_2)$ and $P_i(F_3)$. However, if the probabilities of FOD occur-

Execution Results				PCM-REL Evaluation
A₁	**A₂**	**A₃**	**Result of AS_i**	**Occurrence Probability**
Success	Success	Success	Success	$P_i(\text{Success}) = P_{i1}(\text{Success}) \times P_{i2}(\text{Success}) \times P_{i3}(\text{Success})$
Success	Success	F_3	F_3	$P_i(F_3) = P_{i1}(\text{Success}) \times P_{i2}(\text{Success}) \times P_{i3}(F_3) \approx P_{i3}(F_3)$
Success	F_2	Success	F_2	$P_i(F_2) = P_{i1}(\text{Success}) \times P_{i2}(F_2) \approx P_{i2}(F_2)$
Success	F_2	F_3		
F_1	Success	Success	F_1	$P_i(F_1) = P_{i1}(F_1)$
F_1	Success	F_3		
F_1	F_2	Success		
F_1	F_2	F_3		

Table 5.4: Action Sequence Evaluation Example

rences are small, then the introduced error is also small, as $P_{i1}(Success) \approx 1$ and $P_{i2}(Success) \approx 1$.

5.3.2 Action Types

Each action sequence (see Section 5.3.1) includes a set of individual actions, which belong to the corresponding PCM-REL `ScenarioBehaviour` or `ResourceDemandingBehaviour`. The evaluation of the sequence involves evaluating all of its actions (see Listing 5.7). The Markov transformation distinguishes multiple *action types* and evaluates each action according to its type. Table 5.5 shows the considered action types, as well as the mapping of PCM-REL actions to the action types. *Branches*, *loops*, *forks* and *pointer actions* specify the flow of user behaviour and system execution in the failure-free case. Sections 5.3.3 to 5.3.6 discuss their evaluation. *Computation actions* represent all data processing and computational steps in the system execution (see Section 5.3.7), and *recovery actions* specify the control flow of the system execution when FODs occur (see Section 5.3.8). *Default actions* are all actions that do not exhibit an own potential for failure. This last category includes actions that denote the start and the end of behavioural specifications (namely, the `Start`, `Stop`, `StartAction` and `StopAction`), actions that influence the data flow of the system execution (namely, the `SetVariableAction`), and actions that are part of the PCM behavioural specification language but do not impact system reliability (namely, the Delay, ReleaseAction, and AcquireAction). Listing 5.9 shows how each action in a sequence is evaluated according to its type.

Action Type	User Actions	System Actions
Branch	Branch	BranchAction
Loop	Loop	LoopAction, CollectionIteratorAction
Fork	---	ForkAction
Pointer	EntryLevelSystemCall	ExternalCallAction
Computation	---	InternalAction
Recovery	---	RecoveryBlockAction
Default	Start, Stop, Delay	StartAction, StopAction, SetVariableAction, ReleaseAction, AcquireAction

Table 5.5: Markov Action Types

```
1  // A:         considered action
2  // F:         set of considered failure modes
3  // s:         considered hardware state (optional parameter,
4  //            not used for single−state evaluation)
5  // returns:   basic DTMC for the execution of the
6  //            considered action
7
8  evaluateAction(A, F, s){
9    type := getActionType(A);
10   if(type == BRANCH) {
11     return evaluateBranchAction(A, F, s);
12   } else if(type == LOOP) {
13     return evaluateLoopAction(A, F, s);
14   } else if(type == FORK) {
15     return evaluateForkAction(A, F, s);
16   } else if(type == POINTER) {
17     return evaluatePointerAction(A, F, s);
18   } else if(type == COMPUTATION) {
19     return evaluateComputationAction(A, F, s);
20   } else if(type == RECOVERY) {
21     return evaluateRecoveryAction(A, F, s);
22   } else {
23     return evaluateDefaultAction(A, F);
24 }
```

Listing 5.9: Action Evaluation Procedure

145

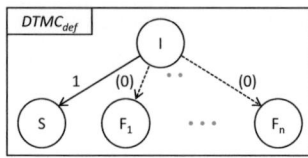

Figure 5.11: Evaluation of Default Actions

```
1  // A_def:     considered default action
2  // F:         set of considered failure modes
3  // returns:   basic DTMC for the execution of the
4  //            considered default action
5
6  evaluateDefaultAction(A_def, F){
7    DTMC_def := initDefaultDTMC(A_def, F);
8    return DTMC_def;
9  }
```

Listing 5.10: Default Action Evaluation Procedure

For default actions, the evaluation is trivial, as shown in Figure 5.11. The corresponding $DTMC_{def}$ is directly created in its basic form, and a transition from the start I to the success S with probability 1 indicates that the action never fails. Listing 5.10 shows the corresponding procedure. The success and failure mode probabilities of the default action execution are:

$$P_{default}(Success) = 1, \quad P_{default}(F_k) = 0 \qquad (5.25)$$

5.3.3 Branch Actions

A branch action A_{branch} is specified through a PCM-REL Branch (Section 2.7.5) or BranchAction (Section 2.7.2). It contains a set of one ore more branch transitions $T := \{t_1, \ldots, t_m\}$, where each transition t_i has an occurrence probability $P(t_i)$ and an associated behaviour, expressed through an action sequence AS_i (the dependency solver resolves any more complex conditional expressions for transitions in the original PCM-REL instance to simple probabilities, see Section 2.7.6). When executing A_{branch}, exactly

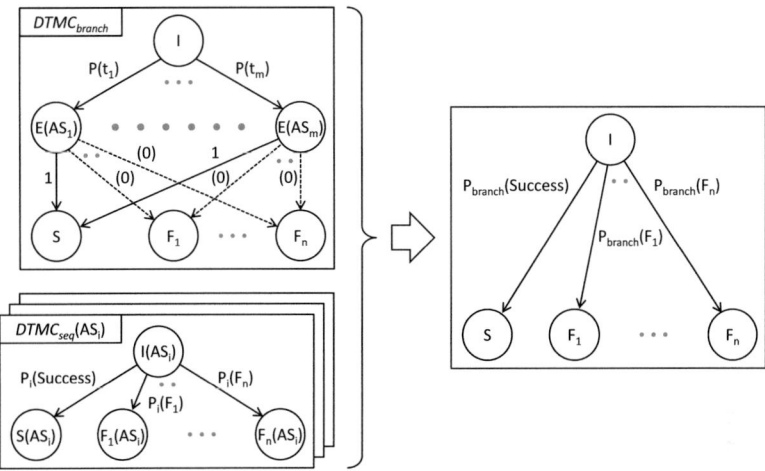

Figure 5.12: Evaluation of Branch Actions

```
1   // A_branch:  considered  branch  action
2   // F:         set  of  considered  failure  modes
3   // s:         considered  hardware  state  (optional  parameter,
4   //            not  used  for  single-state  evaluation)
5   // returns:   basic  DTMC  for  the  execution  of  the
6   //            considered  branch  action
7
8   evaluateBranchAction(A_branch, F, s){
9     DTMC_branch := initBranchDTMC(A_branch, F);
10    T := getSetOfBranchTransitions(A_branch);
11    m := getNumberOfElements(T);
12    for (i = 1; i <= m; i++) {
13      AS_i := getActionSequence(T(i));
14      E_i := getActionSequenceExecutionState(DTMC_branch, AS_i);
15      DTMC_seq_i := evaluateActionSequence(AS_i, F, s);
16      resolve(DTMC_branch, E_i, DTMC_seq_i);
17    }
18    return DTMC_branch;
19  }
```

Listing 5.11: Branch Action Evaluation Procedure

one transition is taken; the transition probabilities sum up to 1:

$$\sum_{i=1}^{m} P(t_i) = 1 \qquad (5.26)$$

The Markov transformation evaluates branch actions as shown in Figure 5.12. Each branch transition t_i and associated action sequence AS_i is represented through a state $E(AS_i)$, and a Markov transition from the initial state I to $E(AS_i)$ with probability $P(t_i)$ denotes the possibility that AS_i is executed. The transformation creates an intermediate $DTMC_{seq}(AS_i)$ for each AS_i and resolves each $E(AS_i)$ accordingly, as shown in Listing 5.11. Hence, each branch transition and associated action sequence is evaluated exactly once by the transformation. The success and failure mode probabilities of A_{branch} can be determined as the weighted sum over each individual branch transition:

$$P_{branch}(Success) = \sum_{i=1}^{m} (P_i(Success) \cdot P(t_i)) \qquad (5.27)$$

$$P_{branch}(F_k) = \sum_{i=1}^{m} (P_i(F_k) \cdot P(t_i)) \qquad (5.28)$$

5.3.4 Loop Actions

Loop actions A_{loop} are specified through PCM-REL Loops (Section 2.7.5), LoopActions or CollectionIteratorActions (Section 2.7.2). A loop contains a body behaviour with a corresponding action sequence AS_b, and – after resolving stochastic expressions and parameter dependencies (Section 2.7.6) – a specification of loop iteration counts $C := \{c_1, \ldots, c_m\} \subset \mathbb{N}$ with occurrence probabilities $P(c_i)$ that sum up to 1:

$$\sum_{i=1}^{m} P(c_i) = 1 \qquad (5.29)$$

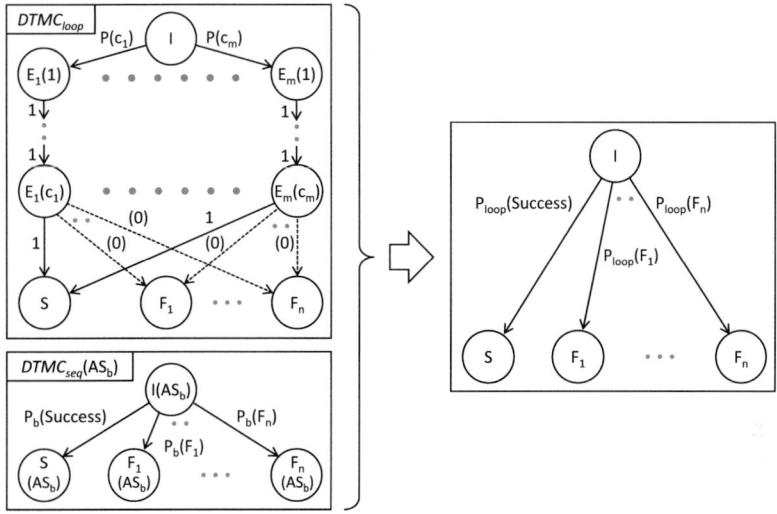

Figure 5.13: Evaluation of Loop Actions

```
1   // A_loop:    considered loop action
2   // F:         set of considered failure modes
3   // s:         considered hardware state (optional parameter,
4   //            not used for single-state evaluation)
5   // returns:   basic DTMC for the execution of the
6   //            considered loop action
7
8   evaluateLoopAction(A_loop, F, s){
9       DTMC_loop := initLoopDTMC(A_loop, F);
10      C := getSetOfLoopIterationCounts(A_loop);
11      m := getNumberOfElements(C);
12      AS_b := getBodyActionSequence(A_loop);
13      DTMC_seq_b := evaluateActionSequence(AS_b, F, s);
14      for (i = 1; i <= m; i++) {
15          for ( j = 1; j <= C(i); j++) {
16              E_ij := getBodyExecutionState(DTMC_loop, i, j);
17              resolve(DTMC_loop, E_ij, DTMC_seq_b);
18          }
19      }
20      return DTMC_loop;
21  }
```

Listing 5.12: Loop Action Evaluation Procedure

149

Each $P(c_i)$ expresses the probability that the loop body AS_b is executed c_i times before the control flow moves on to the successor action of the loop. The Markov transformation must account for the failure potential of each individual execution of AS_b, but evaluates AS_b only once. As Figure 5.13 shows, the initial $DTMC_{loop}$ structure reflects all possible iteration counts c_i by a path leading from the initial state I to a sequence of states $E_i(1)$ to $E_i(c_i)$, where each $E_i(j)$ reflects one execution of AS_b. The transitions starting from I represent the different possible loop iteration counts and have the probabilities $P(c_i)$ attached. From the last body execution states $E_i(c_i)$, transitions lead to the success state S with probability 1. The transformation generates an intermediate $DTMC_{seq}(AS_b)$ and uses it to resolve all of the states $E_i(j)$. Listing 5.12 shows the procedure.

The success and failure mode probabilities of the loop action are:

$$P_{loop}(Success) = \sum_{i=1}^{m}(P_b(Success)^{c_i} \cdot P(c_i)) \qquad (5.30)$$

$$P_{loop}(F_k) = \sum_{i=1}^{m}((\sum_{j=1}^{c_i} P_b(Success)^{j-1} \cdot P_b(F_k)) \cdot P(c_i)) \qquad (5.31)$$

These two equations express the probabilities that, for any loop iteration count c_i, either all c_i executions of the loop body AS_b succeed (Equation 5.30), or that a FOD of type F_k occurs in any of the body executions (Equation 5.31).

The evaluation of loop actions as described here is based on an assumption similar to the evaluation of action sequences (see Section 5.3.1): the first failing execution of the loop body AS_b determines the overall failure mode F_k of the loop. This assumption is necessary to avoid the need for evaluating AS_b multiple times accounting for all possible execution histories. See Section 5.3.1 for a more detailed discussion. Even though – thanks to the described assumption – the Markov transformation evaluates AS_b only once, loop actions can still constitute a scalability issue for the analysis. The $DTMC_{loop}$ which needs to be constructed during the evaluation procedure contains a potentially large number of $c_1 + ... + c_m$ inner Markov states, corresponding to the specified loop iteration counts c_i. However, most modelled loop actions have only a small number of iteration counts, as PCM-REL specifies control flow on a high abstraction level.

5.3.5 Fork Actions

A fork action A_{fork}, specified by a PCM-REL ForkAction (see Section 2.7.2), denotes the parallel execution of m forked behaviours with corresponding action sequences AS_1 to AS_m. After the execution of all AS_i has started, the control flow either moves on to the successor action of A_{fork} immediately, or it waits until the completion of all AS_i, if a SynchronizationPoint has been specified. The Markov transformation abstracts from the involved parallelism and instead evaluates the AS_i as if they were executed sequentially. Figure 5.14 shows the $DTMC_{fork}$ structure initialized with m states $E(AS_i)$ representing the execution of each AS_i, starting from the initial I and finally reaching the success state S. An intermediate $DTMC_{seq}(AS_i)$ evaluates each individual sequence and is used to resolve the corresponding $E(AS_i)$. Hence, the Markov transformation evaluates each forked behaviour exactly once. Listing 5.13 shows the procedure.

The execution of A_{fork} is successful if all AS_i complete without a FOD occurrence. In contrast, a FOD F_k of A_{fork} is the result of F_k occurring within any of the forked behaviours AS_i, leading to the following success and failure mode probabilities of A_{fork}:

$$P_{fork}(Success) = \prod_{i=1}^{m} P_i(Success) \tag{5.32}$$

$$P_{fork}(F_k) = \sum_{i=1}^{m} (\prod_{j=1}^{i-1} P_j(Success) \times P_i(F_k)) \tag{5.33}$$

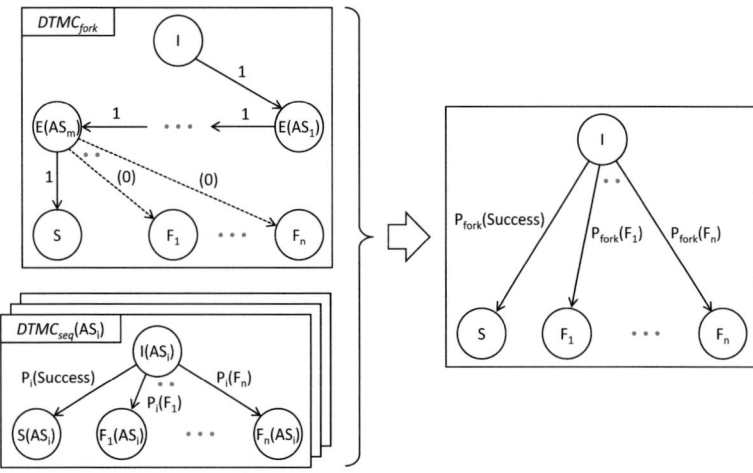

Figure 5.14: Evaluation of Fork Actions

```
1   // A_fork:    considered fork action
2   // F:         set of considered failure modes
3   // s:         considered hardware state (optional parameter,
4   //            not used for single-state evaluation)
5   // returns:  basic DTMC for the execution of the
6   //            considered fork action
7
8   evaluateForkAction(A_fork, F, s){
9     DTMC_fork := initForkDTMC(A_fork, F);
10    B := getSetOfForkedBehaviours(A_fork);
11    m := getNumberOfElements(B);
12    for (i = 1; i <= m; i++) {
13      AS_i := getActionSequence(B(i));
14      E_i := getActionSequenceExecutionState(DTMC_fork, AS_i);
15      DTMC_seq_i := evaluateActionSequence(AS_i, F, s);
16      resolve(DTMC_fork, E_i, DTMC_seq_i);
17    }
18    return DTMC_fork;
19  }
```

Listing 5.13: Fork Action Evaluation Procedure

Due to the involved parallelism, a FOD while executing a forked behaviour AS_i may occur after the surrounding action sequence – or even the whole UsageScenario control flow – has already come to its end. Still, from the reliability prediction point of view, a failing AS_i means a failed A_{fork} and ultimately a failed scenario execution, unless recovery mechanisms are in place (also see the FOD propagation principle described in Section 4.1).

Treating forked behaviours as if they were sequential is possible because the Markov transformation considers all FOD occurrences as being stochastically independent. The success and failure mode probabilities of any forked behaviour AS_i do not depend on the other behaviours or on the relative timing of their execution. While the modeller can generally express a potential for concurrency-related FODs through defining corresponding SoftwareInducedFODTypes and annotating the computation with FOD probabilities, PCM-REL does not explicitly capture how synchronization issues and other problems arise as a result of concurrent system execution. Doing so would shift the focus of the approach towards fault identification and system verification and would require different types of analyses (using time-based synchronisation-aware analysis models).

Based on the sequential treatment of forked behaviours, the transformation assumes that the first failing behaviour AS_i determines the overall failure mode F_k of A_{fork}. This assumption corresponds to the one taken for action sequences (Section 5.3.1) and loop actions (Section 5.3.4). See Section 5.3.1 for a more detailed discussion of the assumption. For fork actions, the additional question arises in which order to consider the forked behaviours (as the behaviours are executed concurrently, there is no natural order given). The Markov transformation chooses an *arbitrary* order, assuming that the order of executed actions or behaviours does not significantly influence the success and failure mode probabilities resulting from the analysis. This assumption is valid as long as the individual FOD probabilities are not too high. As an example, consider a re-ordering of actions A_1, A_2 and A_3 in Table 5.4 – any such re-ordering leads to very

153

similar prediction results, provided that the individual FOD probabilities $P_{ik}(F_k)$ $\forall k \in \{1,2,3\}$ are low.

5.3.6 Pointer Actions

A pointer action $A_{pointer}$ represents an invocation of a service operation. The invocation is triggered by a system user (specified through a PCM-REL `EntryLevelSystemCall`, see Section 2.7.5) or by a service call as part of the system's behaviour (specified through an `ExternalCallAction`, see Section 2.7.2). The invoked service operation may be provided by a software component in the system, or it may be routed to the system's border and provided by a system-external service. In the first case, the called component provides a behavioural specification in terms of a `Resource-DemandingSEFF` for the service operation, and $A_{pointer}$ references the topmost action sequence AS_b representing the `ResourceDemandingSEFF`. In the latter case, the system-external behaviour is regarded as a black-box. A `SpecifiedReliabilityAnnotation` may exist for the system-external call (see Section 4.6) indicating its success and failure mode probabilities[1]. If $A_{pointer}$ represents a service call between two software components that are deployed on different `ResourceContainers`, the invocation involves communication via the `LinkingResource` that connects both containers (see Section 2.7.4).

The Markov transformation classifies pointer actions according to their different targets as *local*, *entry-level*, *remote* and *system-external* pointers, and it applies an individual transformation scheme to each of these classes. Local pointers are invocations between software components deployed on the same `ResourceContainer`. They reference a system-internal behaviour, represented by AS_b, and they do not involve remote communi-

---

[1]More concretely, the target of $A_{pointer}$ is determined depending on the executed *component instance*, which is uniquely identified by the surrounding set of nested `AssemblyContexts`. To avoid overloading the presentation, the passing of `AssemblyContext` hierarchies as parameters is omitted from the presented listings.

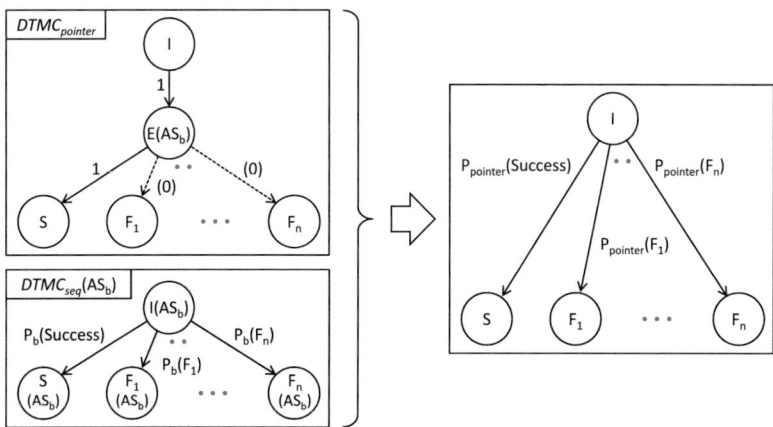

Figure 5.15: Evaluation of Local Pointer Actions

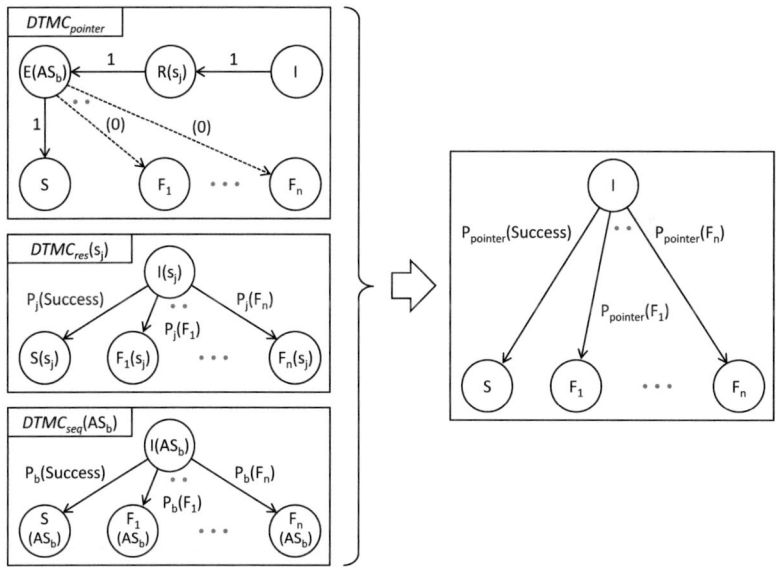

Figure 5.16: Evaluation of Entry-Level Pointer Actions

cation. As shown in Figure 5.15, the initial $DTMC_{pointer}$ contains only one inner state $E(AS_b)$, which is resolved by the intermediate $DTMC_{seq}(AS_b)$ representing AS_b. The success and failure mode probabilities are:

$$P_{pointer}(Success) = P_b(Success), \quad P_{pointer}(F_k) = P_b(F_k) \qquad (5.34)$$

Entry-level pointers represent invocations that are triggered by system users through `EntryLevelSystemCalls`. As an additional required step compared to the evaluation of local pointers, the `ResourceContainer` that hosts the service-providing component must be checked for being operational. The operability check is done before evaluating the invoked service behaviour, as the operability of the container is a precondition for any service execution to take place. The container is operational if all included hardware resources that are strictly required for its operation (as indicated by the `requiredByContainer` attribute of the corresponding `ProcessingResourceSpecification`, see Section 4.4) are available. The evaluation of $A_{pointer}$ varies depending on the way of handling system hardware states, namely through standard or approximated evaluation (see Sections 5.2.2 and 5.2.4) or through single-state evaluation (see Section 5.2.3). With standard or approximated evaluation, $A_{pointer}$ is always evaluated under the precondition of a certain system hardware state s_j. The Markov transformation creates a $DTMC_{pointer}$ as shown in Figure 5.16 with an additional state $R(s_j)$, compared to the local pointer case.

To evaluate the operability of the target container, the transformation creates an intermediate $DTMC_{res}(s_j)$ and resolves $R(s_j)$ accordingly. To this end, the transformation first determines the set of hardware resources $R_{pointer} \subseteq R$ included in the container and strictly required for its operation. If all resources in $R_{pointer}$ are OK under the precondition s_j, a transition from $I(s_j)$ to $S(s_j)$ with probability 1 marks the assured success of the operability check. If one resource $r_i \in R_{pointer}$ is NA, the check fails with the corresponding failure mode F_k (which depends on the selected evaluation level, see Section 5.1.1), denoted by a transition from $I(s_j)$ to $F_k(s_j)$ with probability 1. If there are multiple unavailable resources, it is not predetermined which one causes $A_{pointer}$ to fail. In this situation, the Markov transformation divides the failure potential equally between all unavailable resources. As an example, consider a ResourceContainer with two ProcessingResourceSpecifications of type "CPU" and "HDD", both with their requiredByContainer attributes set to *true*. If both resources are *NA* under a certain state s_j, and if *Type* is selected as an evaluation level, the corresponding $DTMC_{res}(s_j)$ contains two transitions from $I(s_j)$ to two failure states representing a CPU failure and a HDD failure, each with probability 0.5. Overall, the success and failure mode probabilities for entry-level pointers are as follows:

$$P_{pointer}(Success) = P_j(Success) \times P_b(Success) \qquad (5.35)$$

$$P_{pointer}(F_k) = P_j(F_k) + P_j(Success) \times P_b(F_k) \qquad (5.36)$$

Equation 5.35 reflects the fact that a successful completion of $A_{pointer}$ requires a successful operability check of the target container, as well as a successful execution of the invoked service operation. If either of these two factors results in a failure mode F_k, so does $A_{pointer}$ (see Equation 5.36).

Remote pointers are invocations between two physically separated software components. Figure 5.17 shows their evaluation (under standard or approximated evaluation of system hardware states). The evaluation differs from entry-level pointers in that two additional states $E_1(N)$ and $E_2(N)$ represent the transfer of the invocation and return messages over the corresponding network LinkingResource. An additional $DTMC_{comm}(N)$ is used to resolve these two states. It represents the message transfer itself, which may either be successful or result in a transmission failure. The corresponding failure mode F_i depends on the selected evaluation level (see Section 5.1.1). For example, at level 1 (or *Category*), F_i is the "network-induced FOD".

For remote pointers, the success and failure mode probabilities are:

$$P_{pointer}(Success) = P_j(Success) \times P_{comm}(Success)^2$$
$$\times P_b(Success) \qquad (5.37)$$

$$
P_{pointer}(F_k) =
\begin{cases}
P_{comm}(Success) \times P_j(F_k) \\
+ P_{comm}(Success) \times P_j(Success) \times P_b(F_k) & if \ k \neq i \\
\\
P_{comm}(F_k) \\
+ P_{comm}(Success) \times P_j(F_k) \\
+ P_{comm}(Success) \times P_j(Success) \times P_b(F_k) \\
+ P_{comm}(Success) \times P_j(Success) \\
\times P_b(Success) \times P_{comm}(F_k) & if \ k = i
\end{cases}
$$
$$(5.38)$$

Equation 5.37 expresses that the remote pointer action is only successful if both involved transmissions as well as the referenced behaviour AS_b are successfully executed, and if the target ResourceContainer is operational. Equation 5.38 states that failure modes F_k may result from failing transmissions, a failed operability check of the target container, or failing execution of AS_b. If a failure mode does not represent a transmission failure ($k \neq i$), it can only be the result of a failed operability check or failing execution of AS_b after a successful transmission of the service invocation to the target container.

System-external pointers invoke an operation of a system-external service. The corresponding initial $DTMC_{pointer}$ as shown in Figure 5.18 contains a single inner state $E(EC)$ representing the execution of the external call. An intermediate $DTMC_{ext}(EC)$ is directly instantiated with success and failure mode probabilities $P_{ext}(Success)$ and $P_{ext}(F_k)$ determined from the given PCM-REL instance. If a SpecifiedReliabilityAnnotation

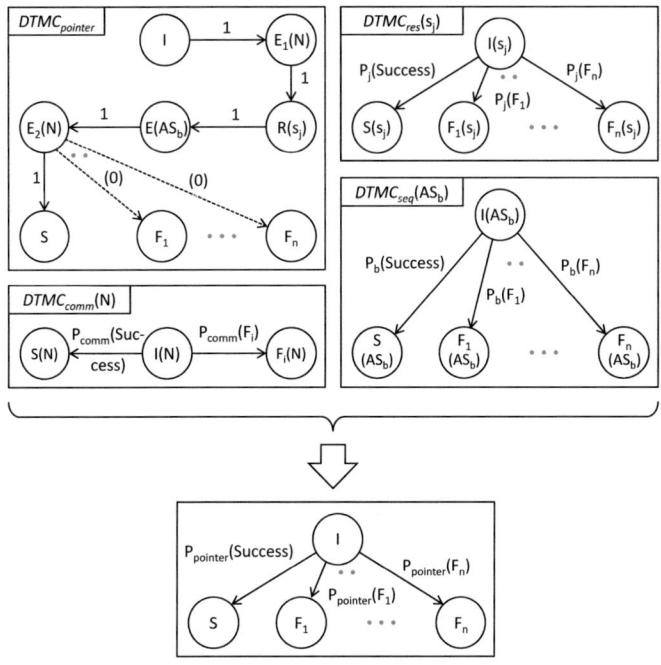

Figure 5.17: Evaluation of Remote Pointer Actions

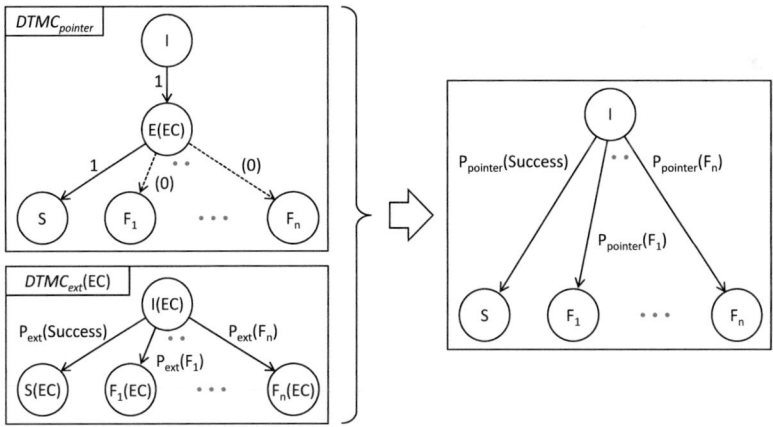

Figure 5.18: Evaluation of System-External Pointer Actions

exists for the call, the probabilities are taken from the annotation. If not, the call is assumed to be fully reliable, namely, $P_{ext}(Success) = 1$ and $P_{ext}(F_k) = 0$. The success and failure mode probabilities of the pointer action are:

$$P_{pointer}(Success) = P_{ext}(Success), \quad P_{pointer}(F_k) = P_{ext}(F_k) \qquad (5.39)$$

Listing 5.14 shows the evaluation procedure covering all types of pointer actions under standard or approximated evaluation of system hardware states.

```
1   // A_pointer:  considered pointer action
2   // F:          set of considered failure modes
3   // s_j:        considered hardware state
4   // returns:    basic DTMC for the execution of the
5   //             considered pointer action
6
7   evaluatePointerAction(A_pointer, F, s_j){
8     type := getPointerType(A_pointer);
9     if(type == LOCAL) {
10       return evaluateLocalPointerAction(A_pointer, F, s_j);
11     } else if(type == ENTRY) {
12       return evaluateEntryPointerAction(A_pointer, F, s_j);
13     } else if(type == REMOTE) {
14       return evaluateRemotePointerAction(A_pointer, F, s_j);
15     } else {
16       return evaluateExternalPointerAction(A_pointer, F);
17     }
18   }
19
20   evaluateLocalPointerAction(A_pointer, F, s_j){
21     DTMC_pointer := initLocalPointerDTMC(A_pointer, F);
22     AS_b := getReferencedActionSequence(DTMC_pointer);
23     E_b := getReferencedExecutionState(DTMC_pointer);
24     DTMC_seq_b := evaluateActionSequence(AS_b, F, s_j);
25     resolve(DTMC_pointer, E_b, DTMC_seq_b);
26     return DTMC_pointer;
27   }
28
29   evaluateEntryPointerAction(A_pointer, F, s_j){
30     DTMC_pointer := initEntryPointerDTMC(A_pointer, F);
31     RC := getTargetResourceContainer(A_pointer);
32     AS_b := getReferencedActionSequence(A_pointer);
33     R_j := getOperabilityCheckState(DTMC_pointer);
34     E_b := getReferencedExecutionState(DTMC_pointer);
35     DTMC_res_j := createOperabilityCheckDTMC(RC, F, s_j);
36     DTMC_seq_b := evaluateActionSequence(AS_b, F, s_j);
37     resolve(DTMC_pointer, R_j, DTMC_res_j);
38     resolve(DTMC_pointer, E_b, DTMC_seq_b);
39     return DTMC_pointer;
```

```
40  }
41
42  evaluateRemotePointerAction(A_pointer, F, s_j){
43    DTMC_pointer := initRemotePointerDTMC(A_pointer, F);
44    LR := getRequiredLinkingResource(A_pointer);
45    RC := getTargetResourceContainer(A_pointer);
46    AS_b := getReferencedActionSequence(A_pointer);
47    R_j := getOperabilityCheckState(DTMC_pointer);
48    E_b := getReferencedExecutionState(DTMC_pointer);
49    DTMC_comm_N := createTransmissionDTMC(LR);
50    DTMC_res_j := createOperabilityCheckDTMC(RC, F, s_j);
51    DTMC_seq_b := evaluateActionSequence(AS_b, F, s_j);
52    for (i = 1; i <= 2; i++) {
53      E_i := getTransmissionState(DTMC_pointer, i);
54      resolve(DTMC_pointer, E_i, DTMC_comm_N);
55    }
56    resolve(DTMC_pointer, R_j, DTMC_res_j);
57    resolve(DTMC_pointer, E_b, DTMC_seq_b);
58    return DTMC_pointer;
59  }
60
61  evaluateExternalPointerAction(A_pointer, F){
62    DTMC_pointer := initExternalPointerDTMC(A_pointer, F);
63    EC := getReferencedExternalCall(A_pointer);
64    E := getReferencedExecutionState(DTMC_pointer);
65    DTMC_ext := createExternalCallDTMC(EC);
66    resolve(DTMC_pointer, E, DTMC_ext);
67    return DTMC_pointer;
68  }
```

Listing 5.14: Pointer Action Evaluation Procedures

The single-state evaluation as introduced in Section 5.2.3 allows for a significantly faster top-level usage scenario evaluation (Figure 5.8) compared to the standard evaluation (Figure 5.7). On the other hand, it requires slightly more effort with respect to entry-level and remote pointer actions. As illustrated by Figures 5.19 and 5.20, the Markov transformation must take into account all possible hardware states $S_{pointer}(t) := \{\bar{s}_1(t), \ldots, \bar{s}_{\bar{m}}(t)\}$ at time t arising from the reduced set of hardware resources $R_{pointer} = \{r_1, \ldots, r_{\bar{n}}\} \subseteq R$ required by the target ResourceContainer of $A_{pointer}$:

$$\bar{s}_j(t) := (\bar{s}_j(r_1, t), \ldots, \bar{s}_j(r_{\bar{n}}, t)) \in \{OK, NA\}^{\bar{n}}$$

$$\forall t > 0, \quad j \in \{1, \ldots, \bar{m}\} \tag{5.40}$$

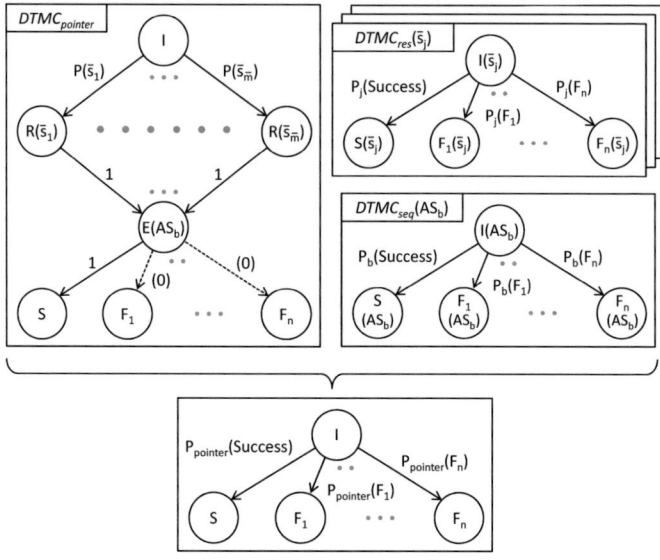

Figure 5.19: Evaluation of Entry-Level Pointer Actions (Single-State)

The probability $P(\bar{s}_j) := P(\bar{s}_j(t))$ of the system being in state $\bar{s}_j$ is determined in analogy to the probabilities of the overall system hardware states (see Equation 5.4), taking into account only the state probabilities of the resources in $R_{compute}$:

$$P(\bar{s}_j(t)) = \prod_{i=1}^{\bar{n}} P(s(r_i,t) = \bar{s}_j(r_i,t)) \;\; \forall t > 0, \;\; j \in \{1,\dots,\bar{m}\} \qquad (5.41)$$

The size $\bar{m}$ of $S_{compute}(t)$ is exponential with respect to the size $\bar{n}$ of $R_{compute}$ (namely, $\bar{m} = 2^{\bar{n}}$), but $S_{compute}(t)$ is significantly smaller than $S(t)$: $\bar{n} \ll n \Rightarrow \bar{m} \ll m$. In practice, $\bar{n} \le 2$ often holds. For example, the case study models used for validation (see Chapter 6) contain at most 2 modelled individual hardware resources per container. This is due to the fact that a resource environment is modelled from a high-level perspective in PCM-REL, following the two-state availability model for hardware resources (see

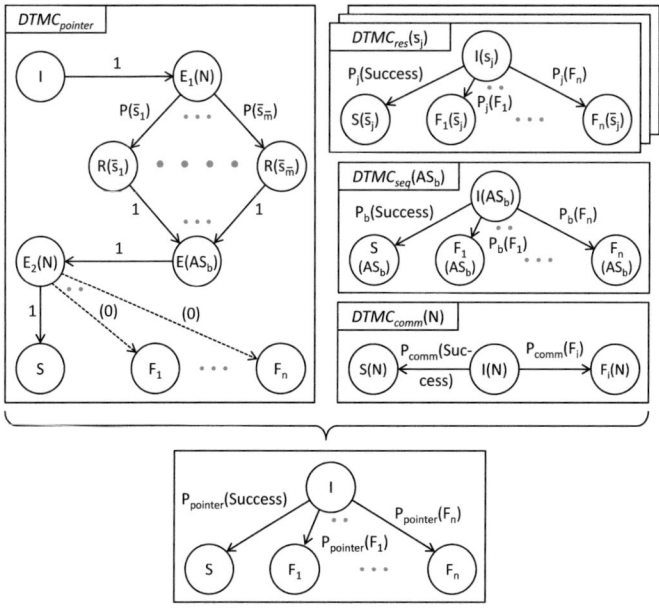

Figure 5.20: Evaluation of Remote Pointer Actions (Single-State)

Section 2.2) rather than focusing on the details of individual hardware elements and their failure behaviour. Hence, the single-state evaluation is generally significantly faster than the standard evaluation, even though some additional effort arises for the evaluation of entry-level and remote pointer actions (as well as computation actions, see Section 5.3.7).

Figure 5.19 illustrates the single-state evaluation of entry-level pointer actions. In contrast to the standard and approximated evaluations, the $DTMC_{pointer}$ contains $\bar{m}$ states $R(\bar{s}_1)$ to $R(\bar{s}_{\bar{m}})$ representing the operability check of the target ResourceContainer of $A_{pointer}$ under the different possible hardware states $\bar{s}_1$ to $\bar{s}_{\bar{m}}$. Each $R(\bar{s}_j)$ is reached from the initial state I with probability $P(\bar{s}_j)$, and it is resolved through an intermediate $DTMC_{res}(\bar{s}_j)$, which is created according to the same rules as the $DTMC_{res}(s_j)$ in the standard and approximated evaluation cases (see

Figure 5.16). A further state $E(AS_b)$ representing the invoked service behaviour is resolved through a corresponding $DTMC_{seq}(AS_b)$ as in the standard and approximated cases. The success and failure mode probabilities of the entry-level $A_{pointer}$ determined through single-state evaluation are:

$$P_{pointer}(Success) = \sum_{j=1}^{\bar{m}} (P_j(Success) \times P(\bar{s}_j)) \times P_b(Success) \qquad (5.42)$$

$$P_{pointer}(F_k) = \sum_{j=1}^{\bar{m}} (P_j(F_k) \times P(\bar{s}_j)) + \sum_{j=1}^{\bar{m}} (P_j(Success) \times P(\bar{s}_j)) \times P_b(F_k)$$

$$(5.43)$$

The calculation is similar to that of Equations 5.35 and 5.36, but it takes into account the different possible hardware states $\bar{s}_j$ that occur each with its specific probability $P(\bar{s}_j)$.

Figure 5.20 depicts the single-state evaluation of remote pointer actions, which is extended compared to the standard and approximated cases (Figure 5.17) in the same way as the single-state evaluation of entry-level pointers (Figure 5.19) compared to their standard or approximated evaluation (Figure 5.16). Instead of a single state $R(s_j)$ for the operability check of the target container, $\bar{m}$ states $R(\bar{s}_1)$ to $R(\bar{s}_{\bar{m}})$ account for the different possible hardware states $\bar{s}_1$ to $\bar{s}_{\bar{m}}$ and are resolved each by its specific $DTMC_{res}(\bar{s}_j)$. Correspondingly, the success and failure mode probabilities of the remote $A_{pointer}$ determined through single-state evaluation are the extended versions of equations 5.37 and 5.38:

$$P_{pointer}(Success) = \sum_{j=1}^{\bar{m}} (P_j(Success) \times P(\bar{s}_j))$$

$$\times P_{comm}(Success)^2 \times P_b(Success) \qquad (5.44)$$

$$P_{pointer}(F_k) = \begin{cases} P_{comm}(Success) \times \sum\limits_{j=1}^{\bar{m}} \left(P_j(F_k) \times P(\bar{s}_j) \right) \\[2ex] + P_{comm}(Success) \times \sum\limits_{j=1}^{\bar{m}} \left(P_j(Success) \times P(\bar{s}_j) \right) \\[2ex] \times P_b(F_k) \hspace{6em} if \; k \neq i \\[4ex] \\ P_{comm}(F_k) \\[1ex] + P_{comm}(Success) \times \sum\limits_{j=1}^{\bar{m}} \left(P_j(F_k) \times P(\bar{s}_j) \right) \\[2ex] + P_{comm}(Success) \times \sum\limits_{j=1}^{\bar{m}} \left(P_j(Success) \times P(\bar{s}_j) \right) \\[2ex] \times P_b(F_k) \\[1ex] + P_{comm}(Success) \times \sum\limits_{j=1}^{\bar{m}} \left(P_j(Success) \times P(\bar{s}_j) \right) \\[2ex] \times P_b(Success) \times P_{comm}(F_k) \hspace{3em} if \; k = i \end{cases}$$

$$(5.45)$$

To complete the consideration of pointer actions, Listing 5.15 shows the evaluation procedure covering all types of pointer actions under the single-state evaluation of system hardware states. For local and system-external pointers, there are no changes compared to the standard and approximated cases, and the details of the corresponding procedures are omitted from the listing.

```
1  // A_pointer:  considered  pointer  action
2  // F:          set  of  considered  failure  modes
3  // returns:    basic  DTMC  for  the  execution  of  the
4  //             considered  pointer  action
5
6  evaluatePointerAction(A_pointer, F){
7    type := getPointerType(A_pointer);
8    if(type == LOCAL) {
9      return evaluateLocalPointerAction(A_pointer, F);
10   } else if(type == ENTRY) {
11     return evaluateEntryPointerAction(A_pointer, F);
12   } else if(type == REMOTE) {
13     return evaluateRemotePointerAction(A_pointer, F);
14   } else {
15     return evaluateExternalPointerAction(A_pointer, F);
```

```
16      }
17   }
18
19   evaluateLocalPointerAction(A_pointer, F){
20      ... // analogous to standard or approximated evaluation
21   }
22
23   evaluateEntryPointerAction(A_pointer, F){
24      RC := getTargetResourceContainer(A_pointer);
25      R  := getSetOfRequiredHardwareResources(RC);
26      S  := determineSetOfHardwareStates(R);
27      P  := determineSetOfHardwareStateProbabilities(R);
28      DTMC_pointer := initEntryPointerDTMC(A_pointer, S, P, F);
29      AS_b := getReferencedActionSequence(A_pointer);
30      E_b  := getReferencedExecutionState(DTMC_pointer);
31      m    := getNumberOfElements(S);
32      for(j = 1; j <= m; j++) {
33         R_j := getOperabilityCheckState(DTMC_pointer, S(j));
34         DTMC_res_j := createOperabilityCheckDTMC(RC, F, S(j));
35         resolve(DTMC_pointer, R_j, DTMC_res_j);
36      }
37      DTMC_seq_b := evaluateActionSequence(AS_b, F, s_j);
38      resolve(DTMC_pointer, E_b, DTMC_seq_b);
39      return DTMC_pointer;
40   }
41
42   evaluateRemotePointerAction(A_pointer, F){
43      LR := getRequiredLinkingResource(A_pointer);
44      RC := getTargetResourceContainer(A_pointer);
45      R  := getSetOfRequiredHardwareResources(RC);
46      S  := determineSetOfHardwareStates(R);
47      P  := determineSetOfHardwareStateProbabilities(R);
48      DTMC_pointer := initRemotePointerDTMC(A_pointer, S, P, F);
49      AS_b := getReferencedActionSequence(A_pointer);
50      E_b  := getReferencedExecutionState(DTMC_pointer);
51      m    := getNumberOfElements(S);
52      for(j = 1; j <= m; j++) {
53         R_j := getOperabilityCheckState(DTMC_pointer, S(j));
54         DTMC_res_j := createOperabilityCheckDTMC(RC, F, S(j));
55         resolve(DTMC_pointer, R_j, DTMC_res_j);
56      }
57      DTMC_comm_N := createTransmissionDTMC(LR);
58      DTMC_seq_b := evaluateActionSequence(AS_b, F, s_j);
59      for (i = 1; i <= 2; i++) {
60         E_i := getTransmissionState(DTMC_pointer, i);
61         resolve(DTMC_pointer, E_i, DTMC_comm_N);
62      }
63      resolve(DTMC_pointer, E_b, DTMC_seq_b);
64      return DTMC_pointer;
65   }
66
67   evaluateExternalPointerAction(A_pointer, F){
68      ... // analogous to standard or approximated evaluation
69   }
```

Listing 5.15: Pointer Action Evaluation Procedures (Single-State)

5.3.7 Computation Actions

Computation actions $A_{compute}$ represent the execution of algorithms, data processing steps and other computations in the system. They are specified through PCM-REL InternalActions (see Section 2.7.2) containing both a set of InternalFODOccurrenceDescriptions (Section 4.3) and a set of required ProcessingResourceTypes. While the former expresses the software failure potentials of the represented computation, the latter indicates the dependencies to hardware resources and the associated failure potentials. As with entry-level and remote pointer actions (see Section 5.3.6), the evaluation of $A_{compute}$ depends on the way the Markov transformation handles system hardware states. With standard or approximated evaluation, $A_{compute}$ is always evaluated under the precondition of a certain system hardware state s_j, and the transformation creates a $DTMC_{compute}$ structure as shown in Figure 5.21. The $DTMC_{compute}$ contains a state $R(s_j)$ expressing the consumption of hardware resources by $A_{compute}$ under the precondition s_j, as well as a state E expressing the computation itself. The consumption of hardware resources is evaluated first, assuming that the computation cannot even start if a required hardware resource is unavailable.

The transformation creates an intermediate $DTMC_{res}(s_j)$ to account for hardware resource consumption and resolves $R(s_j)$ accordingly. The created $DTMC_{res}(s_j)$ considers the set of hardware resources $R_{compute} \subseteq R$ required by $A_{compute}$ through mapping the ParametricResourceDemands of the specified InternalAction to the ProcessingResourceSpecifications of the allocated ResourceContainer[2]. The construction of $DTMC_{res}(s_j)$ based on $R_{compute}$ follows the same rules as with entry-level and remote pointer actions (Figures 5.16 and 5.17) based on $R_{pointer}$: if all required resources are available, $P_j(Success)$ is set to 1; else, an over-

---

[2] As with the invocation target of a pointer action, the mapping of the required resource types of $A_{compute}$ to allocated hardware resources depends on the executed *component instance*. Hence, knowledge about the set of nested AssemblyContexts is again required.

all FOD probability of 1 is equally divided between all unavailable resources.

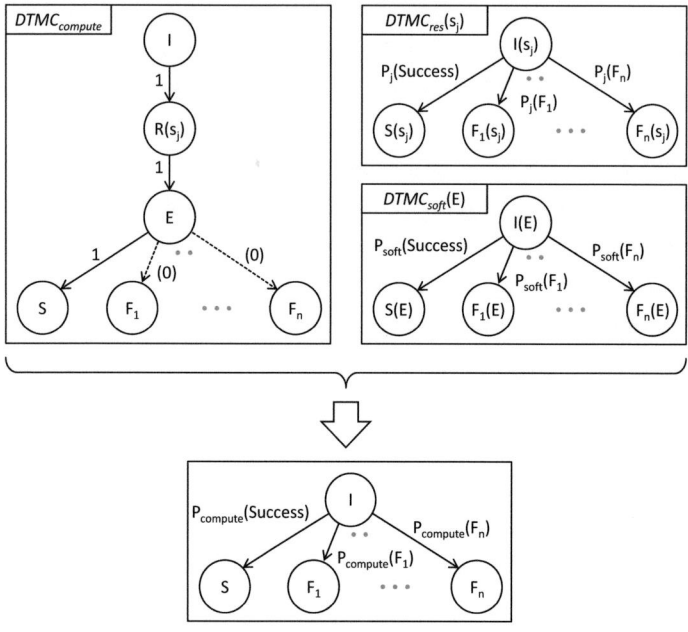

Figure 5.21: Evaluation of Computation Actions

For the computation itself, the Markov transformation resolves the state E with an intermediate $DTMC_{soft}(E)$ which reflects the InternalFODOccurrenceDescriptions of the specified InternalAction. The structure of $DTMC_{soft}(E)$ depends on the FODProbability and the SoftwareInducedFODType of each InternalFODOccurrenceDescription, as well as the selected evaluation level. If no InternalFODOccurrenceDescriptions have been specified, a single transition from $I(E)$ to $S(E)$ with probability 1 denotes the assured success of the computation. In the audio hosting example (Section 1.5), the InternalAction "ParseWebRequest" of the "WebFrontend.DownloadCollection" operation (see Fig-

```
1   // A_compute:    considered computation action
2   // F:            set of considered failure modes
3   // s_j:          considered hardware state
4   // returns:      basic DTMC for the execution of the
5   //               considered computation action
6
7   evaluateComputationAction (A_compute, F, s_j){
8     DTMC_compute := initComputationDTMC (A_compute, F);
9     R_j := getResourceConsumptionState (DTMC_compute );
10    E := getComputationState (DTMC_compute );
11    DTMC_res_j := createResourceConsumptionDTMC (A_compute, F, s_j );
12    DTMC_soft_E := createInnerComputationDTMC (A_compute, F);
13    resolve (DTMC_compute, R_j, DTMC_res_j );
14    resolve (DTMC_compute, E, DTMC_soft_E );
15    return DTMC_compute;
16  }
```

Listing 5.16: Computation Action Evaluation Procedure

ure 2.9) specifies a single `InternalFODOccurrenceDescription` of type "WebRequestFailure" with a probability of 10^{-8} (Figure 4.6). Assuming evaluation level 2 (or *Type*), the corresponding $DTMC_{soft}(E)$ contains two transitions – one from $I(E)$ to $S(E)$ with probability $1 - 10^{-8}$ denoting the success, and one from $I(E)$ to a failure state $F_k(E)$ representing the "WebRequestFailure", with probability 10^{-8}.

According to this description, the success and failure mode probabilities of $A_{compute}$ are as follows:

$$P_{compute}(Success) = P_j(Success) \times P_{soft}(Success) \qquad (5.46)$$

$$P_{compute}(F_k) = P_j(F_k) + P_j(Success) \times P_{soft}(F_k) \qquad (5.47)$$

A successful completion of $A_{compute}$ requires a successful hardware resource consumption and a successful computation; a failure mode F_k in either of the two aspects leads to failure mode F_k as a result of $A_{compute}$. Listing 5.16 shows the evaluation procedure for computation actions under standard and approximated hardware states evaluation.

In the case of a single-state evaluation of system hardware states, a slightly extended evaluation of $A_{compute}$ is required, as Figure 5.22 shows. As with entry-level and remote pointer actions, the extended version takes

169

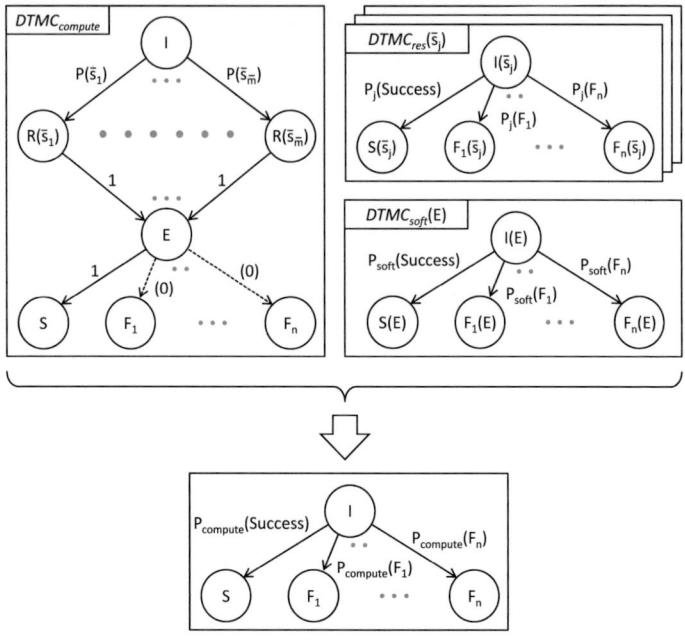

Figure 5.22: Evaluation of Computation Actions (Single-State)

into account a set $S_{compute}(t) := \{\bar{s}_1(t), \ldots, \bar{s}_{\bar{m}}(t)\}$ of possible hardware states at time t, based on the required resources $R_{compute}$ of $A_{compute}$. The correspondingly extended $DTMC_{compute}$ includes $\bar{m}$ states $R(\bar{s}_1)$ to $R(\bar{s}_{\bar{m}})$ instead of a single state $R(s_j)$ only. Each $R(\bar{s}_j)$ is resolved through its specific intermediate $DTMC_{res}(\bar{s}_j)$. The success and failure mode probabilities of $A_{compute}$ determined through single-state evaluation are:

$$P_{compute}(Success) = \sum_{j=1}^{\bar{m}} (P_j(Success) \times P(\bar{s}_j)) \times P_{soft}(Success) \quad (5.48)$$

$$P_{compute}(F_k) = \sum_{j=1}^{\bar{m}} (P_j(F_k) \times P(\bar{s}_j)) + \sum_{j=1}^{\bar{m}} (P_j(Success) \times P(\bar{s}_j)) \times P_{soft}(F_k)$$

$$(5.49)$$

```
1    // A_compute:     considered computation action
2    // F:             set of considered failure modes
3    // returns:       basic DTMC for the execution of the
4    //                considered computation action
5
6    evaluateComputationAction(A_compute, F){
7      R := getSetOfRequiredHardwareResources(A_compute);
8      S := determineSetOfHardwareStates(R);
9      P := determineSetOfHardwareStateProbabilities(R);
10     DTMC_compute := initSingleStateComputationDTMC(A_compute,
11       S, P, F);
12     m := getNumberOfElements(S);
13     for (j = 1; j <= m; j++) {
14       R_j := getResourceConsumptionState(DTMC_compute, S(j));
15       DTMC_res_j := createResourceConsumptionDTMC(A_compute,
16         F, S(j));
17       resolve(DTMC_compute, R_j, DTMC_res_j);
18     }
19     E := getComputationState(DTMC_compute);
20     DTMC_soft_E := createInnerComputationDTMC(A_compute, F);
21     resolve(DTMC_compute, E, DTMC_soft_E);
22     return DTMC_compute;
23   }
```

Listing 5.17: Computation Action Evaluation Procedure (Single-State)

In contrast to Equations 5.46 and 5.47, the calculation takes into account the different possible hardware states $\bar{s}_j$, each occurring with its specific probability $P(\bar{s}_j)$. Listing 5.17 shows the evaluation procedure.

5.3.8 Recovery Actions

Recovery actions $A_{recover}$ are specified through PCM-REL RecoveryActions (see Section 4.7). They express the system's ability to recover from FOD occurrences during service execution by switching to alternative behaviours. More concretely, $A_{recover}$ contains a set of RecoveryAction-Behaviours $B := \{b_1, \ldots, b_m\}$ with each b_i being represented through a corresponding action sequence AS_i. For $i > 1$, each b_i is associated with a set of handled FODTypes, which are mapped to a set of handled failure modes $F_{handled}(b_i) \subseteq F$ for reliability prediction[3]. Moreover, each b_i ref-

---

[3]For evaluation levels 0 and 1, the considered failure modes are more coarse-grained than the individual FODTypes (see Section 5.1.1). Hence, $F_{handled}(b_i)$ cannot be unambiguously determined and is assumed to be empty. As a consequence, alternative behaviours for failure

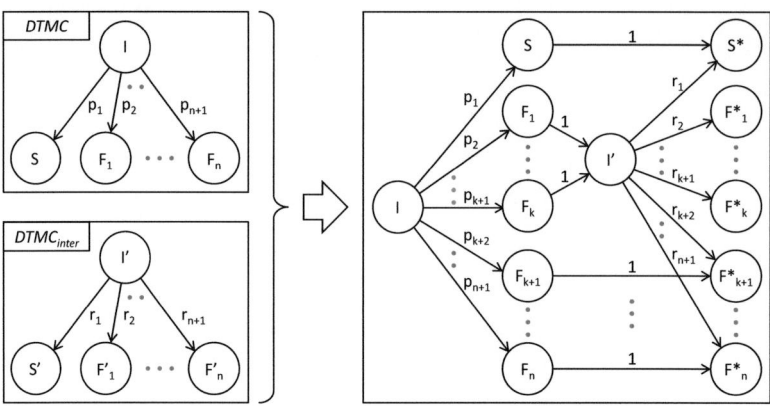

Figure 5.23: Markov Chain Appending (Single DTMC)

erences a set of FODHandlingAlternatives, such that a tree structure arises with each b_i having its FODHandlingAlternatives as its child nodes. The execution of $A_{recover}$ starts with its primaryBehaviour b_1 and proceeds through the tree of recovery behaviours until one b_i either completes successfully or results in a failure mode that is not handled by any of its child nodes.

Recovery actions represent the only actions that can be successfully completed in spite of FODs occurring during their execution. Due to this special ability, the Markov transformation needs two basic operations *chain-appending* and *failure-handling* in addition to the ones described in Section 5.1.3. Figure 5.23 shows the chain-appending operation, which augments an existing *DTMC* with an intermediate *DTMC_inter* by attaching the latter to a subset $F_{handled} \subseteq \{F_1, \ldots F_n\}$ of its failure states. *DTMC_inter* conforms to the basic structure (see Section 5.1.2), and *DTMC* to the generic structure (although the figure shows *DTMC* conforming to the basic structure, this is not a necessary precondition). Without loss of generality, let $F_{handled}$ consist of the first k failure states of *DTMC*, namely $F_{handled} :=$

---

recovery are effectively ignored by the Markov analysis if the evaluation level is switched to 0 or 1.

```
 1  // DTMC:     considered DTMC
 2  // SUCC:     set of successors of considered DTMC;
 3  //           each successor consists of an intermediate
 4  //           basic DTMC and a set of handled failure modes;
 5  //           the sets of handled failure modes of all
 6  //           successors are disjoint
 7
 8  append (DTMC, SUCC){
 9    S := getSuccessState (DTMC);
10    F := getSetOfFailureStates (DTMC);
11    n := getNumberOfElements (F);
12    S_final := createFinalSuccessState (DTMC);
13    F_final := createSetOfFinalFailureStates (DTMC);
14    m := getNumberOfElements (SUCC);
15    for (j = 1; j <= m; j++) {
16      DTMC_inter := getIntermediateDTMC (SUCC(j));
17      F_handled := getSetOfHandledFailureModes (SUCC(j));
18      I_inter := getInitialState (DTMC_inter);
19      S_inter := getSuccessState (DTMC_inter);
20      F_inter := getSetOfFailureStates (DTMC_inter);
21      F_h := getSetOfHandledFailureStates (DTMC, F_handled);
22      q := getNumberOfElements (F_h);
23      for (k = 1; k <= q; k++) {
24        createTransition (DTMC, F_h(k), I_inter, 1);
25      }
26      r_s := getTransitionProbability (DTMC_inter, I_inter,
27        S_inter);
28      createTransition (DTMC, I_inter, S_final, r_s);
29      for (i = 1; i <= n; i++) {
30        r_f := getTransitionProbability (DTMC_inter, I_inter,
31          F_inter(i));
32        createTransition (DTMC, I_inter, F_final(i), r_f);
33      }
34    }
35    createTransition (DTMC, S, S_final, 1);
36    for (i = 1; i <=n; i++) {
37      if (isUnhandled(F(i)) == true) {
38        createTransition (DTMC, F(i), F_final(i), 1);
39      }
40    }
41  }
```

Listing 5.18: Chain-Appending Procedure

$\{F_1, \ldots F_k\}$, $k \leq n$. The append operation includes four individual steps: First, it adds a new set of *final* success and failure states S^* and $F^* := \{F_1^*, \ldots F_n^*\}$ to $DTMC$. Second, it adds transitions with probability 1 from all failure states in $F_{handled}$ to the initial state I' of $DTMC_{inter}$. Third, it adds transitions from I' to all final states S^* and F^* with probabilities corresponding to the original transitions of $DTMC_{inter}$. Finally, it adds transitions with probability 1 from the success state S and the unhandled failure states $F_{unhandled} := \{F_{k+1}, \ldots F_n\}$ of $DTMC$ to their final counterparts. After the operation, the original success and failure states of $DTMC$ are not longer absorbing. Instead, they either lead on to their final counterparts or to further execution as represented through $DTMC_{inter}$. After the operation has been conducted, $DTMC$ has altered success and failure mode probabilities, but it still conforms to the generic structure.

While Figure 5.23 depicts the chain-appending operation with a single intermediate DTMC, the operation more generally copes with a finite set of intermediate DTMCs by repeating the second and third step for each of the DTMCs, based on the precondition that the sets of handled failure modes of all DTMCs are disjoint. Listing 5.18 shows the corresponding procedure.

The failure-handling operation builds upon the chain-appending operation and additionally reduces the intermediate states I', as well as the original success and failure states S and $\{F_1, \ldots F_n\}$ of $DTMC$. In summary, the operation expresses that certain failure modes resulting from a certain part of the execution (represented by the original DTMC) are handled by other execution parts (represented by the set of intermediate DTMCs). Listing 5.19 shows the procedure.

To evaluate $A_{recover}$, the Markov transformation creates a $DTMC_{recover}$ as shown by Figure 5.24. A state $E(AS_1)$ represents the execution of the primary behaviour. Following a recursive procedure, the transformation evaluates the whole tree of recovery behaviours, creating a basic $DTMC_{seq}(AS_i)$ from each behaviour b_i. The evaluation of each b_i involves considering all of its child nodes and using the failure-handling operation for the in-

```
1   // DTMC:      considered DTMC
2   // SUCC:      set of successors of considered DTMC;
3   //            each successor consists of an intermediate
4   //            basic DTMC and a set of handled failure modes;
5   //            the sets of handled failure modes of all
6   //            successors are disjoint
7
8   handle (DTMC, SUCC) {
9      S := getSuccessState (DTMC);
10     F := getSetOfFailureStates (DTMC);
11     n := getNumberOfElements (F);
12     append (DTMC, SUCC);
13     m := getNumberOfElements (SUCC);
14     for (j = 1; j <= m; j++) {
15        DTMC_inter := getIntermediateDTMC (SUCC(j));
16        I_inter := getInitialState (DTMC_inter);
17        reduce (DTMC, I_inter);
18     }
19     reduce (DTMC, S);
20     for (i = 1; i <= n; i++) {
21        reduce (DTMC, F(i));
22     }
23  }
```

Listing 5.19: Failure-Handling Procedure

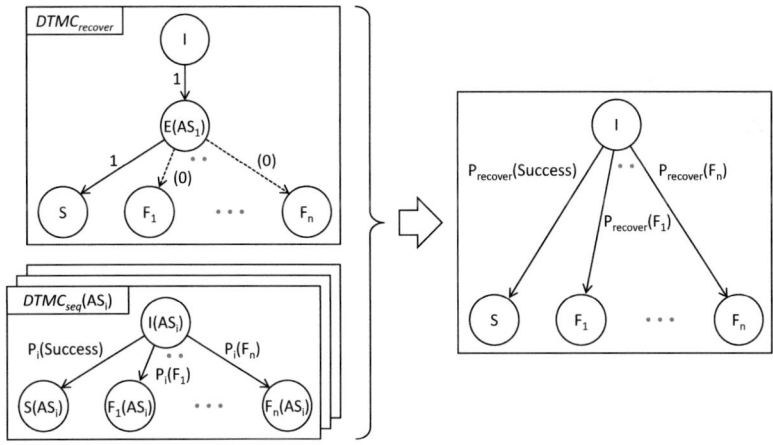

Figure 5.24: Evaluation of Recovery Actions

```
1    // A_recover:    considered recovery action
2    // F:            set of considered failure modes
3    // s:            considered hardware state (optional parameter,
4    //               not used for single−state evaluation)
5    // returns:      basic DTMC for the execution of the
6    //               considered recovery action
7
8    evaluateRecoveryAction(A_recover, F, s){
9      DTMC_recover := initRecoveryDTMC(A_recover, F);
10     E_r := getRecoveryExecutionState(DTMC_recover);
11     B := getPrimaryRecoveryBehaviour(A_recover);
12     DTMC_beh := evaluateRecoveryBehaviour(B, F, s);
13     resolve(DTMC_recover, E_r, DTMC_beh);
14     return DTMC_recover;
15   }
16
17   evaluateRecoveryBehaviour(B, F, s){
18     AS := getActionSequence(B);
19     DTMC_seq := evaluateActionSequence(AS, F, s);
20     ALT := getSetOfAlternativeBehaviours(B);
21     m := getNumberOfElements(ALT);
22     if (m > 0) {
23       SUCC := createEmptySetOfSuccessors();
24       for (j = 1; j <= m; j++) {
25         F_handled = getSetOfHandledFailureModes(ALT(j));
26         DTMC_alt_j = evaluateRecoveryBehaviour(ALT(j), F, s);
27         addSuccessor(SUCC, DTMC_alt_j, F_handled);
28       }
29       handle(DTMC_seq, SUCC);
30     }
31     return DTMC_seq;
32   }
```

Listing 5.20: Recovery Action Evaluation Procedures

tegration of the corresponding failure-handling behaviours. The topmost $DTMC_{seq}(AS_1)$ is then used to resolve $E(AS_1)$. Listing 5.20 shows the involved procedures, which result in $DTMC_{recover}$ conforming to the basic structure. An alternative transformation without Markov state reductions (as introduced in Section 5.1.1) is achieved by replacing failure-handling operations in the listing through chain-appending operations (in analogy to replacing state resolutions through state substitutions in the other transformation listings).

To describe the success and failure probabilities of $A_{recover}$ mathematically, several additional definitions are necessary. To begin with, let $O :=$ $\{Success, F_1, \ldots, F_n\}$ be the set of possible outcomes of each recovery behaviour b_i. A *step* represents the execution of a certain behaviour with a certain outcome:

$$STEP := \left\{ (b_i, o_j) \mid b_i \in B, \; o_j \in O \right\} \qquad (5.50)$$

A function $Beh : STEP \to B$; $Beh((b_i, o_j)) = b_i$ maps each step to its associated behaviour, and $Res := STEP \to O$; $Res((b_i, o_j)) = o_j$ maps each step to its outcome. Furthermore, the semantics of the specified `RecoveryActionBehaviours`, each with its list of `handledFODTypes`, allow for a unique definition of the function $Next : STEP \to B \cup \{x\}$. This function maps any step $s = (b_i, o_j)$ to its next executed behaviour b_k, or to an artificially introduced x, if no other behaviour is executed after s. The overall execution of $A_{recover}$ involves proceeding through its behaviours in a *sequence* of steps. A sequence represents a possible flow of execution, starting with the primary behaviour b_1, proceeding to the next behaviour depending on the outcome of each step, and ending when no more behaviour can be executed:

$$SEQ := \left\{ (s_1, \ldots, s_l) \in STEP^l \left| \begin{array}{l} l \in \mathbb{N}, \\ Beh(s_1) = b_1, \\ Next(s_l) = x, \\ \forall i \in \{1, \ldots, l-1\} : \\ Beh(s_{i+1}) = Next(s_i) \end{array} \right. \right\} \qquad (5.51)$$

Finally, $SEQ(o_j) := \left\{ (s_1, \ldots, s_l) \in SEQ \mid Res(s_l) = o_j \right\}$ is the set of all sequences with result o_j. With these definitions, the success and failure probabilities of $A_{recover}$ can be written as:

$$P_{recover}(Success) = \sum_{seq \in SEQ(Success)} P(seq) \qquad (5.52)$$

$$P_{recover}(F_k) = \sum_{seq \in SEQ(F_k)} P(seq) \qquad (5.53)$$

The occurrence probability of each sequence is the product of the occurrence probabilities of the outcomes of each step:

$$P((s_1, \ldots, s_l) \in SEQ) = \prod_{i=1}^{l} P_{I(s_i)}(Res(s_i)) \qquad (5.54)$$

with $I : STEP \rightarrow \{1, \ldots, m\}$ mapping each step s_i to the index of its associated behaviour.

The evaluation of recovery actions as described here is based on the rule that the action sequence AS_i of each recovery behaviour b_i results in either a success or exactly one failure mode F_k. As Section 5.3.1 discusses, the Markov transformation obeys this rule by assuming that F_k is uniquely determined by the first failing action within AS_i. Although in practice, multiple FODs may occur during the execution of AS_i, such cases are rare and can typically be ignored if FODs occur independently from each other and each one has a low occurrence probability (see the illustrating example in Section 5.3.1).

5.4 Complexity

This section investigates the complexity of the PCM-REL Markov analysis in terms of execution time (Section 5.4.1) and memory consumption (Section 5.4.2). The discussion focuses on the Markov transformation step with Markov state reductions switched on (see Section 5.1). A transformation without reduction operations may be used for special purposes such as comparisons to related approaches, but it is not the generally preferred choice. With state reductions switched on, the transformation results in a basic DTMC. Hence, the following solving step is trivial and can be omitted from complexity considerations. The complexity of parameter dependency solving preceding the Markov analysis (see Section 2.7.6) has been discussed in [Koz08] and is also omitted from consideration here.

5.4.1 Execution Time

The PCM-REL Markov transformation is realized through an algorithm outlined in Sections 5.2 and 5.3. This algorithm consists of several DTMC creation procedures, which follow a general scheme of DTMC initialization and repeated state resolution, and which invoke each other according to an overall hierarchical pattern (see Section 5.1.3). In the following, the execution time of the algorithm is assumed to be proportional to the number of created Markov states. State creation is a heavily repeated atomic step of the algorithm; it involves the effort of initializing a new state object in memory. Other atomic steps include the creation of Markov transitions, as well as the later deletion of states and transitions. The amount of these other steps is roughly proportional to the state creation. A created state is first connected to an existing structure of states through newly created transitions; later, these transitions and the state itself are again deleted as part of a reduction operation.

Table 5.6 lists the DTMC creation procedures involved in the Markov transformation, which can be categorized as procedures for evaluating system hardware states (*SHS*), action sequences (*AS*) and individual actions (*ACT*). Further abbreviations used in the table are as follows:

- F: number of failure modes for a given PCM-REL instance and evaluation level;

- R: number of hardware resources specified for a PCM-REL instance;

- A: number of actions specified for an action sequence;

- B_T: number of branch transition behaviours specified for a branch action;

- $\sum C_i$: sum over all iteration counts specified for a loop action;

- B_F: number of forked behaviours specified for a fork action;

179

- C: number of hardware resources strictly required for the operation of a resource container that represents the invocation target of a pointer action;

- L: number of hardware resources required locally by a computation action;

- B_R: number of recovery behaviours specified for a recovery action.

Each procedure listed in the table includes DTMC-creating calls. Although these calls are not further detailed in the provided Listings 5.4 to 5.20, DTMC sizes and structures follow from the accompanying DTMC illustrations and the textual descriptions. The table indicates the names of the calls, their invocation counts within the procedures and the number of Markov states that they create. Generally, the created DTMCs include $F + 2$ states for start, success and failure modes, as well as further states which are to be resolved through lower-level DTMCs. In most cases, the number of invocations of DTMC-creating calls per procedure is strictly limited to at most 4, and DTMC sizes are bounded by the number of provided model elements. For example, the "evaluateForkAction" procedure creates a single DTMC of size $F + 2 + B_F$, where F is limited by the number of model elements expressing individual failure potentials[4], and B_F is equal to the number of specified forked behaviours. However, some procedures show increased complexity. First, the standard "evaluateScenario" procedure creates a DTMC with exponential size with respect to R. Second, the "evaluateLoopAction" procedure creates a potentially large DTMC reflecting the sum over all specified loop iteration counts $\sum C_i$. Third, the single-state procedures "evaluteEntryPointerAction", "evaluateRemotePointerAction" and "evaluateComputationAction" each create an exponential number of DTMCs with respect to C and L, respectively; each procedure contains one

---

[4]The most differentiated evaluation level 3 (or *PointOfFailure*) includes one failure mode for each specified FODOccurrenceDescription, one for each ProcessingResourceSpecification and one for each CommunicationLinkResourceSpecification.

Type	Listing No. / Procedure	DTMC Creation		Required Lower-Level Procedures	
		DTMC-creating Calls Included in Procedure	Size of Created DTMCs	Count	Type
SHS	(5.4) evaluateScenario [Standard]	1 x initTopLevelDTMC	$F + 2 + 2^R$	2^R	AS
	(5.5) evaluateScenario [Single-State]	1 x initSingleStateTopLevelDTMC	$F + 2 + 1$	1	AS
	(5.6) evaluateScenario [Approximated]	-	-	min: 1 max: 2^R	AS
AS	(5.7) evaluateAction-Sequence	1 x initActionSequenceDTMC	$F + 2 + A$	A	ACT
ACT	(5.10) evaluateDefaultAction	1 x initDefaultDTMC	$F + 2$	-	-
	(5.11) evaluateBranchAction	1 x initBranchDTMC	$F + 2 + B_T$	B_T	AS
	(5.12) evaluateLoopAction	1 x initLoopDTMC	$F + 2 + \Sigma C_i$	1	AS
	(5.13) evaluateForkAction	1 x initForkDTMC	$F + 2 + B_F$	B_F	AS
	(5.14) evaluateLocalPointer-Action	1 x initLocalPointerDTMC	$F + 2 + 1$	1	AS
	(5.14) evaluateEntryPointer-Action	1 x initEntryPointerDTMC 1 x createOperabilityCheckDTMC	$F + 2 + 2$ $F + 2$	1	AS
	(5.14) evaluateRemotePointer-Action	1 x initRemotePointerDTMC 1 x createOperabilityCheckDTMC 2 x createTransmissionDTMC	$F + 2 + 4$ $F + 2$ 3	1	AS
	(5.14) evaluateExternalPointer-Action	1 x initExternalPointerDTMC 1 x createExternalCallDTMC	$F + 2 + 1$ $F + 2$	-	-
	(5.15) evaluateEntryPointer-Action [Single-State]	1 x initEntryPointerDTMC 2^C x createOperabilityCheckDTMC	$F + 2 + 2^C + 1$ $F + 2$	1	AS
	(5.15) evaluateRemotePointer-Action [Single-State]	1 x initRemotePointerDTMC 2^C x createOperabilityCheckDTMC 2 x createTransmissionDTMC	$F + 2 + 2^C + 3$ $F + 2$ 3	1	AS
	(5.16) evaluateComputation-Action	1 x initComputationDTMC 1 x createResourceConsumptionDTMC 1 x createInnerComputationDTMC	$F + 2 + 2$ $F + 2$ $F + 2$	-	-
	(5.17) evaluateComputation-Action [Single-State]	1 x initSingleStateComputationDTMC 2^L x createResourceConsumptionDTMC 1 x createInnerComputationDTMC	$F + 2 + 2^L + 1$ $F + 2$ $F + 2$	-	-
	(5.20) evaluateRecoveryAction	1 x initRecoveryDTMC	$F + 2 + 1$	B_R	AS

Table 5.6: Complexity of DTMC Creation Procedures

DTMC of exponential size. In practice, all of $\sum C_i$, C and L can be assumed to be low enough to keep the number of Markov states created by *ACT* procedures within feasible bounds (see Sections 5.3.4, 5.3.6 and 5.3.7). The approximated "evaluateScenario" procedure is included in the table for completeness but does not create an own DTMC structure.

The overall execution time is not only determined by the complexity of individual procedures, but also by the number of executed procedures during the transformation. As Table 5.6 indicates, a top-level *SHS* procedure invokes one or multiple *AS* procedures. Each *AS* procedure invokes one *ACT* procedure for each action contained in the evaluated sequence. In turn, each *ACT* procedure invokes one *AS* procedure for each behavioural specification referenced by the evaluated action (the table omits intermediate procedures for invocation routing as shown in Listings 5.8, 5.9, 5.14 and 5.15). Default actions, external pointer actions and computation actions do not reference any further behavioural specifications. Hence, their evaluation procedures constitute the lowest level of the DTMC creation hierarchy. Overall, the *AS* and *ACT* procedures consider each action sequence occurrence of a behavioural view (as introduced in Section 4.1) – as well as each action within the sequence – exactly once.

To give an upper bound for the Markov transformation's execution time $T_I(U)$ for a usage scenario U of a PCM-REL instance I, consider the following definitions:

- S: number of Markov states created during the transformation;

- $S_{max}(U)$: maximal number of Markov states created for a behavioural evaluation of the execution of U;

- $S_{max}(AS)$: maximal number of Markov states created by an *AS* procedure;

- $S_{max}(ACT)$: maximal number of Markov states created by an *ACT* procedure;

- C_{AS}: number of action sequence occurrences in the behavioural view of U;

- A_{max}: maximal number of actions in any action sequence belonging to I;

- T_{max}: maximal time effort associated with a created Markov state.

With standard evaluation of system hardware states, $E_I(U)$ is bounded as follows:

$$
\begin{aligned}
T_I(U) &\leq S \times T_{max} \\
&\leq (F + 2 + 2^R \times (1 + S_{max}(U))) \times T_{max} \\
&\leq (F + 2 + 2^R \times (1 + C_{AS} \times (S_{max}(AS) + A_{max} \times S_{max}(ACT)))) \\
&\quad \times T_{max} \\
&= (F + 2 + 2^R \times (1 + C_{AS} \times (F + 2 + A_{max} \times (1 + S_{max}(ACT))))) \\
&\quad \times T_{max} \quad\quad (5.55)
\end{aligned}
$$

Equation 5.55 relates the execution time $T_I(U)$ to the number of created Markov states S. The transformation creates $F + 2 + 2^R$ states at the top level and includes 2^R behavioural evaluations, each with at most $S_{max}(U)$ created states. Each behavioural evaluation requires the consideration of C_{AS} action sequence occurrences with at most $S_{max}(AS) = F + 2 + A_{max}$ states, as well as up to A_{max} individual actions per sequence with at most $S_{max}(ACT)$ states. C_{AS} depends on the number of behavioural specifications (ScenarioBehaviours and ResourceDemandingBehaviours) in I and on the number of pointer actions (EntryLevelSystemCalls and ExternalCallActions) that refer to each behaviour. $S_{max}(ACT)$ depends on the concrete action specifications (see Table 5.6). The most significant factor influencing the execution time is the exponential number of behavioural evaluations, which leads to an overall complexity of $\mathscr{O}(2^R)$ for the Markov transformation with standard evaluation of system hardware states. With single-state evaluation, the factor 2^R is omitted from Equation 5.55, and the complexity can be expressed as $\mathcal{O}(C_{AS})$ relating to the size of the behavioural view instead. The execution time of the approximated evaluation lies between single-state and standard, depending on the specified stop criteria.

5.4.2 Memory Consumption

A second complexity dimension refers to the maximal amount of memory required at a time during the Markov transformation. The discussion is based on the assumption that, at any point in time, the amount of required memory is proportional to the number of currently existing Markov states. Markov transitions require memory as well, but their number can be seen as being roughly proportional to the number of states. Due to the Markov reduction steps performed on-the-fly, the transformation algorithm is highly space-efficient. The discussion reuses definitions and results from the preceding Section 5.4.1 about execution time complexity.

Table 5.6 shows the number and sizes of the DTMCs created by each individual transformation procedure. The specified sizes are the initial ones directly after DTMC creation. They are also the maximal sizes, as each procedure ultimately results in a single basic DTMC with only $F + 2$ states (see Section 5.1.2 for a definition of the basic DTMC structure). All other states are removed during the execution of the procedure through state resolution steps as specified in Listings 5.4 to 5.20[5]. As the procedures invoke each other according to a hierarchical pattern as shown in Figure 5.6, the maximal number of Markov states existing at any time is directly related to the maximal depth of the DTMC creation hierarchy. Let $M_I(U)$ be the required amount of memory for a UsageScenario U of a PCM-REL instance I. Consider further definitions as follows:

---

[5]Although a state resolution step temporarily adds another $F + 2$ states itself, these additional states are the ones created by a lower-level procedure. Hence, the summation over all currently active procedures as done in this section is correct.

- S_T: maximal number of Markov states existing at any step of the transformation;

- D_{max}: maximal depth of nested action sequence occurrences in the behavioural view of U;

- M_{max}: maximal required amount of memory associated with a Markov state.

Additionally, consider $S_{max}(AS)$, $S_{max}(ACT)$ and A_{max} as defined in Section 5.4.1. With standard evaluation of system hardware states, $M_I(U)$ is bounded as follows:

$$
\begin{aligned}
M_I(U) &\leq S_T \times M_{max} \\
&\leq (F + 2 + 2^R + D_{max} \times (S_{max}(AS) + S_{max}(ACT))) \times M_{max} \\
&= (F + 2 + 2^R + D_{max} \times (F + 2 + A_{max} + S_{max}(ACT))) \times M_{max}
\end{aligned}
$$
$$(5.56)$$

Equation 5.56 decomposes the number of existing Markov states S_T into $F + 2 + 2^R$ states at the top level and $S_{max}(AS) + S_{max}(ACT)$ states at each of the D_{max} further levels (each level includes an AS procedure for the sequence and an ACT procedure for a certain action within the sequence). D_{max} depends on the structure of the behavioural view and has a value between 1 and – in the theoretical worst case – C_{AS} (as defined in Section 5.4.1). The space complexity may be dominated either by the 2^R states at the top level or by the D_{max} DTMC creation levels, depending on the nature of I. Hence, it can be expressed as $\mathcal{O}(2^R + D_{max})$. Although this complexity contains an exponential part, the 2^R states in Equation 5.56 are not a multiplied factor as in Equation 5.55. With single-state evaluation, the 2^R states at the top level are omitted and the complexity is $\mathcal{O}(D_{max})$. The same holds for the approximated evaluation, which avoids building a top-level DTMC and instead collects the results in a single data structure (see Section 5.2.4).

5.5 Implementation

The Markov analysis described in this chapter has been implemented and included in the PCM Workbench (see Section 4.8) to allow for evaluating the architectural IT system models created with PCM-REL. The implementation includes the complete Markov transformation and solving of the resulting DTMC. The analysis is triggered through the Eclipse Run Configuration mechanism; each analysis run can be flexibly configured with respect to the options discussed in Section 5.1.1, namely the Markov evaluation level, usage of Markov state reductions and handling of system hardware states. In case of the approximated evaluation (Section 5.2.4), the users can specify one or multiple stop conditions regarding the maximal number of evaluated system hardware states, the minimal required accuracy of the prediction results, or the maximal execution time of the analysis. Then, the analysis run finishes as soon as any of the specified stop conditions is fulfilled. Further configuration options for the analysis refer to the logging of the analysis steps and results.

Figure 5.25 gives an impression of how prediction results are returned as a feedback to the user of the Workbench. The central form of feedback is a report (upper middle part) showing all prediction results for all usage scenarios of the analysed PCM-REL instance. The granularity of the results depends on the selected evaluation level (Section 5.1.1). At the most differentiated level 3 (or `PointOfFailure`), an additional failure impact analysis shows aggregated failure potentials of the specified components and component services, allowing for identifying critical architecture parts at a glance. The Workbench supports persisting the generated report and sharing it with other users. Further parts shown in the figure include a console (lower part) showing the progress of conducted analysis runs, as well as a tree-structured EMF editor (right-hand side, upper part) that shows the contents of the DTMC model resulting from the Markov transforma-

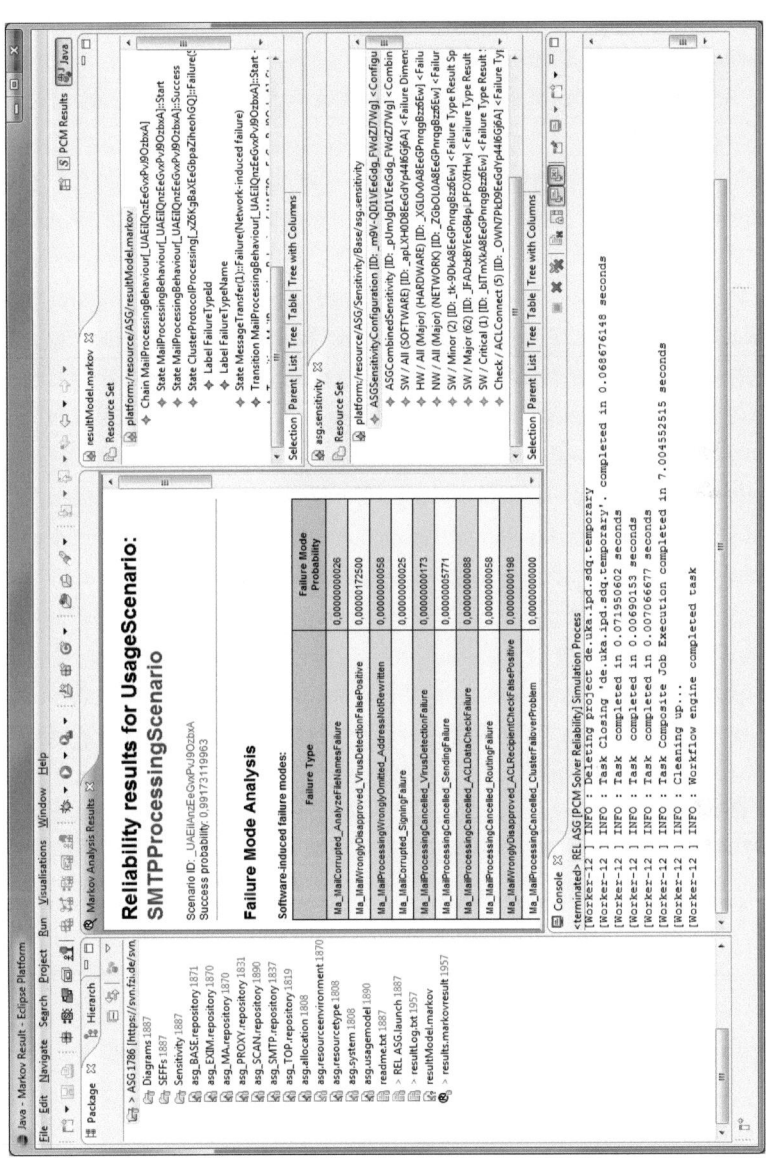

Figure 5.25: PCM-REL Reliability Evaluation Tool Support

tion (the DTMC has a basic structure unless Markov state reductions are switched off, see Section 5.1.1).

A further feature of the implementation is its built-in support for repeated analysis runs over multiple architectural variations of the system under study, thereby supporting sensitivity analyses (see Section 6.1). To this end, an EMF meta-model has been provided capturing variations of individual parameters of an underlying PCM-REL instance. Parameters may refer to PCM-REL entities such as specifications of `VariableUsages` (Section 2.7.5) and reliability annotations. Variations of parameter values are specified in terms of sequences or ranges, based on double or string values, either absolute or relative to the given base values of the PCM-REL instance. Multiple parameter variations can be combined to express more extensive architectural changes. Being provided with a specification of parameter variations, the Workbench automatically conducts a series of analysis runs and adjusts the underlying PCM-REL instance in each run according to the specification. The obtained prediction results allow for assessing the influence of changing architectural properties and usage profile aspects on the system's reliability. In Figure 5.25, a specification of parameter variations for a PCM-REL instance is visualised by a corresponding EMF editor (right-hand side, middle part). Overall, the Workbench provides a comprehensive and flexible environment for reliability evaluation of PCM-REL instances through the built-in Markov transformation and support for sensitivity analyses.

6 PCM-REL Case Studies and Validation

This chapter presents efforts devoted to validate the PCM-REL approach as presented in the thesis. Due to the nature of the approach belonging to the field of architecture-based software reliability prediction (ASRP), established validation tools and methods in this field also form the basic set of means for the validation of PCM-REL. A corresponding review of the state of the art in validating related ASRP approaches is provided by Section 6.1. The following Section 6.2 sets up a list of validation goals along the activities required for applying PCM-REL, assuring that all relevant aspects of the approach are covered by the validation efforts. An overview of these efforts is then given by Section 6.3. At the core of the chapter, Sections 6.4 and 6.5 present two major case studies, applying PCM-REL to concrete IT systems under study. The first one is the audio hosting service used as illustrating example throughout the thesis, with an existing prototypical implementation as its base. The second one is an existing industrial system with e-mail processing functionalities. The studies complement each other and, in summary, provide evidence for the validation of all targeted PCM-REL aspects. The chapter is completed by a short discussion of other existing PCM-REL experiments and case studies in Section 6.6.

6.1 Validating IT System Reliability

This section discusses challenges that PCM-REL has to face for its validation, which to a large extent comply with the general validation challenges of architecture-based software reliability prediction (ASRP). Although validation is an indispensable means of giving evidence for the applicability

Publication Type	Authors	Year	Illustrating Example	Sensitivity Analysis	Prototype Case Study	Real-World Case Study
Methodological	Cheung et al. [Che80]	1980	X	X	-	-
	Dolbec et al. [DS95]	1995	X	-	-	-
	Cortellessa et al. [CSC02]	2002	X	X	-	-
	Gokhale et al. [GT02]	2002	X	X	-	-
	Goseva-Popstojanova et al. [GPHG⁺03]	2003	X	X	-	-
	Reussner et al. [RSP03]	2003	X	X	X	-
	Gokhale et al. [GWHT04]	2004	X	X	-	(X)
	Yacoub et al. [YCA04]	2004	X	X	-	-
	Grassi [Gra05]	2005	X	X	-	-
	Popic et al. [PDAC05]	2005	X	X	-	-
	Rodrigues et al. [RRU05]	2005	X	-	-	-
	Sharma et al. [ST06]	2006	X	X	-	-
	Wang et al. [WPC06]	2006	X	-	-	X
	Cortellessa et al. [CG07a]	2007	X	X	-	-
	Sato et al. [ST07a]	2007	X	-	-	-
	Sharma et al. [ST07c]	2007	X	X	-	X
	Lipton et al. [LG08]	2008	X	X	-	-
	Cooray et al. [CMRK10]	2010	X	X	X	-
	Filieri et al. [FGGM10]	2010	X	X	-	-
Case Study	Goseva-Popstojanova et al. [GPHP05]	2005	-	-	-	X
	Koziolek et al. [KSB10]	2010	-	-	-	X

Table 6.1: Validation of Software Reliability Prediction

of software quality prediction approaches, specific issues arise in the field of reliability prediction. A single – most probably successful – run of a usage scenario or system service invocation gives little insight into the reliability properties of an IT system. Only when a statistical relevant number of failure-related events is observed, reliability can be deduced from the relative occurrence frequencies of those events. The required observation time may be several years or even longer than the system's mission time, which makes reliability measurement experiments in the field impracticable at best, or impossible at worst. Nevertheless, certain means of validation have been established over the years in the ASRP domain. Table 6.1 shows several ASRP publications and their included validation efforts. The table distinguishes methodological papers, which propose a novel prediction approach, and case study papers, which apply existing prediction approaches to specific systems under study. The validation efforts can be categorized as follows:

- *Illustrating examples*: The presentation of an exemplary software architecture, application of the approach to this architecture and interpretation of the results is always conducted to reason for the general plausibility of the approach. Many examples are taken from real-world domains, but there is generally no implementation available against which to check the prediction results.

- *Sensitivity analyses*: Most authors examine the effects of input variations to the prediction results of their approaches, either formally or through repeated prediction runs. If an input variation is chosen such that it represents existing uncertainty regarding input estimations, the prediction results can be checked for their robustness. If the approach allows for drawing conclusions from the prediction results with high confidence in spite of uncertain inputs, an argument for its validity has been established.

- *Prototype case study*: A few authors (such as [RSP03, CMRK10]) apply their predictions to prototypical software implementations of limited complexity and compare prediction results to simulations or measurements. To assure the feasibility of the conducted experiments, several simplifications are introduced compared to a real measurement in the field. Such simplifications may include the injection of artificial faults instead of natural faults, an artificial usage profile that provokes frequent failures-on-demand, substitution of application logic through code skeletons, and others.

- *Real-world case study*: More recently, there are increased efforts to apply predictions to real-world open source or industrial systems, including dedicated case study papers (such as [GPHP05, KSB10]). Although these experiments have strong potential to show the applicability of the examined prediction approaches, they still require certain simplifications. For example, Goseva-Popstojanova et al. [GPHP05] investigate an open source compiler of the C programming language using an artificial usage profile (namely, a regression test suite) that provokes frequent failures due to known software faults. Thus, the authors degrade the reliability of the application to much lower levels than those expected in the field, in order to obtain measured reliability values. Koziolek et al. [KSB10] conduct predictions for a large industrial control system and interpret the results, but do not compare the overall predicted system reliability to measured values.

For PCM-REL, there is an additional validation challenge compared to ASRP in general, as the approach also considers hardware failure potentials. Hardware resources typically only fail after several years of operation. While for software, failure rates can be artificially increased through specific usage profiles, provoking frequent hardware failures is associated with unacceptable costs. Nevertheless, the thesis provides validation experiments that are up to the state of the art in the ASRP domain. The audio hosting example (introduced in Section 1.5) serves as an illustrating example throughout the thesis and as a case study based on a prototypical implementation (Section 6.4). While the reliability measurements do not account for hardware failure potentials, an additional simulation is conducted that takes all failure potentials considered by PCM-REL into account. A second case study applies PCM-REL to an industrial IT system with e-mail processing functionalities (Section 6.5). In both case studies, sensitivity analyses are conducted to examine the robustness of prediction results against uncertain input estimations.

6.2 Validation Goals

This section discusses the validation goals in terms of statements for which the conducted validation experiments shall provide evidence. The top-level goal is to show that PCM-REL can feasibly be applied to predict the reliability of IT systems, and that its application is useful (namely, answers relevant questions regarding system design)[1]. Considering the whole process of applying PCM-REL, including creation of an architectural model, input estimation of reliability annotations, Markov analysis and interpretation of prediction results, the top-level goal includes several sub goals discussed in Sections 6.2.1 to 6.2.4. The validation does not focus on foundational concepts employed by PCM-REL that are commonly established and accepted in the scientific communities of component-based software engineering (CBSE), reliability engineering and architecture-based software reliability prediction (ASRP). More concretely, PCM-REL assumes without further validation that it is generally feasible to represent software failure potentials through independent "per-visit" failure-on-demand (FOD) probabilities, hardware failure potentials through MTTF values, and to view software architectures from a component-based perspective.

6.2.1 Feasibility of Modelling Abstractions

Like every architecture modelling language, PCM-REL includes modelling abstractions which inevitably lead to a simplified view on a represented system under study. The most significant abstractions of the approach refer to the simplified high-level representation of control and data flow, stateless software component modelling and the restriction to synchronous component interactions. More concretely, dependencies of loop iteration counts

---

[1] This goal formulation implies that the validation does not aim at measuring the benefits and costs of a whole system engineering process enriched by continuous reliability modelling and prediction (as introduced in Section 3.2). Rather, the scope of validation roughly corresponds to a system design iteration (see Figure 3.3), focussing not on performance but purely on reliability.

and branch transition probabilities on component-internal state can only be implicitly expressed through probabilistic abstractions. Loop iteration counts are always finite and determined in advance; they may not depend on termination conditions evaluated within the loop bodies. All behavioural specifications are finite and must not contain cyclic invocations of component service operations. Concurrent behaviours are modelled as being independent from each other; synchronisation issues that may lead to effects such as deadlocks, starvation or racing conditions can only be captured through probabilistic abstractions. Invocations of component service operations are generally modelled as being synchronous and blocking.

The two case studies presented in this validation chapter give evidence that, in spite of the discussed abstractions, PCM-REL can feasibly be used to express an IT system under study with all its reliability-relevant aspects. For the audio hosting case study (Section 6.4), the compliance of the model-based reliability predictions with measurements conducted on the implemented system explicitly shows that the simplifications of the model do not prevent the obtained prediction results from being sufficiently accurate.

6.2.2 Feasibility of Estimation of Reliability Annotations

When applying PCM-REL to an IT system under study, the modelled PCM-REL instance includes several reliability-specific annotations in terms of software FOD probabilities, hardware MTTF and MTTR values, as well as network transmission failure probabilities. A central assumption of the modelling step is that input estimations can feasibly be derived for those annotations, with a level of confidence sufficient for trusting the prediction results. In particular, the estimation of software FOD probabilities often constitutes a challenge and is a threat to the validity of ASRP approaches in general (see Section 2.3). In this validation chapter, the Astaro ASG case study (see Section 6.5) explicitly goes through the process of estimating reliability annotations for PCM-REL. The study shows that the required estimations can be achieved based on existing information sources in a typical industrial software development context.

6.2.3 Validity of Markov Analysis

PCM-REL can only be successfully applied if the included Markov analysis is valid – namely, if it produces accurate prediction results when provided with accurate inputs (where "input" refers to the whole architectural model including reliability annotations). Threats to this validity include all known assumptions of the analysis that constitute simplifications compared to reality, as well as any further flaws that might falsify the obtained prediction results. Regarding known assumptions, the Markov analysis abstracts from all time-related aspects. In particular, it treats a system under study as if its mission time was unlimited, and as if all usage scenario runs were instantaneous (namely, having zero time duration). Furthermore, it abstracts from the concrete impact of local FOD occurrences to the subsequent control and data flow, assuming that the first occurred FOD within a `ResourceDemandingBehaviour` determines the result of the behaviour (see Section 5.3.1). The dependency solver, upon which the Markov analysis builds (see Section 2.7.6), additionally neglects stochastic dependencies between multiple variable usages within the same `ResourceDemandingSEFF` (see Figure 2.7), which can lead to incorrect occurrence probabilities of service execution paths.

The validity of the Markov analysis is examined as part of the audio hosting case study, which compares prediction results obtained by analysis with a simulation of the system (Section 6.4.3). The simulation constitutes an alternative evaluation method of the original PCM-REL instance based on a queueing network (QN) formalism; it explicitly considers time-related aspects and is not affected by dependency solver assumptions.

6.2.4 Significance and Robustness of Prediction Results

The prediction results obtained from the application of PCM-REL are only useful if they allow for answering relevant design questions regarding the IT system under study, and if the drawn conclusions are sufficiently stable against existing input estimation uncertainties. To this end, the case studies presented in this validation chapter demonstrate how PCM-REL can be used to determine rankings between the reliabilities of multiple design alternatives and between reliability impacts of different failure potentials throughout the architecture. Moreover, both studies include sensitivity analyses in terms of repeated prediction runs with varying input parameter values to account for the effects of uncertain inputs. The results allow for drawing significant conclusions supporting relevant design decisions and for allocating quality assurance efforts during system development.

6.3 PCM-REL Case Study Features

Out of the set of available case studies conducted for PCM-REL, two studies have been selected and are discussed in detail in this validation chapter, namely the audio hosting case study (Section 6.4) and the Astaro ASG case study (Section 6.5). Together, both studies exhibit a comprehensive set of features, as shown in Table 6.2, to provide convincing evidence for the validity of PCM-REL. The audio hosting study is based on a prototypical implemented system of limited complexity. Illustrative reliability annotation values are chosen to demonstrate the capabilities of the approach. The study features multiple design alternatives and establishes a ranking between those alternatives with respect to reliability, supporting software architects in their design decisions. In addition, predictions are compared to a simulation approach, as well as measurements conducted for the implemented system. The ASG study refers to an industrial IT system and derives input estimations from existing qualitative and statistical failure data. The analysis mainly focuses on the reliability impacts associated with individ-

Feature	Audio Hosting Case Study	Astaro ASG Case Study
Real-world industrial IT system	-	X
Reliability annotations estimated based on existing qualitative and statistical failure data	-	X
Examination and ranking of multiple design alternatives	X	(X)
Examination of reliability impacts of existing architectural failure potentials	X	X
Investigation of robustness of prediction results through sensitivity analyses	X	X
Comparison to simulation	X	-
Comparison to measurements	X	-

Table 6.2: Overview of PCM-REL Case Study Features

ual system processing steps and establishes a ranking between those steps, guiding the allocation of future testing and quality assurance efforts. Due to the high reliability levels of the application, no comparison to simulation or measurements was conducted for the ASG study. However, both studies include sensitivity analyses to examine the robustness of the obtained prediction results against input estimation uncertainties. Other conducted PCM-REL case studies are shortly discussed in Section 6.6.

6.4 Audio Hosting Case Study

This section presents the audio hosting case study, which is based on the scenario introduced in Section 1.5 and on the modelled PCM-REL instance presented throughout Section 2.7. The audio hosting service constitutes an illustrating example and a typical use case for PCM-REL. It features a component-based software architecture whose components can be distributed across multiple computing nodes. Furthermore, its functionality is centred around data storage and processing, which is at the core of many business information systems.

The case study adds additional design alternatives (Section 6.4.1) as a set of known possibilities at the start of a system design iteration. Section 6.4.2 demonstrates how PCM-REL can be used to examine these alternatives and derive relevant insights about the system under study. Further validation of the approach is provided through comparison of prediction results with a queueing network simulation (Section 6.4.3) and with measurements conducted on an implemented prototype (Section 6.4.4). Finally, Section 6.4.5 reviews the case study and its achievements.

The modelled PCM-REL instances of the audio hosting service and its design alternatives are available for download at [BBKR12].

6.4.1 Design Alternatives

To demonstrate the assessment of multiple design alternatives through PCM-REL, this case study does not only consider the initial architectural candidate as presented throughout Section 2.7. Rather, it takes into account a set of architectural improvements which show promise for increased reliability:

- *High-Availability Server* ("ha"): Uses a single server hosting all instantiated components. Replicated hardware resources on the server allow for fast fail-over in case of resource breakdowns. Additionally, the potential for network transmission failures is eliminated as all communications are local on the single server.

- *High-Reliability Audio Processing* ("hr"): Replaces standard algorithms for encoding, watermarking and packaging of audio files by high-quality implementations with significantly reduced FOD probabilities.

- *Replicated Database Server* ("re"): Uses two database servers with synchronized databases so that fail-over between the servers is possible.

These improvements can also be partially combined to further increase the expected reliability of the system. Together with the initial architectural candidate, the case study considers six design alternatives, namely "std" (denoting the initial or standard candidate), "ha", "hr", "re", "ha+hr" (denoting the combined usage of a high-availability server and high-reliability audio processing) and "re+hr" (denoting a replicated DB server and high-reliability audio processing).

From a modelling point of view, all considered design alternatives must be represented through corresponding PCM-REL instances. Thanks to the reuse capabilities built into the modelling language, existing specifications of the "std" alternative can be reused to a large extent for the other alternatives. Other specifications are added as a supplement. For the "ha" alternative, a new ResourceContainer is added to the resource environment model (see Section 2.7.4) representing the high-availability server, with resource MTTR values reduced by factors 20 (for the hard disk) and 200 (for the CPU), accounting for the fast fail-over. A new allocation model maps all component instances from the system definition to the new server. For "hr", new BasicComponents "EncodingHR", "WatermarkingHR" and "PackagingHR" are added to the repository model (Section 2.7.2), along with a new CompositeComponent "AudioProcessingHR", to represent the new high-reliability audio processing. An adjusted system model (Section 2.7.3) instantiates "AudioProcessingHR" instead of "AudioProcessing", and this change is also propagated to the allocation model. Furthermore, the system now relies on its own encoding engine and does not longer need its required role for the "IEncoding" interface. For the "re" alternative, a second database server is added to the resource environment model, and a new linking resource is established connecting the application server and the second database server. Moreover, an additional BasicComponent "DBAccessManagement" includes fault-tolerant data storage and retrieval and is instantiated by an accordingly adjusted system definition. The "UserDBAccess" and "AudioDBAccess" components are both instantiated twice and deployed on the two database servers through an adjusted allocation model. PCM-REL instances for the "ha+hr" and "re+hr" alternatives are obtained by corresponding combinations of the discussed specifications.

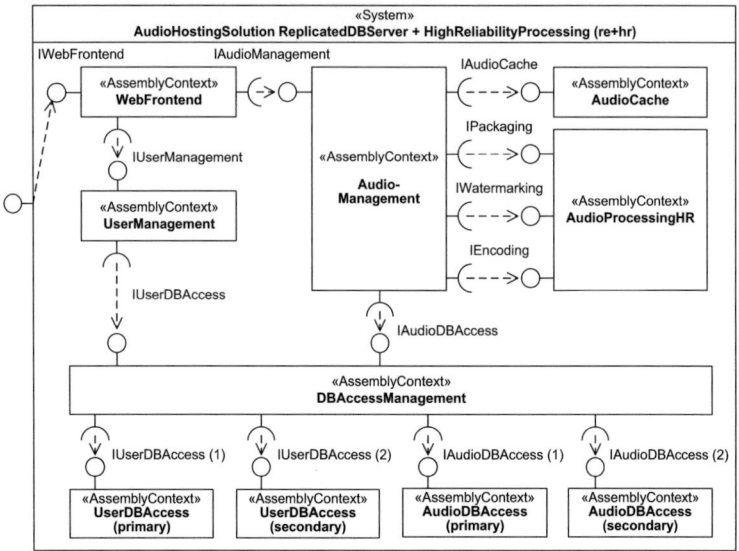

Figure 6.1: Audio Hosting System Model (re+hr)

To further illustrate how the modelled design alternatives emerge from the initial architectural candidate "std", the following figures depict parts of the PCM-REL instance for the "re+hr" alternative. First, Figure 6.1 shows the corresponding system definition. The model differs from the "std" system model (as shown in Figure 2.11) by instantiating "AudioProcessingHR" instead of "AudioProcessing", by omitting the "IEconding" required system role, by duplicating the "UserDBAccess" and "AudioD-BAccess" component instances, and by introducing "DBAccessManagement", which enables fault-tolerant data storage to and retrieval from the two database servers. "DBAccessManagement" provides both "IUserD-BAccess" (to the "UserManagement") and "IAudioDBAccess" (to the "AudioManagement"). In turn, it includes two required roles for each of these interfaces, connected to the individual data accessing components.

Figure 6.2 shows the resource environment and allocation models of the "re+hr" alternative. In contrast to "std" (see Figure 2.13), the environment

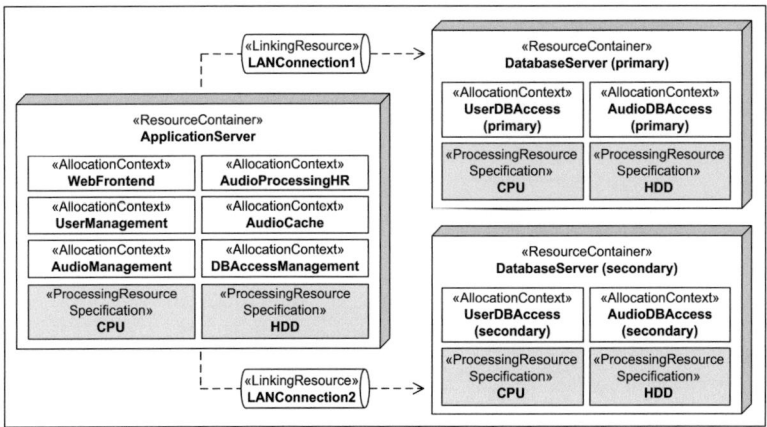

Figure 6.2: Audio Hosting Resource Environment and Allocation (re+hr)

contains two database servers, each with its own allocated "UserDBAccess" and "AudioDBAccess" instances and with a modelled "CPU" and "HDD" (hard disk drive) hardware resource. Both database servers are connected to the application server by two individual linking resources "LANConnection1" and "LANConnection2". The application server hosts the additional "DBAccessManagement" component instance, which controls the propagation of service invocations to the database servers.

As an example for the fault-tolerant behavioural specifications of "DBAccessManagement", Figure 6.3 shows the "RetrieveFile" service operation provided by the component as part of the provided "IAudioDBAccess" interface. The specification contains a RecoveryAction (see Section 4.7) with two inner behaviours. The first behaviour tries to access the primary database server by invoking "IAudioDBAccess_Primary.RetrieveFile". If this invocation fails, a second behaviour performs the same invocation on the secondary server. The represented FT mechanism does not only tolerate a hardware breakdown of the primary server (through its handled HardwareInducedFODTypes "CPUFailure" and "HDDFailure") but also software failure potentials that prevent the data access from being success-

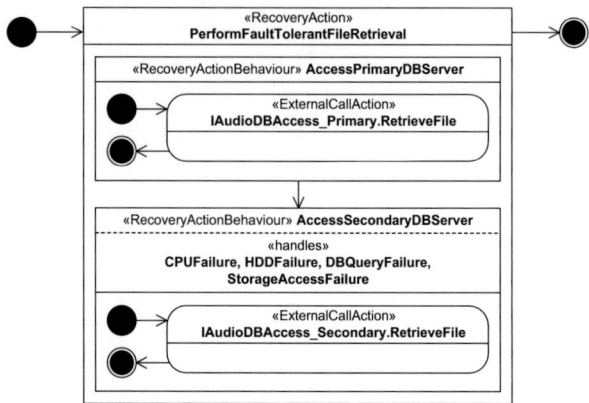

Figure 6.3: RDSEFF "DBAccessManagement.RetrieveFile" (re+hr)

ful (handled `SoftwareInducedFODTypes` "DBQueryFailure" and "StorageAccessFailure"). Hence, the mechanism represents combined software-level and hardware-level FT.

6.4.2 Audio Hosting Reliability Evaluation

This section demonstrates how PCM-REL's Markov analysis can be used to gain insights about the system under study. All analysis runs were conducted with Markov state reductions switched on (see Section 5.1.1) and standard evaluation of system hardware states (Section 5.2.2); the individual runs took less than 5 seconds on a standard laptop computer[2]. Based on the illustratively chosen values of reliability annotations as presented throughout Chapter 4 (including software FOD probabilities, hardware MTTF and MTTR values, and network transmission failure probabilities), PCM-REL predicts the reliability of the audio hosting service as shown in Figure 6.4. Subfigures (a) and (b) show the predicted FOD probabilities $fp\_inter(alt)$ and $fp\_batch(alt)$ of the considered audio hosting

---

[2]The experiments were conducted on a laptop computer with an Intel® Core™i7-620M Processor, 8.0 GB RAM memory and a 64 Bit Windows 7 Professional operating system.

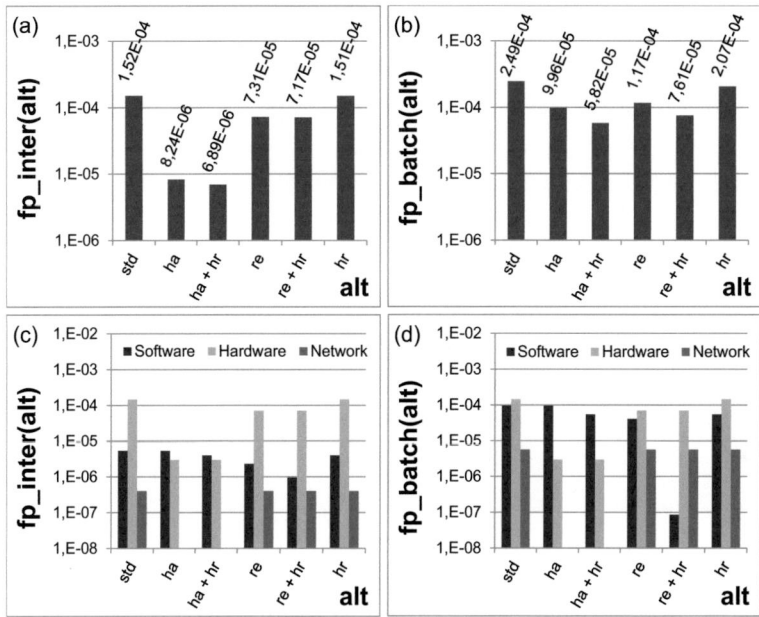

Figure 6.4: Audio Hosting Reliability Predictions by Design Alternatives, Usage Scenarios and Failure Dimensions

design alternatives *alt* (as introduced in Section 6.4.1) for the two existing usage scenarios *inter* and *batch* (see Figure 2.15)[3]. As the figures show, the predicted FOD probabilities range from $6.89 * 10^{-6}$ to $1.52 * 10^{-4}$ for interactive usage and from $5.82 * 10^{-5}$ to $2.94 * 10^{-4}$ for batch usage. Although the concrete predicted values are subject to uncertainty, the figures allow for drawing general conclusions. First, the initial candidate "std" has lowest reliability among all design alternatives, for both modes of usage. This corresponds to the construction of the other alternatives as architectural improvements of "std". Second, the batch mode differs from interactive mode by generally lower reliabilities and smaller differences between

---

[3]The FOD probability is the counterpart of reliability ($fp = 1 - P(Success)$) and is chosen as the displayed metric in the figures of this section. The lower a bar in the presented bar charts is, the higher is the corresponding reliability.

the alternatives. While a significant improvement of more than factor 10 is achieved by "ha" and "ha+hr" (compared to "std") in interactive mode, no such improvements are seen in batch mode. Further observation reveals that "ha+hr" is the best alternative in both modes, and that "hr" and "re+hr" are least affected by a change of mode. In conclusion, the results allow for recommending the "ha" and "ha+hr" alternatives for audio hosting installations whose main mode of usage is interactive. For batch mode, none of the alternatives achieves significant reliability improvements over "std". It may be worthwhile to examine further possible design alternatives especially for this mode.

Subfigures (c) and (d) of Figure 6.4 provide refined information by denoting the individual reliability impacts of the software, hardware and network dimensions. This information is available because the PCM-REL Markov analysis explicitly determines the reliability impacts of failure potentials throughout the system's architecture at different levels of granularity (see Section 5.1.1). The refined perspective allows for further explanation of observations made from Subfigures (a) and (b), and it indicates which failure potentials should be tackled to obtain further reliability improvements. Overall, Subfigures (c) and (d) indicate that the lower reliabilities of the batch mode compared to interactive mode stem from increased software and network failure potentials. This corresponds to the fact that batch downloads include 30 audio files on average (see Figure 2.15) and hence require much more processing and network communication than interactive downloads of a single file. On the other hand, the impact of hardware failure-potentials does not depend on the amount of required software processing, and it stays constant across both modes.

Going further into detail, Subfigure (c) reveals that most design alternatives are dominated by hardware failure potentials in interactive mode. As an explanation for the significant improvements of "ha" and "ha+hr" compared to "std", the figure shows that these two alternatives are the ones lowering the hardware impacts. This corresponds to the usage of a high-availability server in these alternatives (see Section 6.4.1). Furthermore, "ha" and "ha+hr" are single-server solutions and hence do not include any network failure potentials. However, the latter fact is not a significant advantage over the other alternatives, as network-induced FOD probabilities are generally low. Further observation of Subfigure (c) reveals that the "re+hr" alternative has the lowest software-induced FOD probability (approximately 10^{-6}) and promises high reliability, provided that software architects find a way to further modify the alternative and improve it with respect to hardware. Subfigure (d) shows that the reliability impacts of the different dimensions are more balanced in batch mode compared to interactive mode. The "re+hr" alternative has a very low software-induced FOD probability but is dominated by hardware and network impacts. Still, this alternative could significantly benefit from an adjusted resource environment with improved conditions for reliability.

If software architects wish to examine reliability impacts throughout the architecture in detail, PCM-REL supports them by fine-grained prediction results. As an example, Figure 6.5 details the software reliability impacts of the audio hosting service according to the individual modelled SoftwareInducedFODTypes (see Section 4.2). Without going through all aspects shown in the figure, the discussion here focuses on the "re+hr" alternative (combining database server replication and high-reliability audio processing) in batch mode. In Figure 6.4(d), this alternative shows a very low software-induced FOD probability, even though the software impacts of both "re" and "hr" are similar to that of "std". From Figure 6.5(b), it is evident that both "re" and "hr" lower the impacts of a subset of the relevant SoftwareInducedFODTypes, but only "re+hr" lowers all relevant types. The database server replication lowers the occurrence probabilities of database query and storage access failures, and the high-reliability audio processing decreases encoding, watermarking and packaging FOD probabilities.

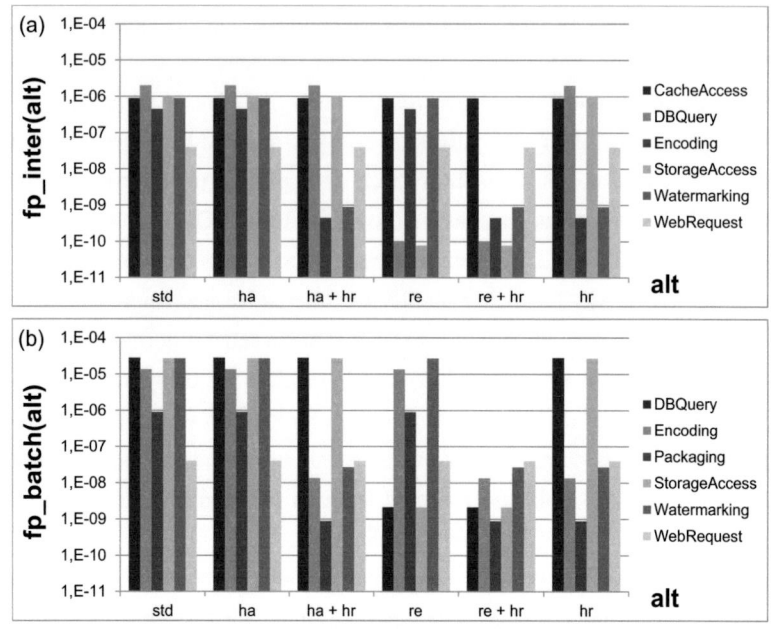

Figure 6.5: Software-Induced Failure-on-Demand Probabilities by Design Alternatives, Usage Scenarios and Failure-on-Demand Types

While the prediction results discussed so far give insight into the reliability characteristics of the audio hosting service, further examination is necessary to determine the robustness of those results in the light of uncertain reliability annotations given as an input to the analysis. To this end, Figure 6.6 shows the results of a sensitivity analysis, focusing on groups of reliability annotations and examining all cases in which one of the groups is off by factor 10. In the example, the granularity of the groups (which, in the general case, should be equal to the granularity of conducted input estimations) is chosen such that all software FOD probabilities of a certain SoftwareInducedFODType (such as cache access failures or database query failures) form each a group, supplemented by the groups of hardware MTTF values, hardware MTTR values and network transmission failure

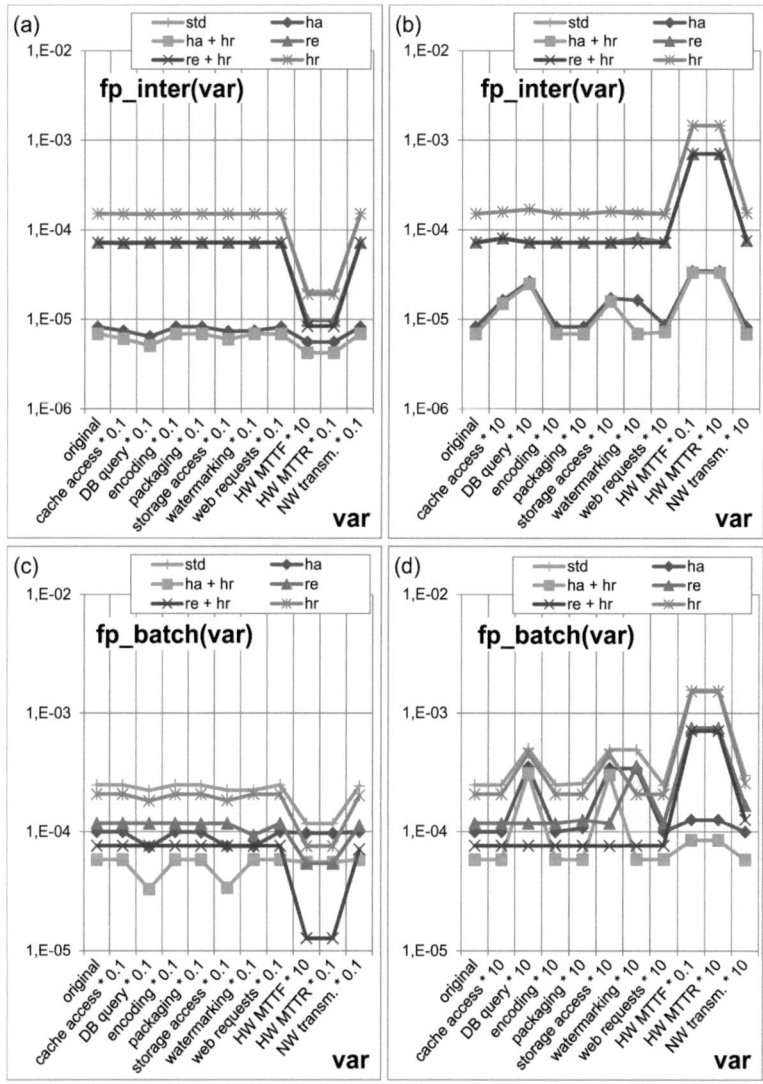

Figure 6.6: Robustness of Ranking of Design Alternatives Against Parameter Group
Variations, Differentiated by Usage Scenarios and Change Directions

probabilities. The figure shows the FOD probabilities $fp\_inter(var)$ and $fp\_batch(var)$ of the audio hosting design alternatives over the individual parameter group variations var for the two modes of usage $inter$ and $batch$. While Subfigures (a) and (c) deal with improvements of individual parameter groups (which means multiplying hardware MTTF values by 10 or other annotations by 0.1), the other two Subfigures (b) and (d) denote degradations of the respective groups. Although the variation scales are discrete, the figure connects the individual predictions through line segments. This presentation allows for recognizing changes in the ranking of design alternatives as crossings of line segments.

The first and most important observation from Figure 6.6 is that the ranking of design alternatives is very stable in interactive mode (no line crossings) and less stable in batch mode. As expected, improvements regarding individual parameter groups – as shown in Subfigures (a) and (c) – also improve the overall reliability of each design alternative, compared to the original setting (namely, each alternative has its highest FOD probability in the leftmost "original" category). Subfigures (b) and (d) show that the argument can be reversed, with degradations of individual parameter groups also degrading the overall reliability of each alternative. Generally, the biggest impacts are caused by changing hardware MTTF or MTTR values. This corresponds to Figures 6.4(c) and 6.4(d) showing that hardware failure potentials have the greatest reliability impact on most design alternatives. The unstable ranking of alternatives in Subfigures (c) and (d) is generally in line with the observation that the differences between the alternatives are only marginal in batch mode, as shown in Figure 6.4(b). Moreover, software-induced FOD probabilities are significantly increased in batch mode compared to interactive mode (Figures 6.4(c) and (d)), which explains why the reliabilities of the design alternatives are more sensitive to software-related input variations in batch mode than in interactive mode. As the improvements obtained by the design alternatives with respect to individual SoftwareInducedFODTypes in batch mode are highly diverse

(Figure 6.5(b)), it is plausible that – especially in the case of software-related degradations (Figure 6.6(d)) – the ranking of the design alternatives changes over the individual variations. In conclusion, the results of the sensitivity analysis support the initial findings: Design alternatives "ha" and "ha+hr" can be recommended in interactive mode with high confidence. In batch mode, no unambiguous recommendation is possible. Instead, further design alternatives should be evaluated.

6.4.3 Comparison with Simulation

While the preceding Section 6.4.2 has demonstrated how PCM-REL can analyse an IT system under study with respect to reliability, the only cause of inaccuracy of prediction results considered so far is the uncertainty of input estimations, whose consequences have been examined through a sensitivity analysis. However, a flawed Markov analysis could likewise lead to inaccurate results, and it might not be possible to detect such flaws just by repeated analysis runs. Therefore, this section compares prediction results obtained through PCM-REL with the results of a simulation-based approach. The simulation is based on the same original PCM-REL instance, but it uses a queueing network (QN) formalism as its simulation model and provides an own transformation from the PCM-REL instance to an instance of the simulation model. Hence, it constitutes an alternative evaluation method of the PCM-REL instance, and the obtained results can be compared to those of the Markov analysis.

Figure 6.7 shows the two evaluation methods, namely the Markov analysis (coloured in grey) and the QN simulation. The latter is an extension of *SimuCom*, an existing PCM discrete-event performance simulation (see [Bec08] for a detailed description). SimuCom takes into account performance-specific annotations which are neglected by the Markov analysis, such as inter-arrival times between consecutive usage scenario runs and resource demand sizes. It observes user behaviour, system execution

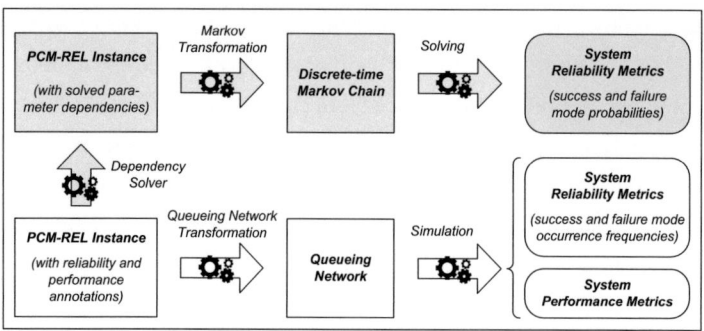

Figure 6.7: PCM-REL Markov Analysis and Simulation

and hardware resource consumptions over a simulated timeline and collects data about the system's performance such as completion times of service execution and the utilization of resources. For validation of PCM-REL, SimuCom was extended to take the reliability-specific aspects of the model into account, and to trigger FOD occurrences according to the modelled failure potentials. The extended simulation represents software FODs through exceptions thrown according to the specified probabilities, drawing samples from a random number generator to decide about the result of each visited potential point of failure (PPOF). The same procedures are employed to trigger network transmission failures. For hardware resources, the simulation uses the given MTTF and MTTR values as mean values of an exponential distribution and draws samples from the distribution to determine actual resource failure and repair times. Whenever service execution requires a currently unavailable hardware resource, it fails with an exception. Overall, the simulation records the execution results of all usage scenario runs, and the so-determined occurrence frequencies of successful and failed scenario runs constitute a benchmark to which the Markov analysis results can be compared.

Besides being an alternative evaluation method, the simulation also differs in its assumptions from the Markov analysis. While the analysis abstracts from time-related aspects, the simulation takes the concept of time explicitly into account. Each simulation experiment observes a system over a limited mission time interval and records a finite number of usage scenario runs during this interval. It tracks hardware resource failures and repairs along the simulated timeline, rather than using an aggregated steady-state availability value per resource (see Section 5.2.1). It is not affected by dependency solver assumptions such as the disregard of stochastic dependencies between variable usages (see Section 6.2.1). Hence, the simulation experiment serves to validate that the additional abstractions of the analysis compared to simulation do not lead to insufficient accuracy of the prediction results.

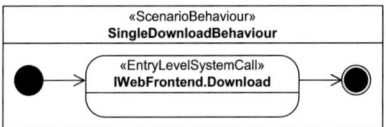

Figure 6.8: Single-Download Usage Scenario for the Audio Hosting Service

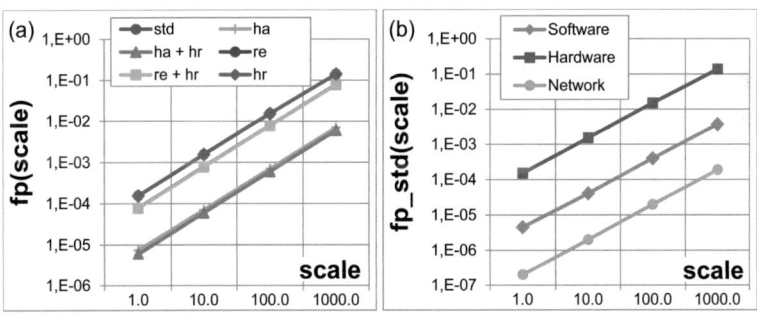

Figure 6.9: Audio Hosting Reliability Predictions with Varying Reliability Annotations, Based on the Single-Download Usage Scenario

The most severe limitation of the simulation is that it consumes significantly more time than the Markov analysis. The time consumption depends on the number of events to be processed during the simulation experiment, which in turn is proportional to the number of observed usage scenario runs and the complexity of the executed behaviour in each run. In the context of this case study, two simplifications are introduced to keep the number of simulation events within feasible bounds. First, a simplified usage scenario as shown in Figure 6.8, which consists of a single-file download only, simplifies the user and system behaviour involved in each scenario run. Second, all reliability annotations in the model are upscaled so that FODs occur more frequently, which allows for observing a statistically relevant number of failure events within fewer usage scenario runs. The upscaling includes multiplying all software FOD probabilities and network transmission failure probabilities with a constant factor, as well as dividing hardware resource MTTF values by the same factor. Figure 6.9 depicts FOD probabilities $fp(scale)$ and $fp\_std(scale)$ obtained through Markov analysis for different scaling factors $scale$, ranging from the original setting 1.0 to 1 000.0. The predictions are based on the singe-download scenario. As the figure shows, the scaling changes the absolute reliability levels of the audio hosting service but preserves the proportions between design alternatives (Subfigure (a)) and failure dimensions (shown by example for the "std" alternative in Subfigure (b)). Hence, the simplifications are introduced in a way such that the fundamental characteristics of the case study scenario are changed as little as possible.

Figure 6.10 shows the result of a series of simulation experiments Exp_1, compared to predictions obtained by the Markov analysis. The series consists of one simulation experiment per design alternative, based on the single-download scenario and upscaled reliability annotations by factor 1000.0. Each experiment includes 10000 usage scenario runs. While Subfigure (a) depicts the overall FOD probabilities $fp\_1000(alt)$ of the design alternatives alt, the other subfigures show the reliability impacts of each of the software, hardware and network dimensions. In spite of the simulation results being based on observed instances of usage scenario runs and thus

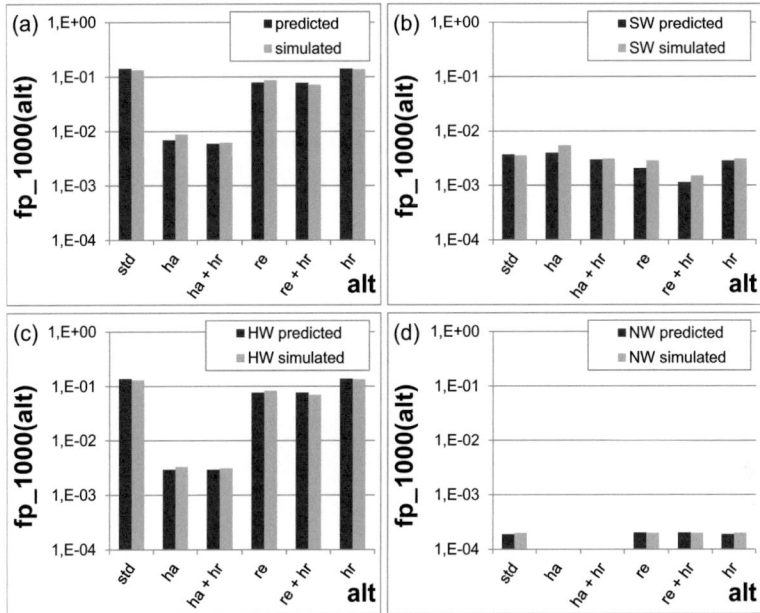

Figure 6.10: Comparison of Reliability Predictions with Simulation by Design Alternatives and Failure Dimensions

subject to statistical variation, prediction results and observations are generally very close. In particular, fundamental findings such as the superior reliability of the "ha" and "ha+re" alternatives are supported by both evaluations. Existing differences vary in sizes and directions and can safely be accredited to the effects of statistical variation.

To give further evidence that the comparison between prediction results and simulation is meaningful in spite of the introduced simplifications, further simulation experiments Exp_2 and Exp_3 were conducted with decreased scaling factors 100.0 and 10.0, which are closer to the original setting. Because of the effects of statistical variation, the achieved degree of compliance of Exp_1 (as shown in Figure 6.10) can only be expected to be upheld if the number of observed usage scenario runs is increased in

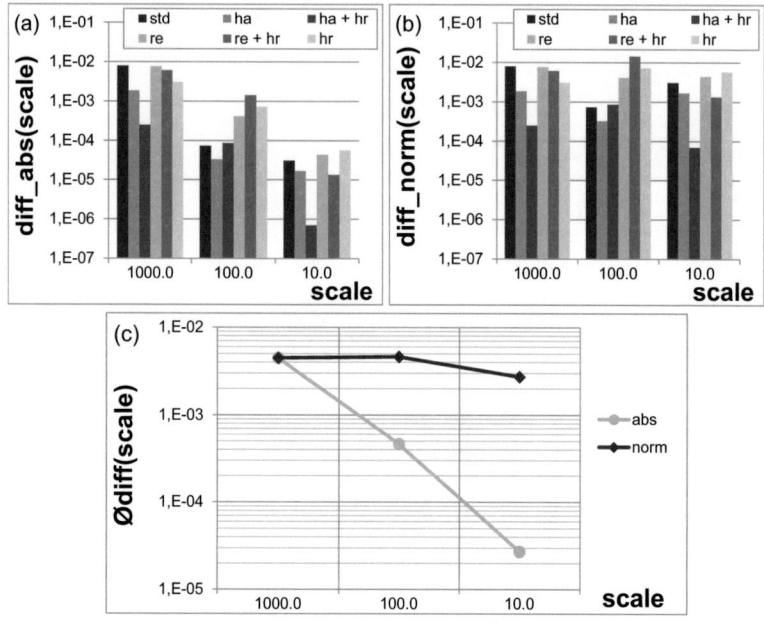

Figure 6.11: Differences Between Reliability Predictions and Simulations, by Scaling Factors and Design Alternatives

proportion to the change of scaling. Hence, each experiment of the EXP_2 series was conducted with 100 000 usage scenario runs, and the EXP_3 series included 1 000 000 scenario runs per experiment. Experiments with further downscaled reliability annotations and accordingly increased scenario run numbers are possible but increasingly difficult to conduct due to time limitations. Figure 6.11 depicts the differences between prediction results and simulation of all experiments Exp_1 to Exp_3 with corresponding scaling factors 1000.0 to 10.0. Subfigure (a) shows the absolute differences $diff\_abs(scale)$ across all scaling factors $scale$ and design alternatives. While the concrete differences are subject to statistical variation, the overall trend clearly shows that the differences decrease together with the scaling factor, due to the increasing number of observed scenario runs per experiment. On the other hand, this trend is actually required to maintain the same degree of compliance across all experiments. To this end, Subfigure (b) shows normalized differences $diff\_norm(scale)$, multiplying each difference in Exp_2 by factor 10 and each difference in Exp_3 by factor 100. The normalized differences are stable across all experiments (apart from the effects of statistical variation). Subfigure (c) further summarizes the findings by showing the absolute and normalized differences $\varnothing diff(scale)$ for the scaling factors, averaged across all design alternatives. In conclusion, the same level of compliance between predictions and simulations could be achieved for all series of experiments Exp_1, Exp_2 and Exp_3, giving evidence for the assumption that validating also high-reliability values by simulation would be possible if the available time for experiment execution was not limited.

The simulation experiments discussed so far do not consider the influence of a limited real-world mission time on the observed system reliability. Exp_1 included 10 000 usage scenario runs over a simulated time interval of 0.6 years (which translates to an average inter-arrival time of approximately 32 minutes between two scenario runs). Due to the increased number of observed scenario runs, system mission times covered by Exp_2 and Exp_3 are 6 years and 60 years, respectively. Such mission times may be unrealistically high for real-world IT systems, which leads to the question if it is possible to validate reliability predictions for systems with limited mission times. For software and network failures potentials, it can be reasoned that the expected number of observed FOD occurrences depends only on the modelled FOD probabilities and the overall number of scenario runs during the system's mission time, but not on the mission time itself. One must only be aware that low input FOD probabilities will not lead to any observed FOD occurrences if the overall number of scenario runs is too low. However, hardware-induced FOD occurrences depend on resource Times-to-Failure (TTF) and Times-to-Repair (TTR). There may not be a statistically relevant number of hardware failure and repair events during a limited system mission time.

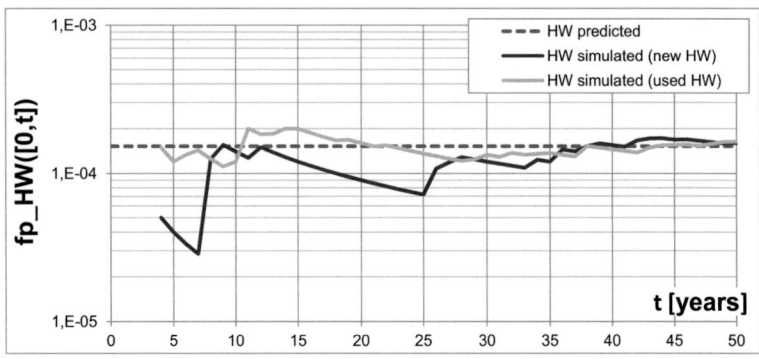

Figure 6.12: Variation of Hardware-Induced Reliability Impacts Depending on System Mission Time

For a closer examination of this question, another experiment Exp_4 is conducted simulating the modelled PCM-REL instance for the "std" alternative in its original setting (namely, without scaling of reliability annotations) based on the single-download usage scenario as shown in Figure 6.8. The system is observed over a theoretical mission time of 50 years with 250000 usage scenario runs. Figure 6.12 shows the hardware-induced FOD probability $fp\_HW([0,t])$ as predicted by the Markov analysis and observed by simulation between system start at $t_0 = 0$ and t. Two separate simulations are conducted, where one simulation assumes new hardware at t_0 and the other one already used hardware[4]. While the predicted value is constant (due to the time-abstracting character of the Markov analysis), the observations by simulation initially differ from this value and eventually converge to it. In the experiment, both simulations do not experience any hardware-induced FOD occurrences in the first three years, leading to $fp\_HW([0,t]) = 0$ during that time. The experiment results suggest that,

---

[4]Both simulations assume exponentially distributed TTFs and TTRs for hardware resources, based on the modelled MTTF and MTTR values.

in spite of a principally valid prediction of hardware-induced FOD probabilities, significant differences from the predicted values may be observed
in practice. This is due to statistical variation, whose impact depends on
the length of the system's mission time, the number of hardware resources
used by the system, as well as the number of observed system installations
(if considering the average results across all installations). All these aspects influence the expected overall number of hardware failure and repair
events. The higher this number, the closer the expected compliance between prediction and observation. An additional finding of the experiment
is that the simulation of the system running with initially new hardware
stays below the predicted threshold, until it eventually converges towards
it. In this case, the assumption of steady-state availability as included in the
Markov analysis (see Section 5.2.1) is not correct in the early stages of the
system's lifetime, which starts with all hardware resources being available
at $t_0 = 0$ with probability 1.0. In conclusion, it has to be noted that observed
hardware reliability impacts may differ from predicted ones for scenarios
with a low number of overall hardware failure and repair events, and that
predictions are rather conservative in cases where a system's mission time
starts with initially new hardware resources.

6.4.4 Comparison with Measurements

The previous discussion of simulation experiments as part of the audio
hosting case study has provided evidence of the validity of the Markov
analysis. However, both the analysis and the simulation have the original
PCM-REL instance as a common starting point and are equally affected
by all abstractions included into the PCM-REL modelling language. This
section provides a supplementary discussion validating those modelling abstractions. To this end, a prototypical implementation of the audio hosting
service has been created which the PCM-REL instance represents. Reliability measurements conducted on the implementation are compared to

predictions to observe if any significant deviations are caused by the modelling abstractions. The implementation is based on Enterprise Java Beans (EJB [Ora12b]) deployed on a GlassFish Application Server [Ora12a] and using an Apache Derby database [Apa12] for storage of user and audio data. For the measurements, the application is executed in a testbed that triggers usage scenario runs and service invocations according to a built-in workload driver and records the results of all scenario runs.

In order to feasibly conduct the measurements, several simplifications had to be included compared to a real-world field experiment. First, the overall number of scenario runs is limited to 4000 (divided into four measurement runs with 1000 scenario runs each). This limitation is due to the fact that the scenarios are executed in real time (unlike the accelerated simulated time in the previous experiments). Second, the implementation comprises only basic functionality for user registration, user login, audio data storage and processing. System reliability is not measured due to real faults but rather to injected ones, with externally controlled FOD probabilities of individual processing steps. Third, the executed system instance is deployed on a single hardware node (ruling out network transmission failures), and this node is assumed to be perfectly available (as the duration of the measurement runs is too short to observe any hardware breakdowns). For comparison between predictions and measurements, a PCM-REL instance is created that represents the specific implemented architectural candidate of the audio hosting service. This candidate corresponds to a modified "std" design alternative with a single computing node hosting all software component instances. While hardware resources possess perfect availability (with MTTF and MTTR values equal to zero), software FOD probabilities are upscaled compared to the original settings by factor 10000. This scaling is done so that a statistically relevant amount of FODs can be observed during the measurements. The single-download usage scenario as shown in Figure 6.8 is employed to represent user behaviour, and it is implemented by the testbed's workload driver.

The most significant modelling abstraction of PCM-REL with respect to the implemented prototype is the abstraction from component-internal state, which, in the implementation, governs certain control flow decisions. For example, the "AudioManagement" component conducts file encoding during download only if the requested bitrate is smaller than the bitrate of the audio file retrieved from the database (see Figure 2.9). The model does not explicitly represent the stored audio files and their bitrates; instead, a BranchAction "EncodingCases" represents the decision using fixed branch transition probabilities of 0.5 for each of the two possible cases (conduct or omit encoding). Similarly, the result of a cache access (which may be a hit or a miss) influences the subsequent control flow and is modelled by PCM-REL through fixed hit and miss probabilities. Both the decisions about encoding and about cache accesses have a potential to influence the resulting system reliability. Omission of encoding eliminates one source of software-induced FOD occurrences during download. A cache hit saves database accesses and most of the required audio processing, thereby significantly reducing the failure potentials of the conducted service operation.

Figure 6.13 shows the results of the conducted measurements as well as the comparison to prediction. Each subfigure depicts one out of four conducted measurement runs with its FOD probabilities $fp\_10000(type)$ for each occurring SoftwareInducedFODType $type$. By manual alteration of the stored cache and database contents for the implemented prototype, different relative frequencies of cache hits and conducted encodings were observed during each of the measurement runs. As the results indicate, these variations have significant impact on the occurrence probabilities of individual FOD types. A high cache hit probability lowers the occurrence probabilities of DB query failures, storage access failures, encoding failures and watermarking failures. Additionally, the occurrence probability of encoding failures rises and falls together with the rate of conducted encodings. Each of the measurement runs is accompanied by a reliability

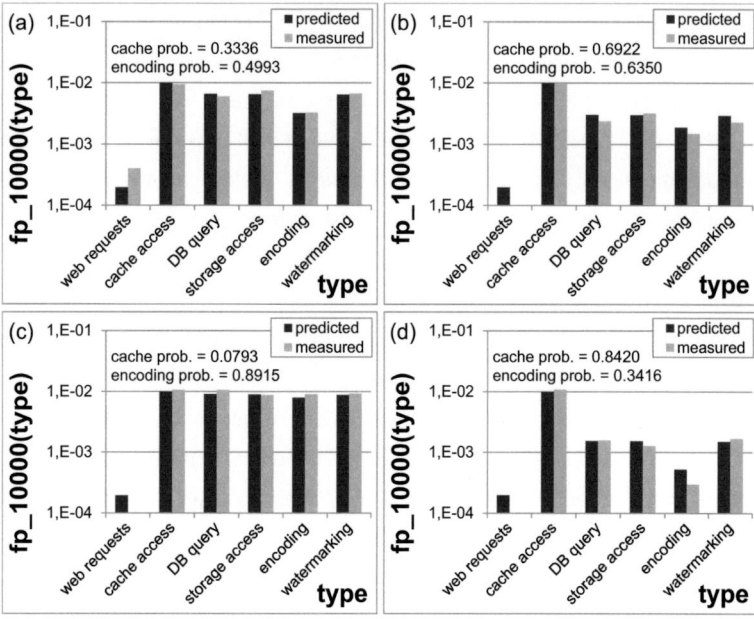

Figure 6.13: Comparison of Reliability Predictions with Simulation by Failure-on-Demand Types and Measurement Runs

prediction with modelled cache and encoding probabilities adjusted to the observed values. The so-calibrated model leads to accurate predictions in all four cases, with deviations that can safely be accredited to statistical variation. As Figure 6.13 shows, the consistent absolute variations across all failure types imply lower relative variations for types with high occurrence probabilities (such as cache access failures) compared to types with low occurrence probabilities (such as web request failures). An increased number of scenario runs per measurement run would be required to further improve the overall compliance to the predicted values.

As the experiment shows, the cache and encoding probabilities have a significant influence on the system's reliability, and accurate predictions can only be achieved with an accordingly calibrated model. However, it is feasible to assume that these probabilities can be estimated by experience or derived from observations obtained from similar systems. The model calibration is not a process of data fitting. No prediction results are used as a feedback for the calibration. Rather, the relevant parameters are directly estimated for the system under study and included in the model.

6.4.5 Case Study Assessment

Within the context of the audio hosting case study, the PCM-REL approach presented in this thesis could successfully be applied to an IT system which features typical characteristics of business information systems with component-based software architectures. A comprehensive set of experiments was conducted that demonstrates the capabilities of the approach and validates several of its assumptions. More concretely, the achievements of the case study with respect to the original validation goals (see Section 6.2) are as follows:

Feasibility of modelling abstractions: Reliability predictions obtained by PCM-REL were compared to measurements conducted for a prototypical implementation which the modelled PCM-REL instance represents. The probabilistic abstraction of control flow dependencies on component-internal state received special attention. While a model calibration step is required estimating the control flow probabilities, such calibration can feasibly be achieved, and the resulting predictions are highly accurate.

Feasibility of estimation of reliability annotations: In this case study, reliability annotations were illustratively chosen. The full process of input estimation is demonstrated by the Astaro ASG study (Section 6.5).

Validity of Markov analysis: Several simulation experiments were conducted and compared to predicted reliability values. The simulation uses an own underlying formalism and is not affected by the known assumptions of the analysis. Simulation and prediction results generally showed a high level of compliance. For hardware-induced FOD probabilities, observed values may deviate from predictions for systems with short mission times or few used hardware resources. Predictions are conservative if the system starts its mission time with initially new resources.

Significance and robustness of prediction results: The results of the Markov analysis could be used to gain several insights into the reliability characteristics of the audio hosting service. Recommendations for choosing between multiple design alternatives could be given with high confidence, based on a sensitivity analysis examining the robustness of the results. Conclusions could be drawn about further potential for improvement which might be exploited in future system design iterations.

6.5 Astaro ASG Case Study

This section presents a PCM-REL case study for the *Astaro Security Gateway* (ASG) [Ast12], a system that enables a secure interconnection between company-internal IT infrastructures and and external communication networks. The system includes functionality in the area of network security (such as a network firewall, remote access capabilities and bandwidth control), mail security (such as spam and virus detection), web security (filtering, reporting and control) and web application security (such as an application firewall). A full installation includes dedicated hardware hosting the system's software on top of a Linux operating system. Multiple replicated hardware nodes may co-operate for improved system performance and availability. Different node sizes are available supporting a recommended number of 10 to 4 000 users per node. The ASG is a product of the Sophos (formerly Astaro) company. There are a worldwide estimated total of 60 000 ASG installations operating in the field.

The case study focuses on a specific part of the ASG's functionality, namely the processing of e-mails received via SMTP. The study includes modelling the involved parts of the software architecture and examining the ASG's reliability with respect to e-mail processing. The description

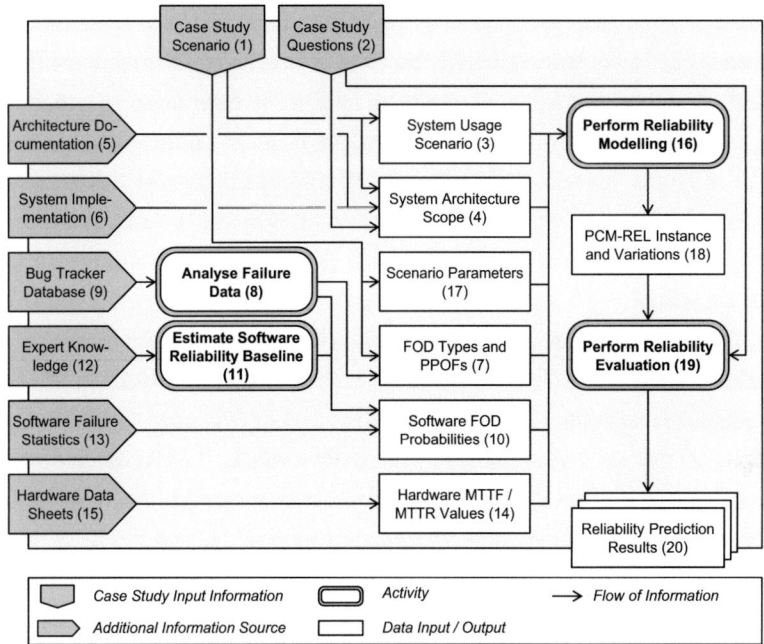

Figure 6.14: ASG Case Study Activities and Information Flows

respects the need for confidentiality and omits several details. However, it is comprehensive in giving evidence for the applicability of PCM-REL to an industrial system such as the ASG. The following gives a general outline of the study (Section 6.5.1), introduces its inputs (Section 6.5.2), describes the modelling activities (Section 6.5.3) including the estimation of required input parameters (Section 6.5.4), illustrates the analysis results (Section 6.5.5) and assesses the case study achievements (Section 6.5.6).

6.5.1 Case Study Outline

This section provides an outline of the ASG case study, which can also more generally serve as a raw model of how to apply PCM-REL to an existing industrial system under study. Figure 6.14 shows the case study's activities and information flows. The study comprises four main activities: failure data analysis, software reliability baseline estimation, reliability modelling and reliability evaluation. There is no need to perform these activities in a strictly sequential order. Rather, there are flows of information between the activities, as well as data outputs of activities that serve as inputs to other activities. A set of information sources provides the required input information, and a set of ASG reliability predictions constitutes the result of the study.

As the figure shows, the starting point of the study is given by the definition of a case study scenario (1) specifying the considered part of the system's functionality and usage, as well as a set of reliability-specific questions (2) that shall be answered by the study's results. The considered system usage scenario (3) specifying relevant system service invocations and input parameters follows directly from the case study scenario. The system architecture scope (4) specifies the relevant part of the system's architecture in terms of software components, interfaces, behaviour and allocation to the hardware resource environment. It is obtained from existing architectural documentation (5) and, as required, reviews of the system's implementation (6). Furthermore, the case study scenario and questions help to determine the relevant fraction and required modelling granularity of the architecture. The considered FOD types and potential points of failure (PPOFs) within the architecture (7) follow mainly from the case study scenario; however, the analysis of failure data (8) from the bug tracker database (9) may reveal additional FOD types and PPOFs not originally considered. Eventually, the specified PPOFs must be annotated with software FOD probabilities (10). In the ASG case study, a mixed approach was chosen to obtain those probabilities, with a baseline estimation (11) for all probabilities determined from expert knowledge (12), enriched by existing failure statistics (13), and further weighted by the results of the bug tracker analysis. Additionally, hardware MTTF and MTTR values (14) are determined from existing hardware data sheets (15).

All gathered data as discussed in the previous paragraph serves as an input to the reliability modelling activity (16). Furthermore, a set of scenario parameters (17) specifying variable aspects of the system's usage and configuration need to be reflected in the model so that their influence on the system's reliability can be examined. The set of relevant parameters follows from the case study scenario definition. The modelling activity produces a PCM-REL instance (18) which serves as an input to the reliability evaluation (19). The evaluation includes repeated Markov analysis runs for the PCM-REL instance and its variations (created to examine the sensitivity of the system's reliability to varying scenario parameters and reliability annotations). A set of reliability prediction results (20) constitutes the output of the evaluation activity and is interpreted to answer the initial case study questions. The following sections discuss the outlined case study inputs, activities and results in detail.

6.5.2 Case Study Scenario and Questions

This section introduces the case study scenario and relevant questions to answer, which emerged from initial discussions with ASG developers and constitutes the first input to the case study (see Figure 6.14). The study focuses on the processing of e-mails received via SMTP, which may be either *incoming* (sent from an external origin to a recipient within the company-internal network) or *outgoing* (sent to an external recipient from an internal origin). The processing includes a series of performed *processing steps* for each e-mail, namely *mail acceptance checks* (such as spam detection) and *mail-handling operations* (such as content encryption). The set of performed processing steps may differ depending on the properties of the e-mail and the ASG's configuration. If an e-mail does not pass an acceptance check, it is not further processed but either rejected or deposited in a *quarantine* storage. In the first case, the ASG returns a rejection notice to the sender. In the second case, an administrator has to decide about the further treatment of the e-mail. If an e-mail passes all acceptance checks, the ASG forwards it to its destination. Information about processed e-mails and processing outcomes is written to the system logs and partially stored in a local ASG database.

The described system functionality provides the context for the definition of the central scenario of the case study, namely the *SMTP processing scenario*. This scenario starts with the arrival of an incoming or outgoing e-mail and includes all processing steps performed on this e-mail. The execution of the scenario has three possible regular outcomes, namely (i) the acceptance and sending, (ii) the rejection or (iii) the quarantining of the processed e-mail. A further (unwanted) outcome is the cancellation of the processing before its completion and loss of the e-mail. The scenario execution is considered successful if all of the following *success criteria* are met:

- *Mail Processing*: Each processing step is performed on the e-mail if and only if it is expected to be performed.

- *Mail Integrity*: Each performed processing step completes without corrupting the e-mail (namely, changing header data or contents of the e-mail in unexpected ways).

- *Mail Classification*: Each performed mail acceptance check produces its expected result (either passing or disapproving the e-mail), leading also to the expected scenario outcome[5].

Minor problems such as wrong logging are not considered as being FODs. Processing delays are only considered as being FODs if they are extreme, such as one day or more. Furthermore, the analysis only considers problems that are directly related to the described scenario. This excludes FODs during the further processing of quarantined e-mails from consideration. Un-

---

[5]Notice that the overall scenario outcome may be as expected even though an individual acceptance check produces a wrong result. It was decided to consider such cases as failed processing. Beyond the overall outcome of the scenario, each individual processing step is expected to perform failure-free.

wanted side effects during e-mail processing (such as writing wrong data to the local database) are not considered as being FODs if they do not violate the defined success criteria of the scenario, even though they might impact the processing of further e-mails or other ASG functionality. However, the analysis must consider the fact that a side effect during the processing of one e-mail may manifest itself as a FOD while processing another e-mail.

The definition of the SMTP processing scenario provides the basis for determining relevant FOD types and PPOFs (as shown in Figure 6.14). From the defined success criteria, it is evident that the PPOFs are connected to the individual e-mail processing steps. Furthermore, FOD occurrences can be categorized according to the type of violation that they constitute:

- *Mail Wrongly Passed*: A mail acceptance check wrongly classifies an e-mail as "OK" instead of "BAD". This may lead to acceptance and sending of the e-mail as an overall unexpected scenario outcome (instead of rejecting or quarantining the e-mail).

- *Mail Wrongly Disapproved*: A mail acceptance check wrongly classifies an e-mail as "BAD" instead of "OK". The e-mail will not be accepted and sent, even if this scenario outcome is the expected one.

- *Mail Corrupted*: A processing step results in a corruption of an e-mail. The e-mail will not arrive at the expected recipient or in its expected form, even if the ASG accepts and forwards it.

- *Mail Wrongly Processed*: A processing step is performed on an e-mail even though it is expected to be skipped. This may have several implications; for example, an e-mail may be rejected instead of accepted.

- *Mail Processing Wrongly Omitted*: A processing step of an e-mail is skipped even though it is expected to be performed. One potential implication is that the e-mail may be accepted instead of rejected.

- *Mail Processing Cancelled*: The processing of an e-mail stops unexpectedly before its completion. The e-mail is lost and can neither be sent nor rejected or quarantined.

Another observation with respect to FOD occurrences during SMTP processing is that they may significantly differ in their criticality; highly critical ones are less tolerable than minor ones. In this respect, FODs can be categorized as follows:

- *Minor*: This category includes spam classification problems due to imperfect spam detection. A non-spam e-mail may be wrongly disapproved as being spam, or a spam e-mail may not be identified as such. Spam detection is a heuristic method performed under high uncertainty. Misclassifications with a certain frequency of occurrence are generally accepted by users and are not particularly critical.

- *Major*: This is the standard category for failed SMTP processing. It includes all FOD occurrences which are neither minor nor critical.

- *Critical*: This category includes the non-identification of virus e-mails due to imperfect virus detection. Undetected viruses may severely and unpredictably damage data and computation within the ASG, and they may further propagate and cause damage at the recipient's side. Hence, FODs of this kind should have very low occurrence probabilities in the field.

For the ASG case study, the described categorization of FOD occurrences according to violation type and criticality guides the specification of FOD types during reliability modelling (see Table 6.3).

The case study questions of interest are centred around two major issues. First, as the development of the ASG's software continues, the question arises which parts of the software are most critical and should receive special attention in terms of quality assurance efforts (which may comprise extended testing, code reviews or even partial re-implementation). Second, the central means to avoid critical FOD occurrences is a redundant virus check of processed e-mails by two independent virus detection engines. The case study shall quantify the relative improvement gained by this redundancy compared to a single-engine check, as a basis for justifying the introduced runtime performance overhead.

6.5.3 ASG Architectural Model

This section introduces the PCM-REL instance created during the reliability modelling activity (see Figure 6.14). The discussion focuses on the model parts that result from the determined system usage scenario (element 3 in the figure), system architecture scope (4), FOD types and PPOFs (7), as well as scenario parameters (17). These inputs follow from the case study scenario (1) and questions (2) as introduced in Section 6.5.2. Additionally, existing architectural documentation (5) was leveraged and the system's implementation was inspected (6) to determine the required information.

6.5.3.1 Model Overview

The PCM-REL instance which represents the SMTP processing part of an ASG installation specifies 16 BasicComponents, 5 CompositeComponents, 8 Interfaces and 3 model-specific DataTypes. Figure 6.15 shows the top-level structure, which consists of 10 AssemblyContexts instantiating the BasicComponents *ClusterProtocol*, *SMTPDatabase* and *CONFDatabase*, as well as the *SMTPProxy* CompositeComponent. The model represents an average-sized cluster ASG installation with triple redundancy. Each of the three *SMTPProxies* implements *IMessageProcessor* so that it can serve e-mail processing requests. The proxies negotiate the distribution of e-mails between them through the cluster protocol. Even though each proxy takes an active part in the protocol, this cannot be directly expressed in PCM-REL, which only allows for modelling passive components. Hence, the model contains a "virtual" *ClusterProtocol* com-

229

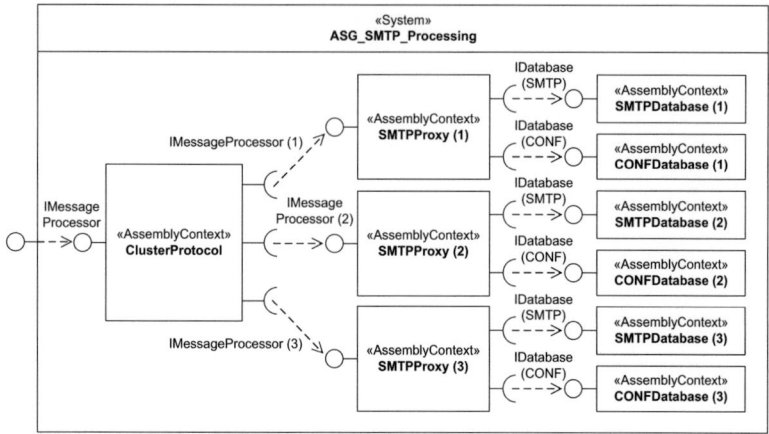

Figure 6.15: ASG SMTP Processing System Model

ponent that receives e-mails first and propagates them to the proxies. This modelling variant is chosen such that it does not change any of the system's reliability characteristics with respect to the context of the case study. Furthermore, the SMTP processing involves two databases whose contents are replicated for each proxy. The *SMTPDatabase* is used to store information about processed e-mails; the *CONFDatabase* contains the ASG's configuration information and is queried to decide about the set and conditions of performed mail acceptance checks and mail-handling operations.

Figure 6.16 shows the ASG resource environment and the allocation of software components to hardware hosts. The model contains four ResourceContainers *ASGSwitch, ASGHost (1), ASGHost (2)* and *ASGHost (3)*. Each of the three hosts contains a full ASG software installation including an *SMTPProxy* and local replica of the *SMTPDatabase* and *CONFDatabase*. Each host receives and sends e-mails via the *ASGSwitch*, which contains the virtual *ClusterProtocol*. Hardware resources within the hosts and the switch are not individually modelled but aggregated to single ProcessingResourceSpecifications per node using two custom ProcessingResourceTypes *ASGHostHW* and *ASGSwitchHW*. Each Pro-

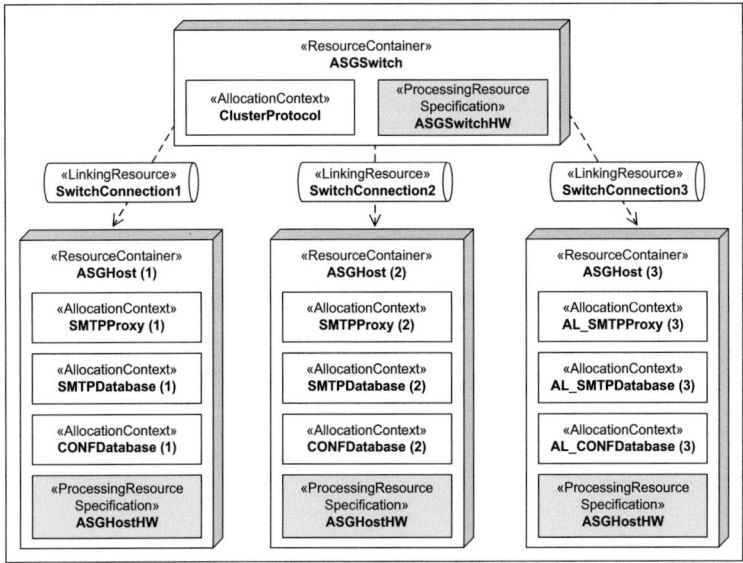

Figure 6.16: ASG Resource Environment and Allocation Model

cessingResourceSpecification has its "RequiredByContainer" flag set to "true" to indicate that the node is only operational when its hardware is available.

Figure 6.17 depicts the ASG usage model, which specifies a single UsageScenario "SMTPProcessingScenario" with a single EntryLevelSystemCall to the "ProcessMessage" operation of the "IMessageProcessor" Interface. Several VariableUsages specify properties of the invoked operation's input parameter "message" and its sub parameters. "Message" is a CompositeDataType contained in the ASG Repository Model, representing the e-mail that is to be processed by the ASG. It has a set of inner declarations to reflect properties that influence its treatment in the system. These properties include the number of recipients of the e-mail, the classification of the e-mail as being spam or containing a virus, containing forbidden expressions in the subject or body, containing crit-

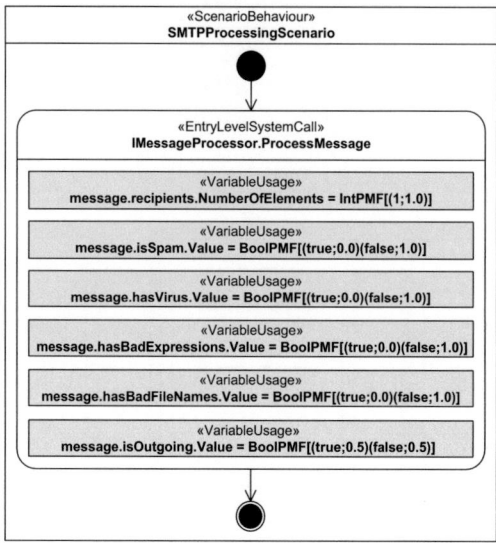

Figure 6.17: ASG Usage Model

ical file name extensions in the set of attached files, as well as being an incoming or outgoing e-mail. Using the PCM-specific *Stochastic Expressions* (StoEx) language [Koz08], Probability Mass Functions (PMFs) of type Integer (IntPMF) and Boolean (BoolPMF) are employed to specify those properties. The figure shows the specification of a processing request for an e-mail with one recipient, which is no spam, does not contain a virus, has no bad expressions or file name extensions, and is either incoming or outgoing, each with probability 0.5. The request properties can be modified during a sensitivity analysis to examine how the system's reliability is influenced by such changes.

The inner structure of the *SMTPProxy* CompositeComponent is shown in Figure 6.18. The proxy makes use of the open source mail transfer agent *Exim* [HWW+12] for the initial handling of received e-mails (realized through the *SMTPServerExim* component), as well as the sending of completely processed e-mails (realized through *SMTPClientExim*). The

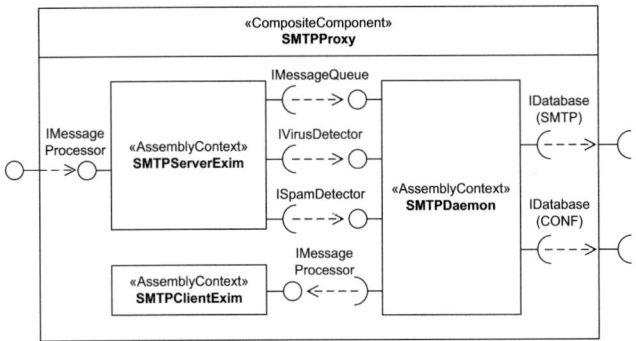

Figure 6.18: ASG SMTP Proxy Model

SMTPServerExim performs initial checks on each received e-mail and either rejects it or passes it on to a message queue for further internal processing by the *SMTPDaemon*. Depending on the configuration of the ASG and the properties of a received e-mail, the *SMTPServerExim* may perform a check for spam or viruses using the spam and virus detection engines of the *SMTPDaemon*. The latter can access the SMTP and configuration databases, and it can hand e-mails over to the *SMTPEximClient* for sending after all processing steps have been completed. The PCM-REL instance further divides the *SMTPServerExim* in two sub components *ServerEximCtrl* and *ServerEximChecks* (not shown in the figure) to distinguish between the control flow that decides over the execution of individual processing steps and the execution of those steps itself.

Figure 6.19 further details the inner structure of the *SMTPDaemon*. The included sub components can be categorized in message queues (namely *InputQueue*, *WorkQueue* and *OutputQueue*, which implement the "IMessageQueue" Interface), message processors (*QueueManager* and *MailAnalyzer*, implementing "IMessageProcessor") and the message deposit *Quarantine* (implementing "IMessageDeposit"). While in reality, the message processors are active components that observe the queues and fetch e-mails from them for processing, this cannot be directly expressed in PCM-

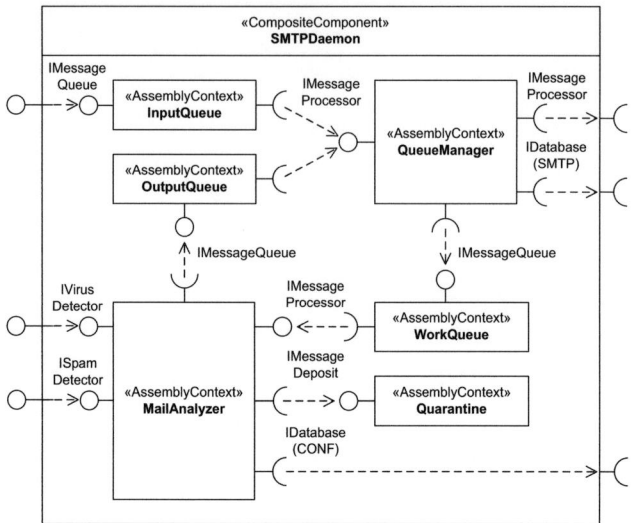

Figure 6.19: ASG SMTP Daemon Model

REL. Instead, the queues are modelled as actively invoking the message processors to trigger the processing of an e-mail. This modelling variant allows for considering the SMTP processing scenario as defined in Section 6.5.2 as a whole and for deriving its overall success probability, rather than only considering the reliability of individual scenario parts. Whenever an e-mail is placed in the *InputQueue* (through the "IMessageQueue" Interface), it is propagated to the *QueueManager*, which stores information about the e-mail in the SMTP database and then places it in the *WorkQueue*. From there, it further propagates to the *MailAnalyzer*, which is the central component responsible for all internal mail processing steps. The *MailAnalyzer* queries the CONF database to decide upon the set of processing steps to be performed for the e-mail. As a result of the executed mail acceptance checks, the *MailAnalyzer* either accepts the e-mail and places it in the *OutputQueue* or disapproves it and places it in the *Quarantine* (through the "IMessageDeposit" Interface). The further processing of quarantined e-mails requires further user interaction. It is excluded from the case study model because it is not part of the considered SMTP processing scenario. From the *OutputQueue*, the e-mail visits the *QueueManager* one more time and is finally passed on to the *SMTPClientExim* for sending (via the "IMessageProcessor" Interface, see Figure 6.18).

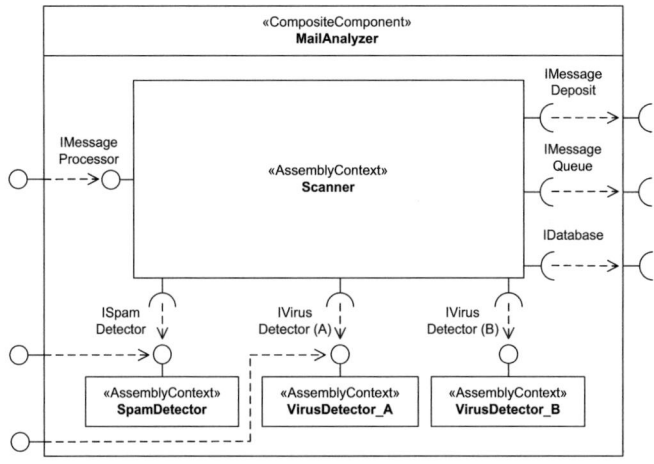

Figure 6.20: ASG Mail Analyzer Model

Figure 6.20 gives further insight in the internals of the *MailAnalyzer* CompositeComponent. The central *Scanner* accepts e-mails via the "IMessageProcessor" Interface and is responsible for performing the required processing steps. The PCM-REL instance further distinguishes two sub components *ScannerCtrl* and *ScannerChecks* of the *Scanner* (not shown in the figure) to separate the decisions about the execution of the individual processing steps from the execution itself. The range of possible processing steps includes checking an e-mail for forbidden expressions and critical file name extensions in the attachments, as well as performing spam and virus detection (if not already done by *SMTPServerExim*, see Figure 6.18). Furthermore, e-mail contents may be encrypted (for outgoing e-mails) or decrypted (for incoming e-mails), and a digital signature may be checked

235

(for incoming e-mails) or created (for outgoing e-mails). For spam and virus detection, the *Scanner* employs the existing engines *SpamDetector*, *VirusDetector_A* and *VirusDetector_B* (the original names of the engines are omitted for confidentiality reasons). Having an e-mail checked by two independent virus detection engines is a fault-tolerance capability of the ASG that decreases the probability of critical FOD occurrences due to undetected viruses. The provided `Interfaces` of the *SpamDetector* and *VirusDetector_A* are not only used internally but also offered as provided `Interfaces` of the *MailAnalyzer*. Hence, the engines can be used by the *SMTPServerExim* if required.

6.5.3.2 Behavioural Specifications

The system behaviour modelled for SMTP processing through the ASG comprises 24 `ResourceDemandingSEFFs`. The core behaviour consists of the execution of mail acceptance checks and mail-handling operations by the *SMTPServerExim* (see Figure 6.18) and *Scanner* (see Figure 6.20). Further relevant aspects include the distribution of e-mails to *SMTPProxies* by the *ClusterProtocol* (Figure 6.15) and the final processing of an accepted e-mail for sending by the *SMTPClientExim* (Figure 6.18). The following exemplary excerpts of behavioural specifications illustrate how the PCM-REL instance captures SMTP processing behaviour.

Figure 6.21 shows part of the "ProcessMessage" `ResourceDemanding-SEFF` of *ServerEximCtrl*. The Exim server performs different mail acceptance checks on each received e-mail based on *Access Control Lists* (ACL). The *ACL Connect Check* and *ACL Data Check* are performed once per e-mail; the *ACL Recipient Check* is performed for each recipient. Each individual check may lead to disapproval and rejection of the e-mail without any further checks being performed. If the e-mail passes all checks, the Exim server places it in the *InputQueue* of the *SMTPDaemon* (see Figure 6.19). The execution of the individual checks by *ServerEximChecks* is triggered within a `RecoveryAction` "PerformACLChecks"

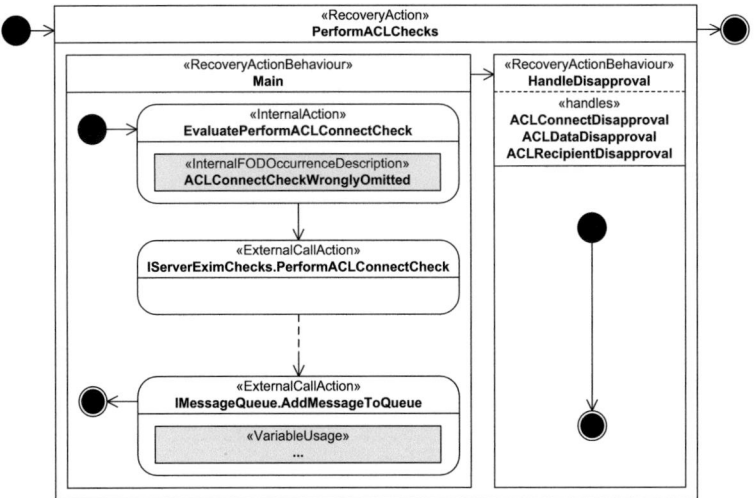

Figure 6.21: RDSEFF "ServerEximCtrl.ProcessMessage" (Excerpt)

(the figure shows only the invocation of the Connect Check and omits the Data and Recipient Check invocations). The model captures the general potential of an ACL check being wrongly omitted through custom FailureTypes (such as "ACLConnectCheckWronglyOmitted") and an additional InternalAction before each check indicating a corresponding point of failure (such as "EvaluatePerformACLConnectCheck"). The final ExternalCallAction places the e-mail in the queue and passes all its relevant properties through VariableUsages on to the called behaviour. When invoked, *ServerEximChecks* indicates any disapproval of the e-mail through one of the SoftwareInducedFODTypes "ACLConnect-Disapproval", "ACLDataDisapproval" or "ACLRecipientDisapproval". In *ServerEximCtrl*, the RecoveryActionBehaviour "HandleDisapproval" specifies that no further checks are invoked after a disapproval, and the e-mail is not passed on to the queue. Hence, the "PerformACLChecks" RecoveryAction does not represent fault-tolerant behaviour in a strict

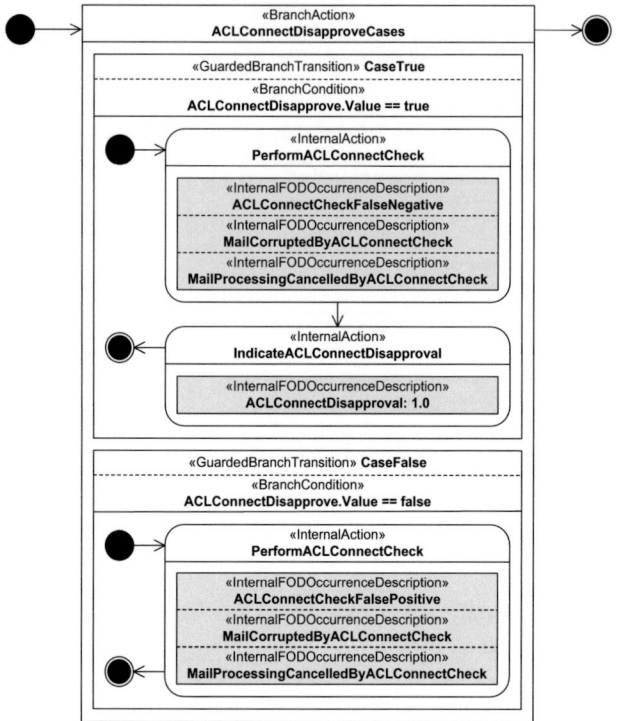

Figure 6.22: RDSEFF "ServerEximChecks.PerformACLConnectCheck"

sense. Rather, it controls the handling of e-mail rejection during the ACL checks.

Figure 6.22 shows the execution of the ACL Connect Check through *ServerEximChecks* as invoked by *ServerEximCtrl*. The specification has to account for the general probability of a reject and the possibility of wrong passing, wrong disapproval, corruption or cancelled processing of the e-mail. The expected result of the check (pass or disapprove) depends on the properties of the e-mail (such as the sender domain) and the configuration of the ASG (such as the set of sender domains that are considered legitimate). However, detailed modelling of all relevant e-mail properties and ASG configuration options would not be feasible. For example, it would not be possible to specify a probability distribution over all possible sender domains as part of the usage model. Instead, the model aggregates all influencing factors into a general probability of rejection specified as a component parameter "ACLConnectDisapprove" of *ServerExim-Checks*, which is directly estimated for a given ASG application scenario. In the behavioural specification, the BranchAction "ACLConnectDisapproveCases" evaluates this parameter to determine the expected result of the check. The check itself is represented by an InternalAction "PerformACLConnectCheck", which may produce an FOD occurrence of one of the types "ACLConnectCheckFalseNegative", "ACLConnectCheckFalse-Positive", "MailCorruptedByACLConnectCheck" or "MailProcessingCancelledByACLConnectCheck". An additional InternalAction indicates the "ACLConnectDisapprove" with probability 1.0 in the case where this result is expected.

Figure 6.23 depicts the e-mail decryption as an example for a mail-handling operation. The operation is invoked by *ScannerCtrl* and carried out by *ScannerChecks*. The specification accounts for the general probability that decryption is to be performed, for the possibility of wrong omission or wrong execution of the operation, as well as FOD occurrences during the operation that lead to e-mail corruption or cancellation of the processing. As decryption is only performed on incoming e-mails, the "isOutgoing" property must be checked to decide about the execution of the operation. Further aspects that influence the probability of decryption are aggregated into a component parameter "PerformDecryption" of *ScannerChecks*. As the figure shows, the BranchAction "PerformDecryptionCases" decides about the execution of the decryption. The probability of a wrong decision is expressed through an InternalAction "EvaluatePerformDecryption" that may produce FODs of type "DecryptionWronglyOmitted" or "DecryptionWronglyPerformed". The operation itself is represented by an

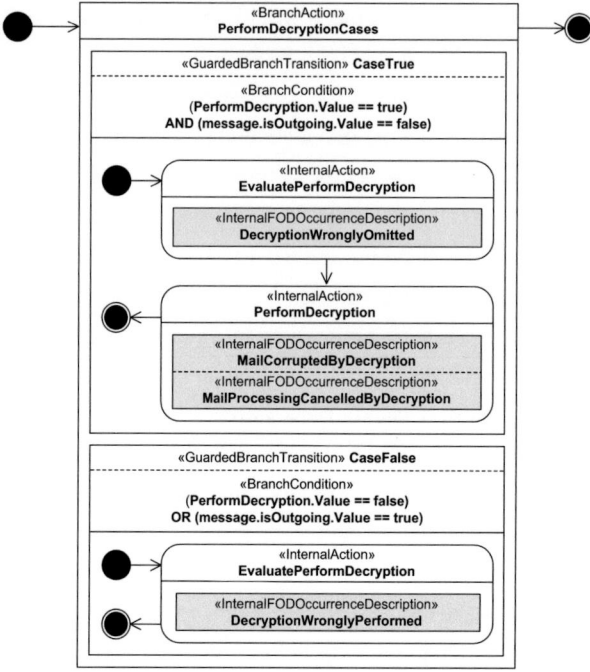

Figure 6.23: RDSEFF "ScannerChecks.PerformDecryption"

InternalAction "PerformDecryption" that may produce a "MailCorrupt-edByDecryption" or a "MailProcessingCancelledByDecryption" FOD.

Figure 6.24 shows part of the "AnalyzeExpressions" operation carried out by *ScannerChecks*, as an example for a mail acceptance check that considers the general probability of the check to be performed, the possibility of wrong omission or wrong execution of the check, wrong mail passing or disapproval as a check result, as well as mail corruption or cancelled mail processing due to the check. The probability that the check is expected to be performed is captured through the component parameter "PerformExpressionsAnalysis". A wrong decision about the execution leads to FODs "ExpressionsAnalysisWronglyOmitted" or "ExpressionsAnaly-sisWronglyPerformed" in the InternalAction "EvaluatePerformExpres-

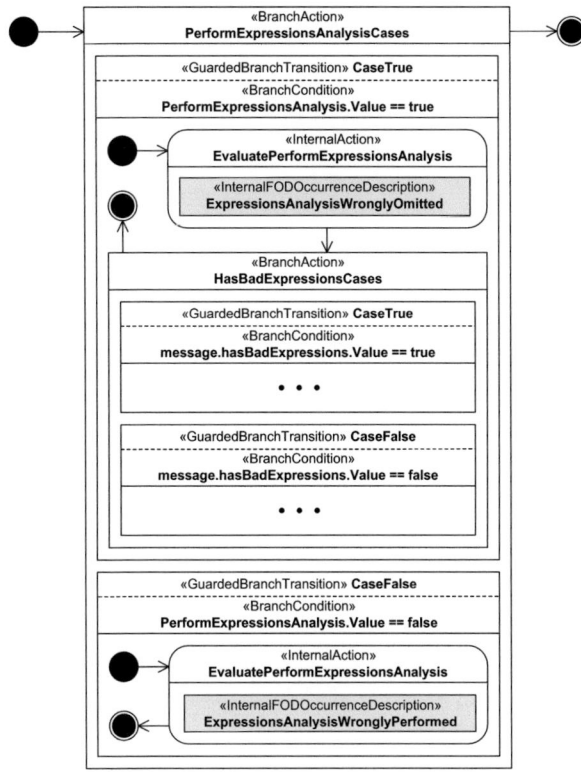

Figure 6.24: RDSEFF "ScannerChecks.AnalyzeExpressions" (Excerpt)

sionsAnalysis". The inner BranchAction "HasBadExpressionsCases" examines the "hasBadExpressions" property of the "message" parameter. Its structure is similar to that of the BranchAction in Figure 6.22, potentially producing FODs of type "AnalyzeExpressionsFalseNegative", "AnalyzeExpressionsFalsePositive", "MailCorrupedByExpressionsAnalysis" or "MailProcessingCancelledByExpressionsAnalysis". Furthermore, the BranchAction indicates an "AnalyzeExpressionsDisapproval" with probability 1.0 (which is handled by the invoking *ScannerCtrl*) in the GuardedBranchTransition "CaseTrue".

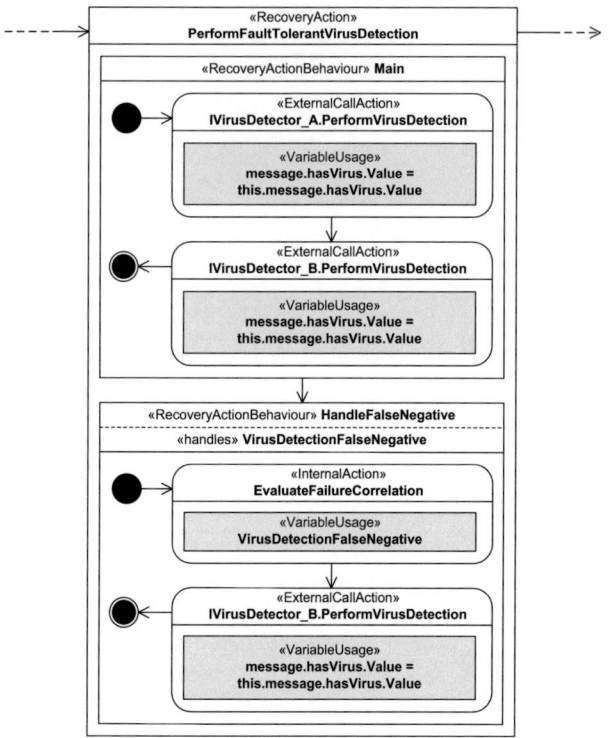

Figure 6.25: RDSEFF "ScannerChecks.PerformVirusDetection" (Excerpt)

The next two figures 6.25 and 6.26 show the parts of the system's behaviour that are related to fault tolerance. First, Figure 6.25 illustrates the fault-tolerant virus detection triggered through the "PerformVirusDetection" operation of *ScannerChecks*. The detection itself is carried out by the engines *VirusDetector_A* and *VirusDetector_B* (see Figure 6.20) and invoked by *ScannerChecks* through corresponding ExternalCallActions. The contamination of an e-mail with a virus is explicitly modelled through the "hasVirus" boolean property of the "message" parameter and passed on to the engines. If the e-mail does contain a virus, the engines indicate this condition through a "VirusDetected" SoftwareInducedFODType, if no mail corruption or cancelled mail processing occurs (the corresponding behavioural specification is similar to that of Figure 6.22). As shown in Figure 6.25, the overall virus detection invokes both engines and can tolerate a single "VirusDetectionFalseNegative" FOD. The execution of the displayed RecoveryAction "PerformFaultTolerantVirusDetection" starts with the "Main" RecoveryActionBehaviour and proceeds as follows:

- If the processed e-mail contains no virus, it may successfully pass both engines, or a "VirusDetectionFalsePositive" may occur, which is not handled by the modelled fault tolerance mechanism.

- If the e-mail contains a virus, the first invoked engine *VirusDetec-tor_A* may indicate this virus through a "VirusDetected" Failure-Type (which is handled outside the displayed RecoveryAction), or it may produce a "VirusDetectionFalseNegative" FOD. The latter case leads to the execution of the "HandleFalseNegative" behaviour, which gives the virus a second chance to be detected by *VirusDe-tector_B*. However, the ability of *VirusDetector_B* to detect the virus may be compromised by failure correlation (taking into account that this virus was already overlooked by *VirusDetector_A*). The additional probability of a second "VirusDetectionFalseNegative" FOD due to failure correlation is expressed through the "EvaluateFailureCorrelation" InternalAction.

- In both discussed cases, *VirusDetector_A* and *VirusDetector_B* may also produce FOD occurrences of type "MailCorruptedByVirusDetection" or "MailProcessingCancelledByVirusDetection". None of these FODs are handled by the modelled fault tolerance mechanism.

A design alternative with only a single virus check can be represented by substituting the displayed RecoveryAction with a single ExternalCall-Action invoking one of the engines. Having both design alternatives modelled enables a quantitative comparison of their reliability and an assessment of the relative improvement gained by the introduction of the second engine.

Further parts of the "PerformVirusDetection" operation of Scanner-Checks, which are not shown in Figure 6.25, deal with the general probability of virus detection to be performed (captured through a *ScannerChecks* component parameter) and with the possibility of wrong omission or wrong execution of the check. The decision about the execution is done individually for each e-mail recipient, but the check itself is executed at most once, as it refers to the e-mail as a whole.

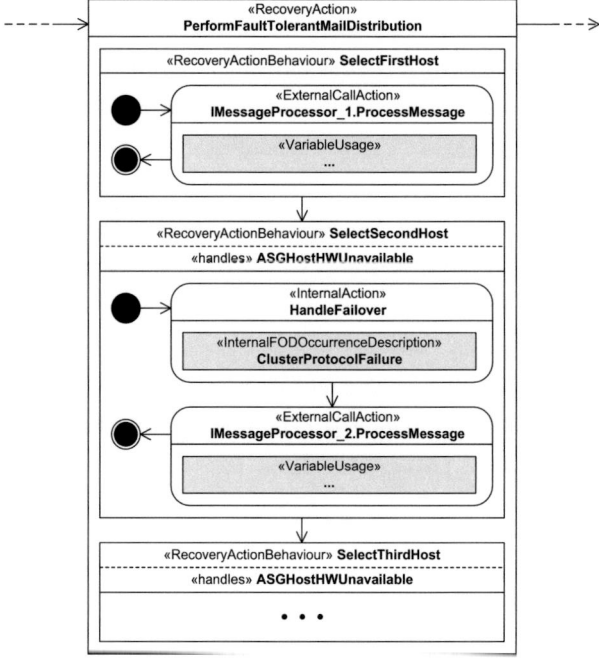

Figure 6.26: RDSEFF "ClusterProtocol.ProcessMessage" (Excerpt)

Figure 6.26 shows how the distribution of e-mails to ASG hosts through the *ClusterProtocol* is modelled in PCM-REL. From the viewpoint of reliability, the most relevant aspect of the cluster protocol is that an e-mail can be processed if at least one of the three ASG hosts is operating. The model abstracts from the details of the distribution of e-mails between multiple operating hosts. Instead, all hosts are targeted in a constant order until the first operating host is detected. A host is deemed operational if its hardware (modelled by `ProcessingResourceSpecifications` of type "ASGHostHW") is available at the moment of the processing request. This modelling reflects the feedback of ASG developers saying that unavailable hardware is the single most important reason for an ASG host being not operational. As the figure shows, the first `RecoveryActionBehaviour` "SelectFirstHost" of the displayed `RecoveryAction` "PerformFaultTolerantMailDistribution" invokes the "ProcessMessage" operation of the first *SMTPProxy* instance, which is allocated to *ASGHost_1* (see Figure 6.16). All relevant message properties are passed as input parameters to the respective `ExternalCallAction` (not fully shown in the figure). A further `RecoveryActionBehaviour` "SelectSecondHost" handles the case that the unavailability of the first host's hardware prevents it from being operational. A corresponding `HardwareInducedFODType` "ASGHostHWUnavailable" has been defined in the ASG Repository model and is pointed out as a `handledFODType` of the behaviour. Beyond the invocation of the second *SMTPProxy* instance, the behaviour also expresses the possibility that the fail-over process triggered by the unavailability of *ASGHost_1* might not be correctly handled by the cluster protocol, leading to an unhandled FOD of type "ClusterProtocolFailure". The last `RecoveryActionBehaviour` "SelectThirdHost" is structured like the second one, invoking the third *SMTPProxy* instance.

6.5.3.3 Model Parametrization

This section introduces the parts of the created PCM-REL instance that refer to failure potentials and scenario parameters (elements 7 and 17 in Figure 6.14), which can be viewed as the dynamic parameters of the model.

245

The software-related reliability annotations comprise a total of 93 software FOD probabilities associated to 65 SoftwareInducedFODTypes and occurring at 57 InternalActions as potential points of failure (PPOFs) during service execution. Table 6.3 shows a list of considered *FOD classes* and gives examples of specified SoftwareInducedFODTypes related to each class. The table distinguishes *initial* classes, which were added to the model according to the initially identified success criteria and violation types of the case study scenario (see Section 6.5.2), and *additional* classes, which were identified during the analysis of the bug tracker database (see Figure 6.14). These additional classes show that a cancellation of e-mail processing can be caused not only by individual malfunctioning processing steps but also by other problems such as complete inoperability of ASG software parts. Beyond the software FOD probabilities, the ASG PCM-REL instance contains further reliability annotations in its ResourceEnvironment model (see Figure 6.16), namely MTTF and MTTR values for each of the four ProcessingResourceSpecifications and network FOD probabilities for each of the three specified LinkingResources). Section 6.5.4 discusses how input estimations for the modelled reliability annotations were derived within the case study process.

The scenario parameters refer to usage and configuration aspects of ASG installations, as well as probabilistic abstractions from ASG-internal states. They constitute the calibration parameters of the model an were estimated by ASG developers from experience. More concretely, the scenario parameters comprise input properties of e-mail processing requests, as well as execution probabilities and expected outcomes of individual processing steps. The former are expressed through VariableUsages in the modelled UsageScenario (see Figure 6.17) and comprise a total of six probability values (modelled as boolean probability mass functions) and one probability distribution (modelled as integer probability mass function). The latter are expressed through a total of 12 component parameters of the *ServerEximChecks* and *ScannerChecks* components, as shown in Table 6.4. Each

Failure-on-Demand Class	Modelled Failure-on-Demand Type(s)
MailCorruptedByProcessingStep: A mail acceptance check or mail-handling operation results in a failure-on-demand and corrupts the e-mail.	• MailCorruptedByACLConnectCheck • MailCorruptedByDecryption • ...
MailProcessingCancelledByProcessingStep: A mail acceptance check or mail-handling operation results in a failure-on-demand and cancels the e-mail processing.	• MailProcessingCancelledByACLConnectCheck • MailProcessingCancelledByDecryption • ...
AcceptanceCheckFalsePositive: A mail acceptance check disapproves an e-mail even though it should pass the e-mail.	• ACLConnectCheckFalsePositive • ExpressionsAnalysisFalsePositive • ...
AcceptanceCheckFalseNegative: A mail acceptance check passes an e-mail even though it should disapprove the e-mail.	• ACLConnectCheckFalseNegative • ExpressionsAnalysisFalseNegative • ...
ProcessingStepWronglyOmitted: A mail acceptance check or mail-handling operation is omitted for an e-mail even though it should be performed.	• ExpressionsAnalysisWronglyOmitted • DecryptionWronglyOmitted • ...
ProcessingStepWronglyPerformed: A mail acceptance check or mail-handling operation is performed on an e-mail even though it should be omitted.	• ExpressionsAnalysisWronglyPerformed • DecryptionWronglyPerformed • ...
MailProcessingCancelledByClusterProtocol: The cluster protocol does not properly operate and the e-mail processing is cancelled.	• ClusterProtocolFailure
MailProcessingCancelledByASGDown: The ASG software is not ready to process e-mails and the e-mail processing is cancelled.	• SMTPDown • ScannerDown
MailProcessingCancelledByDatabaseCorruption: The SMTP or CONF databases cannot be properly accessed and the e-mail processing is cancelled.	• SMTPDatabaseCorrupted • CONFDatabaseCorrupted

The first six rows are grouped under **Initial Classes**; the last three rows are grouped under **Additional Classes**.

Table 6.3: ASG Software-Induced Failure-on-Demand Types

component parameter is modelled as a boolean probability mass function and represents either an expected outcome of a mail acceptance check (such as "ACLConnectDisapprove") or an expected decision about conducting a mail-handling operation (such as "PerformDecryption"). The parameters abstract from ASG configuration options and e-mail properties that are not explicitly modelled to avoid an overly complex specification. The modelled `ResourceDemandingSEFFs` evaluate the component parameters for control flow decisions. For example, Figure 6.22 shows that the "ACLConnectDisapprove" parameter is evaluated to decide about the expected outcome of the ACL Connect Check. The actual outcome may differ from the expected one, as indicated by the modelled "ACLConnectCheckFalseNegative" and "ACLConnectCheckFalsePositive" `FailureTypes` of the "PerformACLConnectCheck" `InternalAction`.

Modelled Component Parameter		Description
ServerEximChecks	PerformVirusDetection	Probability that virus detection is to be performed by SMTPServerExim on a received e-mail.
	PerformSpamDetection	Probability that spam detection is to be performed by SMTPServerExim on a received e-mail.
	ACLConnectDisapprove	Probability that a received e-mail is to be disapproved by the ACL Connect Check.
	ACLRecipientDisapprove	Probability that a received e-mail is to be disapproved by the ACL Recipient Check (evaluated for each recipient).
	ACLDataDisapprove	Probability that a received e-mail is to be disapproved by the ACL Data Check (evaluated based on the precondition that the e-mail is *not* disapproved based on classification as spam or virus).
ScannerChecks	PerformVirusDetection	Probability that virus detection is to be performed by the Scanner on a received e-mail (evaluated for each recipient).
	PerformSpamDetection	Probability that spam detection is to be performed by the Scanner on a received e-mail (evaluated for each recipient).
	PerformEncryption	Probability that a received outgoing e-mail is to be encrypted by the Scanner.
	PerformDecryption	Probability that a received incoming e-mail is to be decrypted by the Scanner.
	PerformExpressionsAnalysis	Probability that expressions analysis is to be performed by the Scanner on a received e-mail.
	PerformFileNamesAnalysis	Probability that file names analysis is to be performed by the Scanner on a received e-mail.
	PerformMessageSigning	Probability that message signing is to be performed by the Scanner on a received e-mail.

Table 6.4: ASG Component Parameters

6.5.4 Estimation of Reliability Annotations

This section describes the estimation of reliability annotations as an input to the reliability modelling activity (see Figure 6.14). The reliability annotations comprise the software FOD probabilities (element 10 in the figure) and hardware MTTF / MTTR values (14). The former part required a major effort analysing failure data (8) from a bug tracker database (9) and combining the results with a software reliability baseline estimation (11) derived from expert knowledge (12), as well as existing failure statistics (13). The latter part could be determined from hardware data sheets (15).

6.5.4.1 Software Failure-on-Demand Probabilities

The estimation of model parameters representing software FOD probabilities constituted the most significant challenge among all input estimations. Due to the high number of modelled parameters (see Section 6.5.3.3), estimations were done for parameter groups (rather than individual parameters) and based on a common software reliability baseline estimation. The most important source of information for the estimations was a bug tracker database that supports the ASG software development. The bug tracker is used to report about the occurrence of software-induced FODs, the identification of underlying implementation faults, as well as the status and responsibilities of fault removal. Failure reports stem from internal software tests as well as external customer feedback for devices operating in the field. The development, test and fault removal of current and new ASG software releases is a continuous process, and each bug tracker entry relates to a certain release version.

While the bug tracker entries describe implementation faults and resulting ASG failures, they provide no direct input for the reliability modelling activity. They describe circumstances of failure, but not the frequency of occurrence of those circumstances. The provided information is qualitative rather than quantitative. Furthermore, existing entries are historical and relate to faults that have already been removed. They do not impact current or future ASG software releases. Hence, the bug tracker data can only serve as a preliminary input that needs further interpretation and analysis to derive quantitative estimations. One way to do this analysis is to use software reliability growth models (SRGMs, see Section 2.3.1) on a component level (more precisely, on a PPOF level). However, the existing ASG bug tracking process significantly violates the underlying assumptions of SRGMs (for example, the software continues to evolve during the data collection), and important input information for the analysis is missing (such as the number of visits to each PPOF per test run). The analysis method had to be adjusted to be applicable to the existing ASG bug tracker data. Like conventional SRGMs, the analysis assumed that current and future failure rates can be deduced from historical failure rates. However, the historical failure rates were not directly available but had to be estimated from the qualitative failure data. Because of the involved uncertainty, the analysis did not aim at determining absolute FOD probabilities but rather relative weights of the individual FOD types and PPOFs. More concretely, the analysis included the following steps:

1. Selection of bug tracker entries to consider;

2. Semantic examination of each selected entry;

3. Deduction of a relative weight for each modelled PPOF (differentiated according to occurring FOD types).

The first step involved the assessment of existing data fields that each entry possesses in order to select a relevant set of entries for the analysis. A *category* field describes the part of the ASG's functionality that is impacted by a certain reported problem. This field is used to reduce the set of considered entries to those related to SMTP processing. A *project* field captures the major release version to which an entry is related. In order to exclude entries which are insignificant due to their age, the analysis was limited to the current and the previous major ASG software release, spanning a time interval of roughly 1.5 years. Within this scope, the SMTP processing architecture as modelled through PCM-REL can be considered stable. Furthermore, each entry has an associated *severity level* that assesses the impact of a certain reported problem. The analysis was limited to the most and second-most severe levels to exclude minor problems such as wrong logging from consideration. After applying all described reductions, 65 entries remained as being relevant for the analysis.

The second step involved an in-depth semantic examination of each relevant entry, covering all contents of the entry. The entries include natural-language discussion threads between several parties (software testers, developers and customer support staff). The relevant information about the nature of occurred FODs, the triggering circumstances, the underlying faults and any actions taken for their removal had to be extracted from these discussions. During the semantic examination, the *validity* of each entry was checked first. The following entries were considered invalid with respect to the case study and excluded from further consideration:

- Entries that are duplicates of other (valid) entries;

- Entries that describe problems resulting from user operation or configuration errors rather than implementation faults;

- Entries that describe feature or documentation requests;

- Entries that are related to security rather than reliability;

- Entries whose included information is incomplete and cannot further be exploited.

After the validity check, 27 entries remained for consideration, each of which describes a distinct SMTP processing problem leading to FOD occurrences, namely violations of the specified success criteria of the case study scenario (see Section 6.5.2). Each of these entries was further examined and categorized as shown in Table 6.5 in order to make more systematic and refined statements about the induced FOD occurrences. The first three categories refer to the *location* within the architecture where the FODs originate. More concretely, FOD occurrences are mapped to one of the InternalActions in the modelled PCM-REL instance (category "Point of Failure"), which is part of an RDSEFF (category "Service Operation") of a BasicComponent (category "Software Component"). The table contains an example in which FODs are located to the "Evaluate-PerformACLConnectCheck" action within the "ProcessMessage" operation of the "ServerEximCtrl" component (see Figure 6.21). Two more

Category	Values
Location — Software Component	e.g. "ServerEximCtrl"
Location — Service Operation	e.g. "ProcessMessage"
Location — Point-of-Failure	e.g. "EvaluatePerformACLConnectCheck"
Type — Failure-on-Demand Class	e.g. "ProcessingStepWronglyOmitted"
Type — Failure-on-Demand Type	e.g. "ACLConnectCheckWronglyOmitted"
Probability of Occurrence — Failure-on-Demand Occurrence Likelihood	• <u>Very low</u> (*not expected to occur in practice*) • <u>Low</u> (*may occur in practice under specific cirumstances*) • <u>Medium</u> (*likely to occur for a few customers and installations*) • <u>High</u> (*likely to occur for a considerable number of customers and installations*) • <u>Very high</u> (*occurs for all customers and installations*) • <u>Unknown</u>
Probability of Occurrence — Failure-on-Demand Persistence	• <u>Single</u> (*single failures-on-demand without further impact*) • <u>Transient</u> (*disrupted processing for limited period of time*) • <u>Until ASG restart</u> • <u>Until ASG reconfiguration</u> • <u>Until ASG version update</u> • <u>Unknown</u>
Configuration Dependencies	e.g. spam detection enabled, expression filters configured, ... (can be "none" or "unknown")
Request Dependencies	e.g. mail with >100 recipients, mail with special characters, ... (can be "none" or "unknown")

Table 6.5: Semantic Categorization of ASG Bug Tracker Entries

categories refer to *type* information, selecting a certain class of FODs (as listed in Table 6.3) and a modelled SoftwareInducedFODType. Together, the type and location categories unambiguously select a certain FODOccurrenceDescription within the modelled PCM-REL instance.

The remaining categories serve as indications for the *probability of occurrence* of the FODs, namely the "FODProbability" attribute of the modelled FODOccurrenceDescriptions (see Figure 4.5). First, the category "FOD Occurrence Likelihood" specifies the fraction of existing customers and ASG installations that are expected to experience FODs due to the reported problem, with values ranging from "very low" (namely, no FODs are expected to occur in the field) to "very high" (namely, FODs are expected to occur for all customers and installations). The category "FOD Persistence" describes the system behaviour after a FOD has occurred. There may be no consequences on further e-mail processing requests (value "single"), or the processing may be temporarily disrupted and then function again (value "transient"). Alternatively, the processing may be permanently disrupted until administrative action is taken (values "until ASG restart / reconfiguration / version update"). The two remaining categories "Configuration Dependencies" and "Request Dependencies" describe preconditions of FOD occurrences in terms of ASG configuration options and request properties. For example, a reported problem may only lead to FODs if the ASG is configured to perform spam detection, and if an e-mail contains specific characters in its body message. All categories contain an additional value "unknown" in case that the bug tracker entry does not contain enough information to determine a concrete value.

(1) Baseline Estimation	(2) Bug Tracker Analysis		(3) Resulting Software Failure-on-Demand Probability
	Conditions	Weight	
1.0E-b	• At least 4 reported problems • At least 1 reported problem with occurrence likelihood "low" (or higher) OR persistence "restart" (or higher) OR occuring for all configurations and requests	3	1.0E-(b-3)
1.0E-b	• At least 2 reported problems • At least 1 reported problem with occurrence likelihood "low" (or higher) OR persistence "transient" (or higher)	2	1.0E-(b-2)
1.0E-b	• At least 1 reported problem with occurrence likelihood "low" (or higher)	1	1.0E-(b-1)
1.0E-b	All other cases	0	1.0E-b

Table 6.6: Determination of Software Failure-on-Demand Probabilities

As a result of the semantic examination of the bug tracker entries, each FOD type occurring at a PPOF (represented by a FODOccurrenceDescription in the modelled PCM-REL instance) is associated with a set of zero or more entries. As Table 6.6 shows, the corresponding software FOD probability is determined by a baseline estimation 10^{-b} and adjusted by a relative weight $w \in \{0,..,3\}$ resulting in 10^{-b+w} (the actual probabilities are omitted for confidentiality reasons). The weight values w were deduced in a third and final step of the bug tracker analysis. They are a relative indication of the estimated historical FOD probabilities connected to each PPOF and FOD type. The exact range of weight values and the conditions of each value result from a manual assessment of the whole considered failure data set; they may vary for other data sets in similar case studies. Generally, the assigned weights depend on the number of associated entries, the FOD occurrence likelihood, the degree of FOD persistence, as well as the degree of existing configuration and request dependencies. The adjustment of the baseline estimations by the determined weights is based on the assumption that historical FOD probabilities can be extrapolated to the future – the higher a historical FOD probability for a certain PPOF and FOD type is, the higher is also its current and future FOD probability expected to be. The baseline estimation value b is the same for all software FOD probabilities. It was manually contributed by ASG developers and is subject to relatively high uncertainty. For this reason, the reliability evaluation done for the case study refrains from absolute statements about the ASG's reliability (see Section 6.5.5).

In addition to the described bug tracker analysis, some software FOD probabilities related to false negatives and false positives during spam and virus detection were directly estimated from existing statistical failure data. The corresponding FODs are not caused by implementation faults in a strict sense, and they are not reported in the bug tracker database. Rather, they result from natural limitations of the existing detection engines, which cannot achieve perfect success rates. Corresponding failure statistics are commonly available (for example, see failure statistics of commercial anti-virus engines in [AV-10]). Likewise, concrete FOD probabilities for the ASG's spam and virus detection engines could be determined from existing failure statistics.

6.5.4.2 Further Reliability Annotations

Besides the software failure potential of the ASG's SMTP processing, there is also a failure potential stemming from the system's resource environment (see Figure 6.16) that impacts its reliability. To this end, different hardware configurations are available for the ASG hosts with specified data sheet

MTTF values between 50 000 and 100 000 hours. In the modelled PCM-REL instance, MTTF values were set to 60 000 hours reflecting a common default installation. The MTTF value for the ASG switch was also taken from data sheet specifications and set to 200 000 hours. MTTR values of all hardware devices depend on the repair times of each specific customer and installation. For the case study, average values of 12 hours were assumed. As a local ASG installation does not contain any complex or long-range network communication technology, network transmission failure probabilities were set to a low value of 10^{-9}.

6.5.5 ASG Reliability Evaluation

This section presents the results of the reliability evaluation done for the ASG case study through Markov analysis (see Figure 6.14, element 19). The evaluation is based on the PCM-REL instance (18) created by the modelling activity (16). From the overall set of possible analysis experiments, those experiments were chosen that can answer the relevant case study questions (2), which have been described in Section 6.5.2. For sensitivity analysis, the existing PCM-REL instance was altered with respect to the variable model parameters identified in Section 6.5.3.3. All presented result diagrams denote FOD probabilities on the vertical axis on a logarithmic scale to the power of ten. The actual probability values are omitted for confidentiality reasons. The analysis runs were conducted with Markov state reductions switched on (see Section 5.1.1) and standard evaluation of system hardware states (Section 5.2.2). Each run took approximately 4 seconds on a standard laptop computer.

First, Figure 6.27 presents the results of a single analysis run without any model variations, aggregated according to different categories of interest. Subfigure (a) shows the general distinction of failure potentials according to the software, hardware and network dimensions *dim*. While overall, software-induced FODs clearly dominate the other dimensions, Subfigure

255

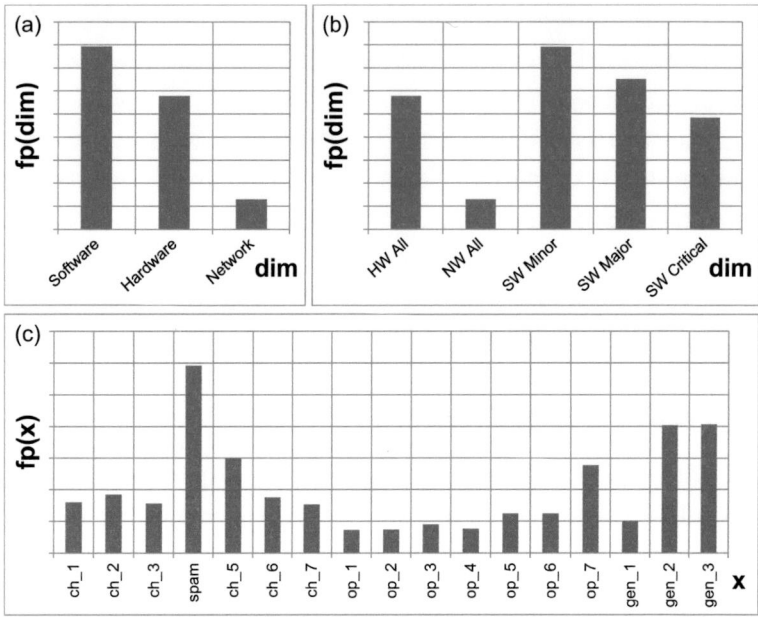

Figure 6.27: ASG Reliability Predictions by Failure Dimensions and Mail Processing Steps

(b) presents a more fine-grained distinction according to criticality (see Section 6.5.2). When focussing on major and critical FOD occurrences, it turns
out that reliability impacts of similar significance are caused by the hardware and software dimensions (assuming that hardware and network FOD
occurrences are generally "major"). Subfigure (c) further differentiates the
software failure potential according to individual mail acceptance checks
ch_1 to ch_7, mail handling operations op_1 to op_7 and generic failure
potentials gen_1 to gen_3 which cannot be associated with a single check
or operation (the original names have been altered for confidentiality). Each
distinguished category x includes a list of modelled FOD types. For example, a check ch_i may be wrongly conducted or wrongly omitted, it may
wrongly pass or wrongly disapprove an e-mail, and it may cause corrup-

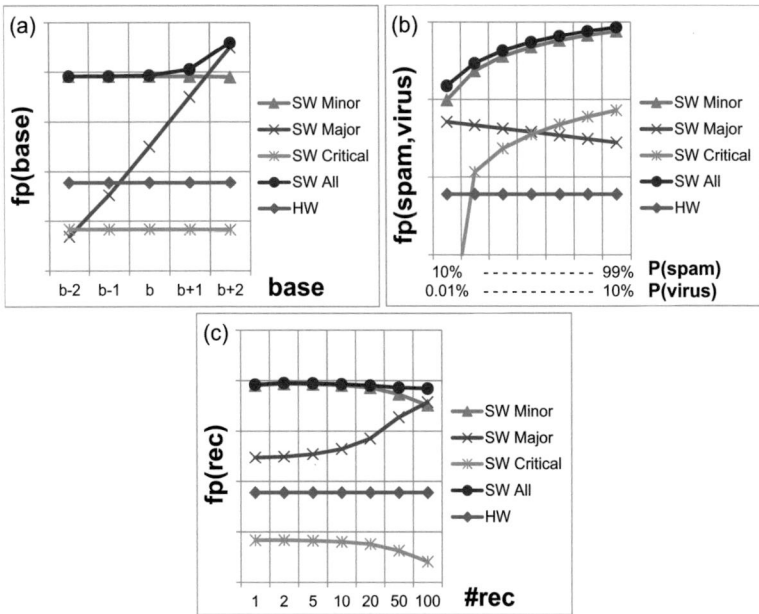

Figure 6.28: Robustness of Ranking of Failure Dimensions Against Software Baseline and Usage Profile Variations

tion of the e-mail or even the cancellation of its processing. As the figure shows, the spam detection, *gen_2*, *gen_3*, *ch_5* and *op_7* contain the most significant failure potentials. The specifically high FOD occurrence probability associated with the spam detection is acceptable as it causes only minor FODs. In summary, the analysis results indicate to which dimensions and individual mail processing steps future quality assurance efforts should predominantly be allocated.

To further investigate how existing input uncertainties and varying usage properties influence the expected reliability of SMTP processing, Figure 6.28 shows reliability impacts differentiated according to criticality and failure dimensions (excluding network) over varying model parameters. The biggest uncertainty in the model is caused by the estimation of software

FOD probabilities relative to a baseline value b, yielding probability values 10^{-b+w} ($w \in \{0, .., 3\}$) (see Section 6.5.4.1). Subfigure (a) varies these probabilities on a logarithmic scale between 10^{-b+w-2} and 10^{-b+w+2} to account for the uncertainty of the baseline estimation. As the figure indicates, the results allow for stable statements about the "minor" and "critical" failure categories, and the baseline variation affects only the "major" category. This is due to the fact that the "minor" and "critical" categories refer to spam and virus detection, for which baseline-independent estimations were possible due to available statistical failure data. The figure further shows that one can assume the "major" potential to be in an acceptable range between "minor" and critical" (only for the border case of $b + 2$, the "major" category overtakes the "minor" one). Subfigure (b) introduces another variation regarding the probability of malicious inputs (namely, spam or virus e-mails). For different customers and installations, this probability varies, depending on the trustworthiness of the involved communication partners and transmission paths. More concretely, the figure varies the probability of spam e-mails between $P(spam) = 10\%$ and $P(spam) = 90\%$ and the probability of viruses between $P(virus) = 0.01\%$ and $P(virus) = 10\%$ (each on a linear scale). As the figure shows, the variation affects mainly the "minor" and "critical" categories, while leaving "major" relatively stable. For high probabilities of malicious content, the "critical" category rises to levels above the "major" one. Hence, it may be worthwile to increase efforts avoiding critical FODs specifically for environments with many malicious inputs. Subfigure (c) varies the average number of recipients #rec per e-mail between 1 and 100 to examine the influence of this usage parameter. More recipients require more processing, as some processing steps have to be repeated for each recipient. However, major influences on the resulting failure potentials can only be observed for #rec $\geq$ 20. Interestingly, the "minor" and "critical" categories even decrease with increasing #rec. A possible explanation is that each recipient may trigger spam and virus detection (if not already done for the current e-mail), lowering the probability

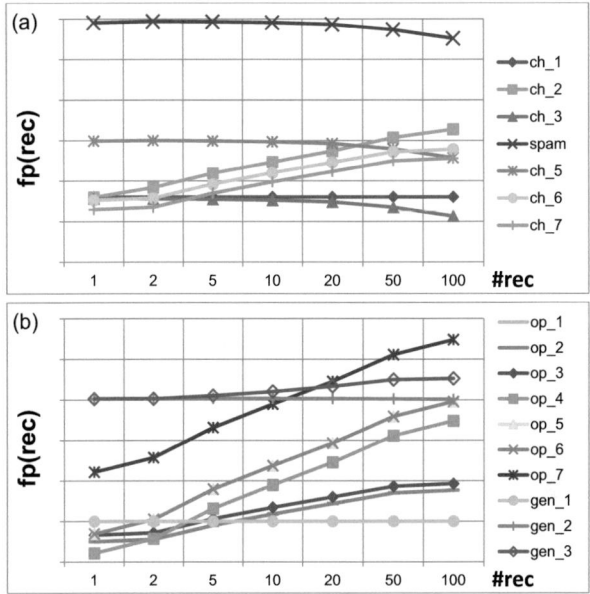

Figure 6.29: Robustness of Ranking of Processing Step Reliability Impacts Against Usage Profile Variations

of undetected malicious inputs. In sum, the software-induced reliability impact is stable and hence independent from the number of recipients.

While the sensitivity analysis presented so far only distinguishes the main failure dimensions, Figure 6.29 goes one step further and shows the influence of a varying model parameter – namely, the number of e-mail recipients – on the reliability impacts of the individual processing steps. Depending on the concrete step, increasing #*rec* has a slightly negative effect (*ch_2*, *ch_6*, *ch_7*, *op_1* to *op_3*), a strongly negative effect (*op_4* to *op_7*), no effect (*ch_1*, *gen_1* to *gen_3*), or even a slightly positive effect (*spam*, *ch_3*, *ch_5*). Apart from the spam detection, *gen_3* and *op_7* may rise to relatively high levels and should be specifically tested for e-mails with many recipients. Overall, the results support the findings of Figure 6.27(c) about which processing steps have the most significant fail-

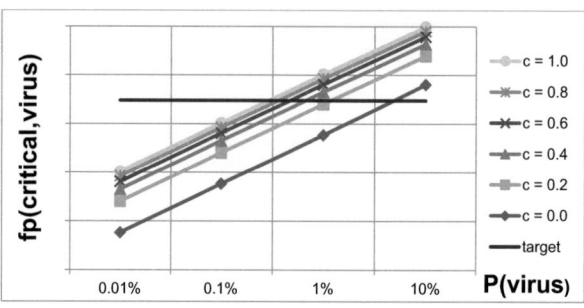

Figure 6.30: Effectiveness of Redundant Virus Detection

ure potentials. The variation of #rec additionally reveals that ch_5 is more critical for lower numbers of recipients than for higher ones.

Figure 6.30 presents the results of another experiment that specifically focuses on the redundant virus detection which the ASG performs during e-mail processing. To this end, the figure depicts the occurrence probability of critical FODs and varies the most important influencing factors – namely, the probability of a virus e-mail (between $P(virus) = 0.01\%$ and $P(virus) = 10\%$) and the conditional probability that a virus not detected by the first engine is also missed by the second one (between $c = 0.0$ and $c = 1.0$). The border case of $c = 1.0$ corresponds numerically to the design alternative with only one virus engine. With both the x-axis and the y-axis being logarithmic, the occurrence probability of critical FODs presents itself as a steadily increasing. The relative benefit of using a second engine is stable against the occurrence probability of viruses and only depends on the degree of correlation between both engines, with a FOD probability reduced by up to approximately one power of ten in case of complete independence $c = 0.0$. For an example target value as shown in the figure, determining an envisioned upper bound for critical FOD occurrences, the second engine is required for $P(virus) \geq 1\%$, and even further measures for avoiding critical FODs should be considered for $P(virus) \geq 10\%$.

6.5.6 Case Study Assessment

The ASG case study is an important milestone providing evidence of the applicability of PCM-REL to an industrial IT system. The approach could successfully be used to model the ASG's SMTP processing part with all aspects relevant for reliability prediction. Based on this model, the conducted analysis could answer the relevant case study questions. This section reviews the most important aspects of the case study process and results along the line of the validation goals presented in Section 6.2.

Feasibility of modelling abstractions: Even though the ASG's architecture does not follow a component-based paradigm as strictly as assumed by PCM-REL, it could be adequately represented by a PCM-REL instance providing a valid base for reliability prediction. Some adaptations were necessary to build the model (such as substituting the asynchronous queue-based e-mail processing through a chain of synchronous component calls) but did not impact the reliability calculations or the flexibility of the model. The behavioural specifications were capable of expressing all required details of the ASG's behaviour. Future potential remains to reduce the size and complexity of the specifications through more advanced modelling constructs (for example, encoding parameter conditions directly in `FailureOccurrenceDescriptions` could save the effort of duplicate `InternalActions` with surrounding `BranchActions` and `BranchConditions`, as seen in Figure 6.22).

Feasibility of estimation of reliability annotations: The available input information sources of the case study as shown in Figure 6.14 can be deemed typical for many industrial software development projects. While for the ASG, enough information was available to conduct the case study, more significant and detailed analysis results would be possible with more comprehensive and stable failure data. Improved input data could be gathered through measures such as extended statistical tests of ASG products or extended collection of failure data in the field. The process of extracting estimates of FOD probabilities from a bug tracker database (see Section 6.5.4) was subject to high uncertainty and could only provide relative estimates; more research on how to extract the statistical FOD probabilities required for PCM-REL would be desirable.

Validity of Markov analysis: Validation of Markov analysis was not in the focus of this case study. For a validation of this aspect, see the audio hosting study (Section 6.4).

Significance and robustness of prediction results: Experiments could be conducted that answered the relevant case study questions. Sensitivity analysis was applied to gain further evidence about the robustness of the results in the light of existing input uncertainties. Even though the estimation of most software FOD probabilities was only relative to a baseline estimation value (see Table 6.6), it was possible to reveal the most critical processing steps and the relative benefits of redundant virus detection with high confidence (see Section 6.5.5). Due to the high number of variable model parameters (see Section 6.5.3.3), considerable effort was required to identify the most significant ones with the respect to the case study questions. Further automation to support the identification of significant parameters would be desirable.

Further findings of the case study are related to scalability and efforts: The created PCM-REL instance did not pose any scalability issues to the analysis, with individual analysis runs requiring less than 5 seconds on a standard laptop computer. The overall effort for conducting the case study was acceptable; interaction with ASG developers and architects was required to establish the case study scenario and questions, to analyse the bug tracker database, to evaluate the relevant information sources and to conduct a baseline estimation for the software FOD probabilities. The interaction comprised five interview sessions and further e-mail communication with four involved ASG team members. The main work took approximately two weeks (one week for analysing the bug tracker database and one week for reliability modelling and evaluation). This does not include initial learning efforts on how to apply PCM-REL in an industrial context and how to leverage the relevant information sources, nor the documentation of the study for the thesis.

6.6 Further PCM-REL Case Studies

Besides the two case studies presented in this chapter, further studies have been conducted for the PCM-REL approach, based on modelled system architectures of a web-based media store product line [BBKR11], an industrial control system [BKBR11], a distributed business reporting system [BKBR11] and a sales support system for retail chains [KB09]. The experiments conducted within these case studies include ranking multiple design alternatives, assessing quantitative improvements gained by different fault tolerance mechanisms, identifying critical architectural components and processing steps, as well as assuring the robustness of obtained prediction results. To give an impression of one of the conducted studies, Figure 6.31 gives an overview of the PCM-REL instance modelled for the business reporting system, which generates management reports from business data collected in a database. The model features multiple usage scenarios reflecting different user roles (accounting manager, sales manager and administrator), multiple servers with dedicated computing tasks, as well as fault-tolerant design in terms of triple redundancy of certain software and hardware parts of the architecture. Beyond the mentioned case studies, further conducted experiments give evidence of the scalability of the Markov analysis and of the savings that can be realized in terms of model size by using parameter dependencies as offered by PCM-REL [BKBR11]. Due to space limitations, the details of the mentioned case studies and experiments are omitted from this thesis. Further information and case study models for download can be found at [BBKR12].

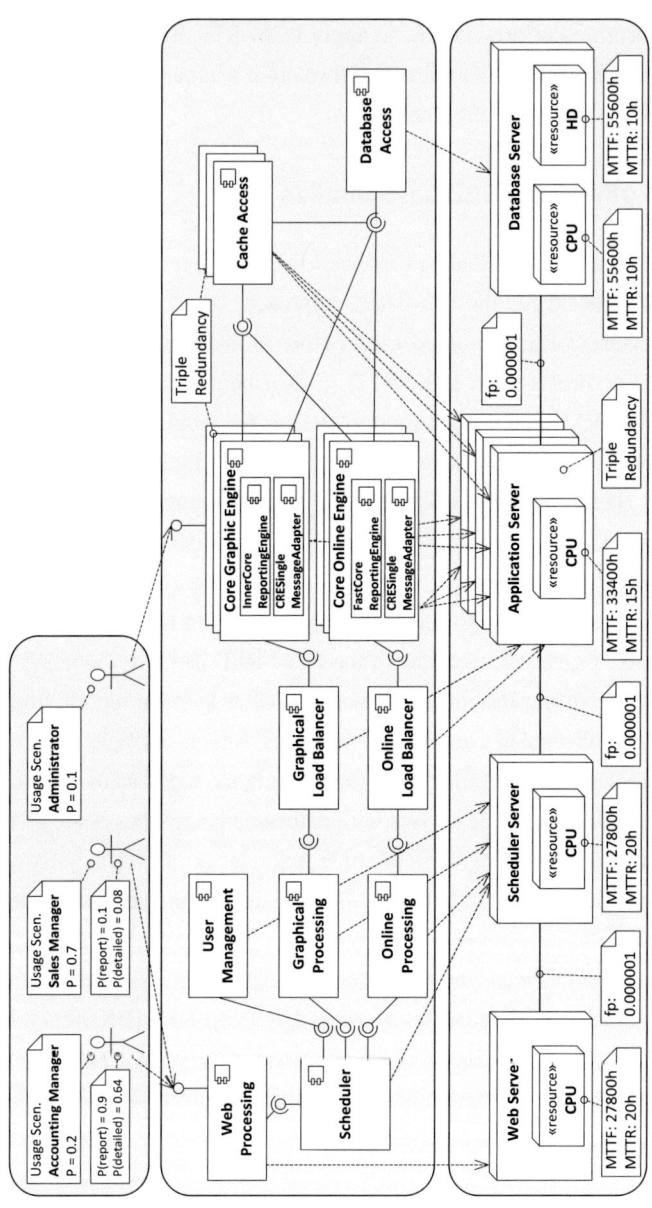

Figure 6.31: Business Reporting System (Overview)

7 Related Work

The PCM-REL approach presented in this thesis belongs to the field of architecture-based software reliability prediction (ASRP). While the approach benefits from the experiences gained in this field, it also presents unique features that enhance the state-of-the-art. The main distinguishing aspects of PCM-REL are the combined consideration of software and hardware failure potentials (Section 7.1), the consideration of fault tolerance capabilities (Section 7.2), as well as usage profile modelling and input parameter propagation (Section 7.3). The covered related work mostly belongs to the field of ASRP, but further approaches are also mentioned that are related to PCM-REL in one or multiple specific aspects. A final discussion in Section 7.4 includes a general assessment of PCM-REL against the state-of-the-art in the field of ASRP.

7.1 Combined Consideration of Software and Hardware Failure Potentials

One of the factors that make PCM-REL unique is the way how the approach integrates failure potentials of software components and hardware resources into a common analytical model and derives a system reliability value that accounts for both dimensions. If only software failure potentials are considered for ASRP, the prediction results are over-optimistic, neglecting the potential for failure-on-demand (FOD) occurrences due to unavailable hardware resources. If, on the other hand, software and hardware failure potentials are analysed independently, it remains unclear how an overall system reliability value should be derived. Only an integrated analysis can consider the circumstances under which a hardware resource is actually used by the service execution, such that its hardware failure results in a system level FOD (see Section 4.4).

In spite of the relevance of hardware failures to system reliability, and although mathematical foundations for a combined consideration were presented by Laprie et al. already in 1992 [LK92], until today many ASRP approaches and related case studies focus purely on software [CG07b, DS95, GWTH98, GPHP05, KSB10, PEO11, RSP03, ST07b, ST07c, WPC06, YCA04, KM97]. However, some approaches have made steps towards an integrated consideration of hardware and software failure potentials. A closer investigation of those approaches reveals that they do not match the generality and comprehensiveness of the combined software/hardware consideration as done by PCM-REL. The following Sections 7.1.1 to 7.1.4 discuss existing strategies and approaches for the combined consideration, within the field of ASRP and beyond.

7.1.1 MTTF/MTTR Model for Software Components

A number of approaches exist that aim at reusing hardware-oriented analyses for combined software/hardware considerations [DW04b, DW04a, KMT09, RS07, STTA08, TWH$^+$08]. These approaches extend the scope of the standard failure model for hardware resources (see Section 2.2) by applying it also to software components. Hence, software and hardware components in a system are treated in a unified manner, annotated each with a pair of MTTF and MTTR values, from which a steady-state availability Av can be derived. Formalisms such as fault trees can be used to express static relations between components such as "component C_1 requires component C_2". A component is regarded as ready for service only when it is available, and when all its required components are also available. One or several components are marked as being top-level (namely, providing the system-level services), and the system is by definition ready for service when all its top-level components are. Standard combinatorial calculation yields the fraction of time in which the system is ready, or – under a slightly different interpretation – the probability that the system is ready for service when accessed at an arbitrary point in time, hence delivering service as expected. As this calculation is based on component availabilities, most authors speak of *system availability prediction*, rather than reliability prediction.

While the discussed strategy seems intuitive and therefore attractive, its applicability to software-intensive systems is limited. Probably the most severe limitation is the missing consideration of transient FOD occurrences of software components. As an extreme example, consider a software component C that does not have any permanent failures but produces wrong computational results for 50% of all service invocations. The proposed approaches would mark C as being perfectly available even though it has a very high failure rate. Musa [Mus04] restricts software availability considerations to "major software failures" such as crashes or hang-ups, which require system restarts and possibly data recovery actions before the system is again ready for service. However, such a policy certainly captures only part of the possible failure behaviours of software.

A further drawback is the fact that the approaches do not cover the relation of system availability or reliability to the system usage. Software component availability and component interdependencies are statically formulated without taking into account any usage parameters. The authors do not even implicitly account for usage aspects when determining software MTTF and MTTR values in their demonstrating examples [KMT09, STTA08, TWH+08].

Another distinguishing aspect of PCM-REL and the discussed approaches is that most of them focus on special kinds of IT systems, such as virtualized systems [KMT09, RS07], blade server systems [STTA08] or the IBM© SIP Application Server [TCD+08]. Only Das et al. [DW04b, DW04a] provide a generalized architectural modelling formalism.

7.1.2 Usage Period Model for Hardware Resources

A few approaches have proposed to account for hardware failures in ASRP by considering hardware failure rates and usage periods during service execution [Gra05, GMS07, Hap04]. The approaches explicitly model the individual requests for hardware resource consumption by software. The time needed by the resource for processing each request is directly annotated to the model [Hap04] or can be calculated from a given requested processing amount and resource processing speed [Gra05]. Based on the given resource failure rates, the probabilities that the required resources complete their processing without failure are determined per request [Gra05] or over all requests of a resource [Hap04]. The system's reliability is determined as the probability that no software and no hardware failures occur during service execution.

The main drawback of this strategy is that it treats hardware resources as if they were non-repairable entities. The failure probability for each resource request is calculated under the precondition that the resource is non-failed at the beginning of the request. Hence, the predicted system reliability is the probability that service execution at a point in time t succeeds if all resources of the system have survived until t. Furthermore, a general system reliability value R independent from t can only be calculated under the assumption of exponential hardware TTFs, which has been demonstrated to be a rather inaccurate approximation in practice [SG07]. Although the significance of the prediction results is questionable in light of these limitations, the authors do not discuss them. In contrast, the PCM-REL prediction yields the probability of successful service execution at an arbitrary point in time t, accounting for the fact that hardware resources can fail and be repaired or replaced over the system's lifetime.

7.1.3 Alternative Modelling Approaches

Beyond the approaches discussed so far, several other works aim at system reliability or availability prediction based on modelling formalisms featuring a combined consideration of software and hardware components [CMRK10, KKM03, KOBMP99, KOB00, MRKE09, MKK03, RKK07, RFKK08, ST06, ST07a, WT05]. However, these approaches focus on specific failure scenarios, they do not make the influence of software and hardware failures explicit in the model, or they do not take both dimensions into account for predicting system reliability.

Kaaniche et al. [KKM03] and Martinello et al. [MKK03] examine the availability of services provided over the Internet. They focus on replication schemes for web servers [MKK03] and on the example of a web-based travel agency [KKM03]. The consideration of failures is limited to special failure types, namely overflowing service request buffers as software failures and unavailability of computer hosts as hardware failures. Due to this special focus, the authors avoid explicit modelling of software architecture and components. Instead, they use queueing theory to directly calculate the reliability impact of the considered failure potentials.

Wang [WT05] combines a *system availability model* (SAM) with a *user behaviour graph* (UBG) to determine the probability that user sessions are successfully completed in spite of the risk of the system becoming partially or totally unavailable. The SAM is a CTMC capturing the different possible availability states of the system under study. However, the author does not give any general rule how to construct the SAM. Hence, the reader is left alone with the exercise to express software and hardware failures and their effects implicitly in the states of the SAM.

The specific domain of mobile applications is targeted by the approaches of Malek et al. [MRKE09] and Cooray et al. [CMRK10]. The authors introduce the notion of the *context* of mobile devices and software components executed on them. The context includes all aspects of the frequently changing environment, such as the location, reachability of other hosts, available network bandwith, battery charge, and others. Hence, the context includes software and hardware aspects. The authors propose continuous reliability prediction during system operation based on component reliability models (see Section 2.3.3) with the dynamically changing context properties implicitly encoded in the transition probabilities. However, the context properties are only generically specified as a vector of numeric parameters. No further instruction is given as to which individual context properties should actually be considered, and how they should be encoded in the vector. Furthermore, the main focus is on context changes due to mobility rather than failures in the software or hardware environment.

The approach of Sato et al. [ST07a] is close to PCM-REL in that it predicts the reliability of a system with software services and hardware resources, explicitly taking into account the usage of the resources by the service execution, as well as the hardware-specific failure potentials. The approach models the software architecture as a DTMC whose states represent service invocations and resource usages. The availability states of each resource are captured through a CTMC. The central difference to PCM-REL is that Sato et al. do not consider software failure potentials. Their approach assumes that all service failures are due to hardware resource unavailability. Consequently, the approach yields over-optimistic prediction results for systems with imperfect software.

The approach of Sharma et al. [ST06] predicts the software reliability of a component-based system subject to software failures during service execution, as well as operating system (OS) and hardware failures in the execution environment. A DTMC captures the software components and their failure behaviour; hardware and OS failures are expressed through a CTMC per involved machine. Based on the assumption that a failing machine does not lead to a service failure but only to a delayed service execution (where the delay is caused by the waiting time of service requests until the machine is rebooted and again ready for service), machine failures are not taken into account for reliability prediction, but only for the performance-related evaluation of the *goodput*, namely the rate of successfully completed service requests per unit of time. Hence, the reliability prediction only accounts for the software failures in the system.

Kanoun et al. [KOBMP99, KOB00] provide an alternative approach to availability modelling and prediction of IT systems using *Generalized Stochastic Petri Nets* (GSPN), which can be viewed as an evolution of the strategy discussed in Section 7.1.1. Instead of providing a single MTTF and MTTR value per software and hardware component, the approach flexibly models failure and repair processes with multiple stages and transition rates through a dedicated GSPN per component. Additional interaction GSPNs capture relations between components, where a state change in one component impacts the behaviour of other components. Rugina et al. [RKK07, RFKK08] build upon these results and provide a transformation from the *SAE Architectural Analysis and Design Language* (SAE-AADL) to the GSPNs for IT system availability prediction. While these approaches offer detailed modelling capabilities for software and hardware availability states and interactions, they still share significant shortcomings with those discussed in Section 7.1.1. First, they do not consider purely transient FOD occurrences but only failures that lead a component into an error state with a non-zero duration. Second, they do not account for system usage and its reflection in the component and interaction models.

7.1.4 Combined Software/Hardware Consideration in General

Several approaches exhibit a combined consideration of software and hardware components and their failure potentials, but differ in their scope and their goals from the field of ASRP [BMP09, DJP96, DL93a, DL93b, DDPH94, GHK$^+$99, GI93, HLL$^+$05, KOBMP99, KP00, SL88, VPMM05].

Bernardi et al. [BMP09] present a dependability profile as part of UML MARTE [Obj07] offering comprehensive capabilities for modelling soft-

271

ware and hardware failures and their effects. The main focus of this work is on modelling rather than prediction and on dependability rather than reliability only. The authors demonstrate a transformation from a case study design model to a *deterministic and stochastic Petri net* (DSPN) and conduct availability prediction for the case study, but they do not propose a transformation and prediction method for the general case.

Several authors [DJP96, GI93, HLL^{+}05] have proposed approaches for the simulative or analytical evaluation of software behaviour over imperfect hardware resources. Considered hardware faults are low-level (such as destructed memory bits or CPU registers), and metrics of interest are fault detection times and coverages rather than system reliability. The approaches aim at improving given hardware designs; software behaviour is not modelled through an architecture but captured in terms of types and frequencies of hardware requests, thus functioning as a hardware usage profile.

An early work of Shin et al. [SL88] proposes an architectural model for systems composed from *modules*, where a module may refer to either software, hardware or a combination of both. However, the approach is concerned with error propagation times rather than system reliability.

Vilkomir et al. [VPMM05] evaluate the availability of a system with software and hardware failures and multiple recovery procedures. Instead of modelling the system architecture, the approach constructs a DTMC representing multiple system failure levels and considers the sojourn times and failure and restauration probabilities at each level. Similarly, Stark [Sta87] presents a specific DTMC with 6 system availability states (of which 2 are deemed failure states) and estimates transition probabilities for a Shuttle Mission Simulator (SMS) in order to evaluate its availability and reliability. Section 7.2.1 contains a related discussion of non-architectural availability and reliability evaluation of fault tolerance mechanisms and structures; most of the approaches mentioned there include combined software/hardware consideration.

A further class of approaches deals with the problem of finding optimal redundancy allocations for components in a system (see [KP00] for a survey). These approaches belong to the field of reliability optimization. A system is defined as a sequential or parallel structure of redundant components, where each component may refer to software, hardware or both dimensions. Each component is associated with a time- and usage-independent reliability value, and the overall system reliability is optimized using genetic algorithms or other methods, subject to a set of constraints. The focus is on the efficiency and quality of the employed optimization algorithms rather than a differentiated system reliability model.

7.2 Consideration of Fault Tolerance Capabilities

This section discusses the ability of PCM-REL related work to model fault tolerance (FT) capabilities of an IT system under study, and to quantitatively evaluate their influence on its reliability. FT capabilities are commonly included in IT systems (see Section 2.6) and constitute an important means to improve reliability. Therefore, PCM-REL explicitly considers such capabilities in terms of failure recovery during service execution (see Section 4.7). The approach allows software architects for taking FT-related measures into consideration during system design, as demonstrated in both the audio hosting case study (Section 6.4) and the Astaro ASG case study (Section 6.5).

In contrast, many other ASRP approaches do not provide any modelling constructs to express FT [Che80, CSC02, DS95, GWTH98, GT02, GWHT04, GPK03, GPHG+03, GPHW06, KM97, LG08, PEO11, RSP03, ST07a, ST07c, YCA04, ZL10] or have only basic FT expressiveness (see Section 7.2.3). Further approaches provide more detailed FT analysis, but their scope is limited to individual FT mechanisms and structures considered in isolation (see Section 7.2.2). PCM-REL is unique in combining highly expressive FT modelling with an architectural scope, analysing how individual FT capabilities employed in different parts of a system's architecture influence the overall reliability of the system. The following Sections 7.2.1 to 7.2.4 give a detailed overview of PCM-REL related work with respect to FT modelling and analysis.

7.2.1 Availability Evaluation of Fault-Tolerant System Architectures

Several approaches target system availability rather than reliability but are still closely related to the field of ASRP [DW04b, DW04a, KOBMP99, KOB00, KMT09, RKK07, RFKK08, STTA08, TWH$^+$08]. Typically, they treat software and hardware components in a unified manner, assigning MTTF and MTTR values to each component (also see Section 7.1.1). Especially for software components, MTTR annotations may indicate FT capabilities either within the components or in their execution environment (which may, for example, have the ability to restart components upon detection of an error). However, component repair may also be an act of maintenance carried out by an external agent [ALRL04]. The MTTR annotation does not distinguish between both cases, and it does not explicitly denote any FT capabilities which lead to component repair. Hence, the possibility to account for FT through MTTR annotations is limited to a basic level.

Some approaches have enriched the standard availability evaluation with specific constructs for considering FT. One possibility of doing so is to extend inter-component relationships from simple "C_1 requires C_2" relations to "C_1 requires C_2 OR ...OR C_n" relations [DW04b, DW04a, STTA08, TWH$^+$08]. Such relations express that a system contains redundancy, stating that only 1 out of the set of hardware and / or software components $\{C_2,..,C_n\}$ has to be ready for service so that C_1 can deliver its respective service.

While the consideration of *OR* relationships is still limited to special kinds of FT capabilities, the approaches of Kanoun et al. [KOBMP99,

KOB00] and Rugina et al. [RKK07, RFKK08] (which have been discussed in Section 7.1.3) offer a highly expressive availability evaluation including detailed FT modelling capabilities. The modeller is free to specify each component and each inter-component dependency through a dedicated *Generalized Stochastic Petri Net* (GSPN), capturing system structure and functional interactions between components, as well as reconfiguration and maintenance activities.

Compared to PCM-REL, all discussed approaches are limited in that they only evaluate the availability impact of the modelled FT capabilities, thereby leaving their influence on system reliability unclear. For example, wait-and-retry strategies can significantly improve the reliability of distributed applications with purely transient network transmission failures. However, as the availability of the network is not impacted by the transient failures, availability-tailored approaches cannot evaluate the benefits of the wait-and-retry. Moreover, the approaches do not take the system's usage into consideration (see also Section 7.1.1). Hence, they cannot account for the usage dependencies of the fault-tolerant service execution (see Section 4.7).

7.2.2 Non-Architectural Fault Tolerance Modelling and Prediction

A substantial amount of work focuses on availability and reliability evaluations of individual FT mechanisms and structures – examples include [BDT+87, CLL78, DT89, DL93a, DL93b, DDPH94, DL95, GHK+99, GLT97, KKB+93, LKBK91, MSHT92, TG83, YSP09, YSP11]. The evaluation is done based on DTMCs, CTMCs, *Stochastic Petri Nets* (SPNs) or variations of these formalisms. However, the formalisms are not used as architectural models, denoting components and transitions of control flow between them. Rather, they denote a set of different availability states and the possible transitions between those states, annotated with transition probabilities or rates. While the expressiveness of such modelling approaches with respect to the targeted FT mechanisms or structures may be as high or even higher than that of PCM-REL, their scope is limited to system fractures rather than whole system architectures. Even though some authors speak of "system" availability or reliability as an achieved prediction result, they assume that the considered structure essentially forms the system. This assumption holds for specific systems under study, but it is generally infeasible with respect to modern distributed and heterogeneous system architectures. Moreover, approaches targeted at reliability evaluation mostly focus on the time-dependent probability that a considered FT structure "survives" from a defined start $t_0 = 0$ up to a point in time t without visiting any failure states, which differs from the goal of PCM-REL to predict the probability of successful service execution at an arbitrary point in time.

Costes et al. [CLL78] examine the availability and reliability of single or redundant *units* or *elements* that may be affected by both software and hardware failures. The authors take maintenance activities into account, namely hardware replacements and software fault removal (thereby accounting for software reliability growth processes). Laprie et al. [LKBK91] take a similar approach, but more generally consider n redundant or non-redundant components.

Further approaches [DL93a, DL93b, DDPH94, DL95] examine certain variations of well-established FT mechanisms, namely *Distributed Recovery Blocks* (DRB), *N-Version Programming* (NVP) and *N-Self-Checking Programming* (NSCP). The authors aim at a combined consideration of software and hardware failures through *Markov Reward Models* (MRM) and *Fault Trees*. Gokhale et al. [GLT97] propose an alternative evaluation through simulation instead of analysis. Kanoun et al. [KKB⁺93] use *Generalized Stochastic Petri Nets* (GSPN) to evaluate the reliability of *Recovery Blocks* (RB) and NVP.

Garg et al. [GHK⁺99] focus on *Passive Replication Schemes* and evaluate the performance and reliability of server applications with either *Cold*

Replication or *Warm Replication*. For the evaluation, the authors include hardware and software failure and repair events in a common CTMC. Muppala et al. [MSHT92] evaluate the availability of VAX-cluster systems using *Stochastic Reward Nets* (SRN) as a variation of the SPN formalism. Other authors [BDT$^+$87, DT89, TG83] introduce the notion of *behavioural decomposition* as a two-level modelling formalism, including high-level case-specific fault trees or CTMCs representing the availability states of a considered FT structure, as well as lower-level CTMCs or *Extended Stochastic Petri Nets* (ESPN) representing fault detection and recovery processes within each FT structural element.

Yusuf et al. [YSP09, YSP11] propose the *Recovery-Aware Component* (RAC) pattern for grid applications and employ *Parameterized Markov Models* (PMM) to evaluate the pattern's reliability. In contrast to other approaches discussed in this section, the authors introduce RACs explicitly as an architectural pattern, and they propose a reference architecture based on RACs. The reference architecture includes specific components designated to the FT management of grid applications. In contrast to PCM-REL, the authors focus on the specific domain of grid applications, as opposed to IT systems in general.

7.2.3 Architectural Reliability Prediction Considering Fault Tolerance

This section discusses approaches that evaluate software architectures regarding reliability, considering certain FT capabilities of a system under study [CG07a, CG07b, FGGM10, GLT98, GL05, Gok05, Gra05, MZ08, PDAC05, ST06, WWC99, WPC06]. Although the goals of these approaches are closely related to PCM-REL, their FT expressiveness is significantly more limited than that of PCM-REL (which has been presented in Section 4.7).

The approach of Sharma et al. [ST06], which has also been discussed in Section 7.1.3, takes the possibility of component restarts and application retries into consideration. More concretely, if a software component exhibits a FOD during service execution, it may be either visited again (interpreted as a component restart), or the whole service execution may be repeated from start (interpreted as application retry), or the service execution results in failure (denoting that the component FOD could neither be handled by component restart nor application retry). Fixed probabilities for component restart, application retry and system failure are annotated per component to the architectural DTMC. The authors also consider hardware failures and repairs, but they do not take them into account for reliability prediction (see Section 7.1.3). Compared to PCM-REL, the approach lacks FT expressiveness in several respects, including individual recovery behaviours in response to FOD occurrences, multi-stage recovery, multi-type recovery, as well as influencing aspects of service usage and recovery from hardware failures.

Wang et al. [WWC99, WPC06] propose several architectural styles, including a *fault-tolerant architectural style*, and use an extended architectural DTMC to evaluate the reliability of system architectures incorporating those styles. Similar to the *OR* relation discussed in Section 7.2.1, the FT architectural style considers a set of n redundant software components $\{C_1, \ldots, C_n\}$. Only 1 out of the n components is required to be ready for service for an overall successful service execution. The FT architectural style is the only FT capability considered by the authors.

Gokhale et al. [GLT98, GL05] propose a simulation approach to evaluate an architectural DTMC for reliability. The simulation takes individual *FT configurations* per software component into account. An FT configuration may refer to FT structures such as *N-Version Programming* (NVP) or *Distributed Recovery Block* (DRB). In contrary to PCM-REL, the approach does not take into account hardware failures and recovery, system usage influences on FT execution, nor any FT structures that involve multiple components. Other aspects such as limited FT coverage, imperfect recovery, multiple recovery stages and types might be realized by the simulation procedures but are not explicitly discussed by the authors. Moreover, the authors do not discuss the scalability of the approach, which may be critical with respect to failure probabilities. While in practice, failure probabilities may be as small as 10^{-9}, the demonstrating examples in [GL05] only show reliability values between 0.69 and 0.96.

Another approach of Gokhale [Gok05] proposes to annotate software components in an architectural DTMC with an additional *coverage factor* per component that indicates the possibility of component-level FOD occurrences to be recovered from before resulting in an overall service execution failure. This approach provides only basic FT capabilities compressed into a single FT-specific value per component.

Cortellessa and Grassi [CG07b, Gra05] focus on reliability prediction for service-oriented architectures (SOA). They consider recursively composed services, where each service may invoke multiple external services in order to complete its own execution. The approach conducts an algorithmic evaluation of the probability of successful execution of a top-level user-invoked service. Similarly to previously-discussed approaches, the authors introduce the *OR completion model* denoting the possibility that a composed service requires only 1 out of n invoked external services to be successful in order for its own execution to succeed.

Several ASRP approaches enrich their analysis by explicit consideration of error propagation [CG07a, FGGM10, MZ08, PDAC05], relaxing the prevalent assumption of each component-level FOD automatically resulting in a system-level FOD. They introduce specific concepts such as multiple failure types and error propagation probabilities, which may be used to express the masking or conversion of FOD occurrences, representing FT capabilities of the modelled system. In contrast to PCM-REL, these approaches do not model FT mechanisms and structures explicitly. Instead, they rely on direct estimation of the additional error propagation probabilities, which may be hard to acquire in practice. Moreover, the approaches do not reflect the influence of system usage or hardware failures and recovery on the FT-related component behaviour.

7.2.4 Further Fault Tolerance Considerations

This section shortly discusses approaches that consider FT capabilities of IT systems but differ in their goals and scope from PCM-REL [BMP09, CL04, CLV05, EL85, KP00, LM89, PSMK03, TST02, Wol10]. Some of these approaches focus on specific problems related to FT and provide detailed accounts of these. For example, Eckhardt, Littlewood, Popov et al. [EL85, LM89, PSMK03] examine the theoretical effects of failure correlation on the overall failure probability of multi-version software. Cai et al. [CL04, CLV05] complement these considerations through empirical studies and experiments. Wolter [Wol10] examines the *timeout selection problem*, aiming at a good choice for the frequency of periodic FT activities such as restart, rejuvenation and checkpointing.

The work of Trapp et al. [TST02] targets embedded systems and specifically focuses on the data flow throughout a system's architecture. The authors explicitly consider how the quality of input data (such as the accuracy of a measured temperature value) affects the operation of the system and its produced outputs. An *object-oriented hierarchical Petri net* is used to represent the system with its components and performed tasks. As with approaches considering error propagation (see Section 7.2.3), the approach can be used to implicitly reflect FT capabilities of the system under study.

Further approaches, which have been introduced in Section 7.1.4, include FT considerations: Bernardi et al. [BMP09] provide capabilities for modelling redundant system structures; Kuo et al. [KP00] provide an overview of reliability optimization, covering the *redundancy allocation problem* as a specific component-level redundancy pattern.

7.3 Usage Profiles and Input Parameter Propagation

This section assesses the capabilities of approaches related to PCM-REL for consideration of system usage aspects. As discussed in Section 2.1.2, the usage profile may heavily affect the reliability of a software-intensive system in non-intuitive ways. Hence, it is an important factor that should be explicitly considered for reliability modelling and prediction.

PCM-REL is particularly strong in its consideration of usage aspects. Based on the capabilities of the existing PCM approach [BKR09], it offers an explicit meta-model capturing a system usage profile with multiple usage scenarios, as well as an explicit specification of input parameter properties for individual system service invocations (see Section 2.7.5). The specification of system behaviour includes parameter dependencies (Section 2.7.6) to account for the influence of input parameter properties on the service execution. A sophisticated *Stochastic Expressions* (StoEx) language [Koz08] allows for specifying the properties through arbitrary probability distributions rather than single values only. Moreover, user and system behavioural specifications are strictly separated to assure the independence of developer roles and the reusability of model artefacts (Section 2.7.1). While these features are essentially part of the existing PCM approach for software performance prediction, they are highly innovative and unique for reliability predictions and the ASRP field. In the thesis, experiments conducted for the Astaro ASG case study (Section 6.5) show how usage profile changes can significantly influence the expected reliability of an IT system (Figures 6.28 and 6.29).

The following Sections 7.3.1 to 7.3.5 examine capabilities of PCM-REL related work for consideration of usage profiles aspects, including the number and sequence of system service invocations, as well as input parameter properties of individual invocations and their influence on service execution.

7.3.1 Usage-Agnostic Prediction Approaches

Several approaches, which typically speak of predicting software availability rather than reliability, have been proposed that do not take any usage aspects into account [DW04b, DW04a, KOBMP99, KOB00, KMT09, RS07, RKK07, RFKK08, STTA08, TWH+08]. Many of these approaches assign MTTF and MTTR values to software and hardware components and have been discussed in Section 7.1.1. Their applicability is essentially limited to the consideration of crash failures and other permanent failure situations whose occurrence frequencies do not depend on specific usage patterns. While some of the approaches [KOBMP99, KOB00, RKK07, RFKK08] (see Section 7.1.3) are more expressive in modelling failure and repair processes, they still share the principal disadvantage of neglecting usage aspects. With these approaches, modellers have no means to determine which parts of a created system model are affected by changes in the envisioned system usage; analysing a system under a different usage profile requires restarting the modelling activity from scratch.

7.3.2 Implicit Consideration of Usage Profiles

Most of the related approaches of PCM-REL fall under the category of implicit usage profile consideration [CG07a, CG07b, Che80, FGGM10, GLT98, GT02, GWHT04, GL05, GPK03, LG08, RSP03, RPS03, ST07a, ST06, ST07c, WWC99, WPC06, ZL10, GWTH98]. These approaches employ either an architectural model expressing the transfer of control between the services or components of a system, or a workflow model expressing the flow of execution within "composite" services or components, invoking further "basic" or "atomic" services. Modelling formalisms of choice are either equal or closely related to DTMCs, or they include explicit control flow constructs such as branches, loops or forks. All models include probabilistic annotations, such as DTMC transition probabilities, branch transition probabilities and loop iteration counts. These annotations influence the set and occurrence probabilities of possible sequences of visited components or steps during service execution. Hence, the annotations merge aspects of system behaviour (namely, the implementation) and system usage (namely, input parameter properties). Although several approaches call their models "usage profiles" or "operational profiles", they express system behaviour influenced by its usage, rather than user behaviour. However, by considering the topmost level of composition as being the usage scenario itself, it is actually possible to represent the behaviour of system users. In conclusion, the main differences between the discussed approaches and PCM-REL are that (a) their modelling formalisms do not explicitly distinguish between user and system behaviour, and that (b) they do not explicitly reflect how input parameter properties of service invocations influence service execution; instead, they merge system and usage aspects when modelling the service execution. Hence, the approaches suffer from significantly reduced reusability with respect to usage profile changes.

The following gives a short overview of the approaches in this category. A well-known representative approach is the Cheung model [Che80] (see Section 2.4), which expresses inter-component control flow through an absorbing DTMC and encodes the system's usage profile into the transition probabilities. Cortellessa et al. [CG07a] and Filieri et al. [FGGM10] build upon the same formalism and additionally superimpose error propagation models. Wang et al. [WWC99, WPC06] extend the formalism to capture heterogeneous software architectures that incorporate different architectural styles. Further approaches building upon the Cheung model are [GWTH98, GLT98, GT02, GWHT04, GL05, GPK03, LG08, ST06, ST07c]. Reussner et al. [RSP03, RPS03] employ the Rich Architecture Definition Language (RADL) for model creation but build upon the same underlying theory as Cheung for model resolution and reliability prediction. Cortellessa et al. [CG07b] (Section 7.2.3) and Sato et al. [ST07a] (Section 7.1.3) use the absorbing DTMC formalism to express execution workflows of composite services with the states representing external service invocations, internal operations or resource usages. Zheng et al. [ZL10] employ a workflow description for composite services with sequences, loops and parallel structures.

7.3.3 Scenario-Based Software Reliability Prediction

Several approaches can be subsumed as being *scenario-based* [CSC02, GPHG+03, PDAC05, RRU05, YCA99, YCA04]. These approaches share the idea that systems experience different *scenarios* occurring with different frequencies or probabilities, and that system reliability should be expressed averaged across all scenarios. Yacoub et al. [YCA99, YCA04] specify scenarios through *component sequence diagrams* (similar to UML sequence diagrams) and attach an occurrence probability to each scenario. An overall *component dependency graph* (which extends the DTMC formalism through variable state sojourn times and transition reliability values) is deduced from the given scenario specifications and used as a basis for reliability prediction. Cortellessa et al. [CSC02] and Popic et al. [PDAC05] employ annotated UML use case diagrams to specify system users, use cases and occurrence probabilities, as well as UML sequence diagrams to specify a set of scenarios per use case. The authors predict the success probability of scenario execution averaged over all specified scenarios, considering per-visit FOD probabilities of the involved software components and network transmission failure probabilities for remote inter-component invocations. Goseva-Popstojanova et al. [GPHG+03] use a similar method but additionally differentiate multiple failure severities from *minor* to *catastrophic* and derive *risk factors* from component state charts, predicting an overall system risk factor across all specified scenarios and use cases. Rodrigues et al. [RRU05] specify scenarios through *basic message sequence charts* (BSMCs) and use an overall *high-level message sequence chart* (HMSC, similar to an absorbing DTMC) to capture possible sequences of scenario executions and their occurrence probabilities.

While scenario-based approaches provide modelling concepts (such as use case diagrams) or annotations (such as scenario occurrence probabilities) that explicitly refer to usage aspects, they still merge system and usage aspects in their scenario specifications, because component invocation sequences are generally influenced by input parameter properties of the scenario-triggering system service invocations. None of the discussed approaches keeps track of parameter properties and their propagation throughout the invocation sequences. Hence, the approaches are significantly limited compared to PCM-REL with respect to usage profile consideration.

7.3.4 Parametrized Reliability Prediction Approaches

A few approaches explicitly deal with the effect of input parameter properties on the service execution and provide a correspondingly parametrized service specification [HMW01, Gra05, GMS07]. One of these approaches is provided by Hamlet et al. [HMW01], whose main focus is on the *data flow* throughout a component-based software architecture, rather than its control flow. The approach considers service execution as a sequence of component executions, where each component takes an *input* (from the system user or the previous component) and produces an *output* (which is, in turn, the input of the next component). The set of possible component execution sequences is specified through a *reliability algebra* that can express linear sequences, loops and branches. Moreover, each component visit may trigger a FOD; the approach predicts the probability of successful execution of the overall sequence. The authors explicitly consider parameter properties by breaking down the overall *input domain* (namely, the set of possible input values) into a set of disjoint *subdomains*, and by expressing the FOD probability of each component, as well as its produced output, as a function of the subdomain of its received input. A set of occurrence probabilities of the individual subdomains characterizes the initial user input and hence constitutes a usage profile for the service execution. The most significant disadvantage of the approach is that the authors do not provide any means to capture the component-internal mapping from input to output domains through modelling; instead, they rely on software architects to assemble and execute the system under study in order to derive the mapping. This method may be associated with very high efforts and effectively prevents the application of the approach at early system design stages.

The approach of Grassi [Gra05] is very close to the approaches discussed in Section 7.3.2, especially to the one of Cortellessa et al. [CG07b] (also see Sections 7.1.2 and 7.2.3), expressing execution workflows of composite services through absorbing DTMCs. Additionally, Grassi explicitly reflects input parameter properties of the composite service invocation, their propagation to external service invocations, and the resulting influence on the FOD probabilities of atomic services. The same concepts are reused by Grassi et al. [GMS07], who propose the *Kernel Language for Performance and Reliability Analysis* (KLAPER). Compared to PCM-REL, limitations still exist in that user and system behaviour are not explicitly distinguished, and the DTMC transition probabilities still merge both aspects.

7.3.5 Further Usage Profile Considerations

Besides the previously discussed categories, a few further approaches exhibit capabilities for consideration of usage aspects [BMP09, KKR01, KKM03, WT05]. Kaaniche et al. [KKR01, KKM03] (see Section 7.1.3) provide a dependability modelling framework, allowing for combining different modelling formalisms and prediction methods. They distinguish multiple modelling levels, namely *user, function, service* and *resource*. In a demonstrating example of a web-based travel agency, the authors model the user level through a DTMC-style *operational profile graph*, with states representing the execution of functions. In turn, each function is modelled by an *interaction diagram* expressing possible sequences of invocations of services. The interaction diagrams include branches, loops and parallel structures, with probabilistic annotations for branch transition probabilities and loop iteration counts. Hence, the approach is similar to those discussed in Section 7.3.2 but additionally distinguishes user and system behaviour explicitly.

The approach of Wang et al. [WT05] (see Section 7.1.3) also explicitly expresses user behaviour through its *user behaviour graph* (UBG). However, the approach does not consider input parameter properties of service invocations, and it specifies the system through a set of availability states rather than an architectural model. Bernardi et al. [BMP09] (Section 7.1.4) demonstrate the combination of annotated UML use case diagrams, deployment diagrams, sequence diagrams and statecharts for availability prediction in their reported case study.

7.4 PCM-REL and Architecture-Based Software Reliability Prediction

This section reviews the overall degree of innovation of PCM-REL compared to existing ASRP approaches. As discussed in the previous Sections 7.1 to 7.3, the main scientific contributions of the approach are the combined consideration of software and hardware failure potentials, the consideration of fault tolerance (FT) capabilities for reliability prediction and the explicit modelling of usage profiles and input parameter propagation. Although these are individual contributions, they are related to each other, and PCM-REL combines them to significantly advance the support that software architects can get from ASRP during system design. To this end, the consideration of hardware failures could be misleading if a system's ability to recover from them was not considered as well. On the other hand, the consideration of FT capabilities should not be limited to the software level only and benefits from an integrated software/hardware view.

In addition, both the software/hardware integration and the FT modelling benefit from the explicit consideration of usage profiles and input parameter propagation. The system's usage influences the service execution paths taken throughout the architecture and the involved accesses to hardware resources, as well as the alternative behaviours executed for failure recovery. Together, the modelling and analysis capabilities of PCM-REL allow for a differentiated view on an IT system and a comprehensive assessment of relevant questions during system design, as shown by the audio hosting and Astaro ASG case studies reported in the thesis (see Chapter 6).

Table 7.1 provides an overview of ASRP approaches and assesses these with respect to the innovative features of PCM-REL. The focus of this overview is narrowed down compared to the discussion in the previous sections to ASRP approaches in a strict sense only (see Section 2.5), excluding further discussed approaches (such as the ones predicting a system's availability rather than its reliability). Furthermore, the overview omits publications with a main focus on reporting experiments and case studies rather than new methodologies, as well as survey and overview papers. Any entry in parentheses indicates that an approach exhibits capabilities with respect to a certain feature but is limited compared to PCM-REL.

As the table shows, related ASRP approaches are generally limited compared to PCM-REL with respect to its main scientific contributions (which are listed in the first three feature columns). All approaches exhibit certain capabilities for usage profile considerations; most of them implicitly include usage aspects in probabilistic annotations to their underlying modelling formalisms (see Section 7.3.2). Several approaches provide basic consideration of FT capabilities (Section 7.2.3), and a few approaches provide some form of differentiation between software and hardware failure potentials (Sections 7.1.2 and 7.1.3). Overall, the approaches of Grassi [Gra05], Grassi et al. [GMS07] and Sharma et al. [ST06] are close to PCM-REL in that they exhibit capabilities in all three aspects. Sato et al. [ST07a] show conceptual similarity to PCM-REL as they consider a ser-

Authors	Year	Combined HW/SW Consideration	FT Consideration	Usage Profile Consideration	Network/Connector Failures	Multiple Failure Modes	Flexible PPOF Modelling	Design-Oriented Modellnig	Developer Roles	Tool Support
Cheung et al. [Che80]	1980	-	-	(X)	-	-	-	-	-	-
Dolbec et al. [DS95]	1995	-	-	(X)	-	-	-	-	-	-
Gokhale et al. [GWTH98]	1998	-	-	(X)	-	-	-	-	-	(X)
Gokhale et al. [GLT98]	1998	-	(X)	(X)	-	-	-	-	-	(X)
Wang et al. [WWC99]	1999	-	(X)	(X)	-	-	-	-	-	-
Yacoub et al. [YCA99]	1999	-	-	(X)	X	-	-	(X)	-	-
Cortellessa et al. [CSC02]	2002	-	-	(X)	X	-	-	X	-	-
Gokhale et al. [GT02]	2002	-	-	(X)	-	-	-	-	-	-
Goseva-Popstojanova et al. [GPHG+03]	2003	-	-	(X)	X	X	-	X	-	(X)
Goseva-Popstojanova et al. [GPK03]	2003	-	-	(X)	-	-	-	-	-	(X)
Reussner et al. [RSP03]	2003	-	-	(X)	X	-	-	X	-	(X)
Reussner et al. [RPS03]	2003	-	-	(X)	X	-	-	X	-	(X)
Gokhale et al. [GWHT04]	2004	-	-	(X)	-	-	-	-	-	(X)
Yacoub et al. [YCA04]	2004	-	-	(X)	X	-	-	(X)	-	-
Gokhale et al. [GL05]	2005	-	(X)	(X)	-	-	-	-	-	(X)
Gokhale [Gok05]	2005	-	(X)	(X)	-	-	-	-	-	-
Grassi [Gra05]	2005	(X)	(X)	(X)	X	-	(X)	-	-	-
Popic et al. [PDAC05]	2005	-	(X)	(X)	X	-	-	X	-	X
Rodrigues et al. [RRU05]	2005	-	-	(X)	-	-	-	(X)	-	(X)
Sharma et al. [ST06]	2006	(X)	(X)	(X)	-	-	-	-	-	(X)
Wang et al. [WPC06]	2006	-	(X)	(X)	-	-	-	-	-	-
Cortellessa et al. [CG07a]	2007	-	(X)	(X)	-	-	-	-	-	-
Cortellessa et al. [CG07b]	2007	-	(X)	(X)	X	-	X	-	-	-
Grassi et al. [GMS07]	2007	(X)	(X)	(X)	X	-	(X)	(X)	-	(X)
Sato et al. [ST07a]	2007	(X)	-	(X)	(X)	-	-	-	-	-
Sato et al. [ST07b]	2007	-	-	(X)	-	-	-	-	-	-
Sharma et al. [ST07c]	2007	-	-	(X)	-	-	-	-	-	(X)
Lipton et al. [LG08]	2008	-	-	(X)	X	-	-	-	-	-
Mohamed et al. [MZ08]	2008	-	(X)	(X)	-	X	-	(X)	-	-
Cooray et al. [CMRK10]	2010	(X)	-	(X)	-	-	-	(X)	-	X
Filieri et al. [FGGM10]	2010	-	(X)	(X)	-	X	-	-	-	-
Zheng et al. [ZL10]	2010	-	-	(X)	-	-	-	-	-	(X)
Palviainen et al. [PEO11]	2011	-	-	(X)	-	-	-	X	-	X

Table 7.1: Feature Overview of ASRP Approaches

vice execution flow (modelled through a DTMC) and its accesses to a set of independent and potentially unavailable hardware resources. Furthermore, Bernardi et al. [BMP09] (Section 7.1.4) provide very comprehensive reliability modelling capabilities; their work is not mentioned in the ASRP overview table as the authors do not target automated transformation and reliability prediction for general specified architectures.

Looking beyond the central contributions, the table indicates that several but not all approaches share with PCM-REL the ability to express failure potentials related to component interoperations. While PCM-REL assigns transmission failure probabilities to network links (Section 4.5), FOD probabilities have also been assigned to component connectors or interfaces by related approaches. Furthermore, several approaches allow for modelling architectures in a design-oriented way, rather than directly using DTMCs or related formalisms. On the other hand, a distinction between multiple failure modes (Section 4.2) is rarely offered by related approaches. The same holds for a flexible modelling of *potential points of failure* (PPOFs) that are not strictly related to the software components or invoked services of an architecture (see Section 4.3). Moreover, the issue of a separation of modelling concerns along the lines of multiple developer roles (in order to support a truly distributed software development process, see Section 2.7.1) is – to the best of the author's knowledge – not explicitly discussed and considered by any of the related ASRP approaches. Regarding tool support, several but not all approaches point out tools and implementations created or used for realizing the presented methodologies. However, most presented tool support is limited in that it covers only part of the methodology (such as only the prediction but not the modelling part), it focuses on accompanying tasks rather than the centre of the approach (such as test coverage tools for deriving component reliability values), or there is no reference to any publicly available version of the tool. The most comprehensive tool support is provided by Popic et al. [PDAC05], Cooray et al. [CMRK10] and Palviainen et al. [PEO11].

In conclusion, none of the related ASRP approaches matches PCM-REL in its overall set of innovative features, which are targeted at providing comprehensive and differentiated ready-to-use support for software architects during IT system design. While Table 7.1 lists a set of features relevant for this goal, related ASRP approaches have presented other kinds of contributions. To this end, some approaches investigate alternative modelling formalisms such as *Markov reward models* (MRM) [ST07a] or *Bayesian networks* (BN) [CSC02], focus on prediction through simulation [GLT98, GL05], integrate ASRP and *software reliability growth modelling* (SRGM) [GL05], conduct reliability optimization [LG08, FGGM10], offer combined predictions of multiple quality attributes [GT02, ST07b, ST06, ST07c], focus on *service oriented architectures* (SOA) [CG07b, Gra05, ZL10], describe methods for deriving reliability annotations [ZL10, GWTH98, GWHT04, PEO11] and provide closed-formula considerations of input uncertainties and the corresponding sensitivity of analysis results [GT02, GPK03]. In future work, PCM-REL may benefit from adopting those contributions and integrating them with its existing achievements.

8 Summary and Outlook

This chapter concludes the thesis, providing a summary of the presented contents and achievements (Section 8.1), an overview of completed and ongoing research efforts associated with the PCM-REL approach (Section 8.2), a discussion of promising directions for future developments (Section 8.3), as well as a final assessment of the approach and its benefits (Section 8.4).

8.1 Summary of Contents

This thesis has presented PCM-REL, an approach to integrated software architecture-based reliability prediction for IT systems. PCM-REL offers a design-oriented modelling language that comprehensively integrates the different reliability-influencing factors into an overall architectural specification of a system under study. A corresponding analysis method evaluates the architectural specification and obtains the probability of successful service execution as a prediction result. Overall, the following aspects are explicitly expressed by the modelling language and considered for the analysis:

- the structure of an IT system in terms of its included software component instances and their interconnections;

- the provided and required interfaces of each software component, as well as its internal (high-level) control and data flow;

- the resource environment of the system with its computing nodes, their interconnections and included hardware resources;

- the allocation of software components to computing nodes and the usage of hardware resources during service execution;

- the usage of system-external services for providing the system's own services;

- the system's usage profile in terms of a set of usage scenarios, where each scenario specifies the sequences of invoked system services and their input parameter properties;

- the software, hardware and network failure potentials that the system comprises;

- the failure potentials associated with system-external service invocations;

- the capabilities of service execution to recover from local failure occurrences and to prevent them from reaching the system's boundaries.

With the help of PCM-REL, software architects can assess multiple design alternatives of a system under study and rank them with respect to their expected reliabilities. They can identify reliability-critical parts in the architecture or processing steps during service execution, and they can assess the influence of envisioned changes in a system's architecture and usage on its reliability. The application of PCM-REL does not require the actual system being assembled and executed; hence, the approach can already be applied at early system design stages, when the most fundamental architectural decisions are to be made.

While a broader scientific context of PCM-REL is given through the existing fields of *reliability engineering, software reliability engineering* and *component-based software engineering*, the approach more concretely belongs to the field of *architecture-based software reliability prediction* (ASRP). The state-of-the-art in this field is advanced by PCM-REL through the following central contributions:

- *Combined consideration of software and hardware failure potentials:* PCM-REL allows for modelling both software components and hardware resources with their specific failure potentials. The approach considers how unavailable resources affect service execution, and it derives an overall reliability value accounting for both dimensions of failure.

- *Consideration of fault tolerance capabilities:* PCM-REL offers modelling constructs to express how service execution can recover from local failure-on-demand (FOD) occurrences by carrying out alternative behaviours, thereby avoiding the occurrence of system-level FODs. Failure recovery can compensate for FOD occurrences induced by software, hardware and network failure potentials. The definition of system-specific FOD types allows for precisely describing which failure situations are handled by a modelled recovery construct.

- *Explicit consideration of usage profiles and the propagation of input parameter properties:* PCM-REL explicitly specifies a system's usage profile as a set of usage scenarios, describing possible sequences of system service invocations and their occurrence probabilities. Service invocations can be annotated with stochastic specifications of input parameter properties, and control flow constructs within the service execution are specified depending on those properties. Hence, the approach explicitly considers how the input parameter properties of system service invocations influence the service execution.

In contrast, related ASRP approaches provide none or only limited capabilities in these respects, thereby significantly reducing the reusability of model artefacts and the decision support offered to software architects. Further innovative aspects of PCM-REL include the consideration of network transmission failures, the flexible specification of potential points of failure

(PPOFs) within the service execution control flow, as well as its design-oriented modelling language providing a consequent separation of modelling concerns along the lines of multiple envisioned developer roles. In addition, the approach offers comprehensive tool support including a graphical modelling environment and automated analysis capabilities.

To realize the set of features discussed above, PCM-REL builds upon the existing Palladio Component Model (PCM), which allows for modelling component-based software architectures, as well as its associated tool support. The approach extends the PCM meta-model by the specification of software, hardware and network failure potentials, as well as modelling constructs for failure recovery. Furthermore, PCM-REL adds a Markov analysis that transforms a modelled PCM-REL instance to an absorbing discrete-time Markov chain (DTMC) and resolves this DTMC by applying existing Markov theory. As a result, the analysis delivers the probability of successful execution of each specified usage scenario, as well as the occurrence probabilities of potential failure modes differentiated according to the software, hardware and network categories, individual FOD types or individual PPOFs. Compared to the use of DTMCs in related ASRP approaches, PCM-REL's Markov analysis is innovative in that it includes the user behaviour, the intra-component control flow, the state of the system's hardware resources and multiple failure modes in its DTMC representation. A time- and space-efficient transformation procedure compensates for the significantly increased size of the resulting DTMC models. The transformation has been implemented and included in the tool environment, allowing for a fully automated Markov analysis and the display of the obtained prediction results as a visual feedback.

The thesis includes two major case studies, which demonstrate the capabilities of the approach and validate that PCM-REL can feasibly be applied to predict the reliability of IT systems. More concretely, the validation gives evidence of the feasibility of the included modelling abstractions, the feasibility of estimating the required reliability annotations, the validity of the Markov analysis itself, as well as the significance and robustness of the obtained prediction results. The first case study is about a system providing audio hosting functionality. The study assesses and ranks multiple design alternatives, compares the prediction results to those obtained by a simulation approach and to measurements conducted for an implemented system prototype. The second case study features the Astaro Security Gateway (ASG), a well-established industrial IT system, focussing on the system's SMTP processing functionality. The study creates an architectural system model based on existing documentation and feedback from developers, derives input estimations for the required reliability annotations from existing qualitative and statistical failure data, and it assesses the reliability impacts associated with individual system processing steps, as well as the quantitative reliability improvements achieved by the system's included fault tolerance capabilities. While the conducted case studies generally support the validity of the approach, they also reveal certain potentials for future work, such as further research devoted to the input estimation of reliability annotations, as well as further extensions of PCM-REL's modelling capabilities to allow for a more intuitive representation of system behaviour. Moreover, occurrence frequencies of hardware-induced FODs observed over a limited system mission time interval may deviate from the predicted values if the expected number of hardware failure and repair events during the observation period is small.

8.2 Research Overview

The PCM-REL approach and its contributions have been described in multiple peer-reviewed publications [BZ09, BKBR10, BBKR11, BKBR11]; a preliminary integration of parameter dependencies in component reliability specifications has been developed in [KB09]. The most significant work is an article in the *IEEE Transactions on Software Engineering* (TSE) journal [BKBR11], which is currently accepted for publication and available in an online pre-print version. The article describes the combined consideration of software and hardware failure potentials by PCM-REL, as well as its capabilities for usage profile modelling and input parameter propagation. Two reported case studies demonstrate and validate the approach for a business reporting system and an industrial control system. PCM-REL's capabilities for fault tolerance consideration are specifically covered in [BBKR11].

Further completed and ongoing research efforts build upon the approach or include it as part of a broader methodology. The European research project SLA@SOI [SLA12] has focused on the comprehensive and consistent management of *service-level-agreements* (SLAs) across the stages of an IT-based service life cycle. Within the context of this project, methods for automated SLA negotiation have been developed, using PCM performance predictions and PCM-REL reliability predictions for determining feasible SLA parameters. Corresponding prediction functionality has been integrated in an open source SLA management framework that constitutes the main technological outcome of the project. Furthermore, methodologies for reliability assessment of web services and mashups have been created based on PCM-REL, and corresponding tool support has been integrated in a mashup composition platform developed by the German research project COCKTAIL [COC12]. PCM-REL is also employed by an approach to multi-criteria optimization for automated improvement of software architecture models [Koz11], and it is included in the corresponding *PerOpterix* optimization framework [KRKB12]. Other research efforts are targeted at an integrated consideration of business process and IT system reliability; this research is ongoing and has not yet resulted in a publication. Finally, PCM-REL is integrated in the overall open source PCM tool environment [FZI12], allowing for being used and further enhanced by any interested third parties.

8.3 Future Work Potentials

While PCM-REL constitutes a comprehensive solution for architecture-based reliability prediction of IT systems, several new research questions emerged during the development of the approach, and various aspects lend themselves to being further explored. These aspects can be roughly grouped into the following categories: (a) advanced methods for input estimations, (b) extended modelling capabilities, (c) extended analysis capabilities, (d) advanced evaluation of prediction results and (e) long-term future work potentials.

Regarding input estimations (a), each PCM-REL instance includes reliability annotations (namely software FOD probabilities, hardware MTTF and MTTR values and network FOD probabilities), and it can include further parameters for model calibration (encoded in component parameters or otherwise included in the model). The ability to conduct all required input estimations with sufficient confidence is a crucial prerequisite for a successful application of the approach. An exemplary process of obtaining input estimates has been demonstrated for the Astaro ASG case study, but the development of systematic estimation methods is not in the scope of the thesis itself and remains as an open task for future work. In spite of existing research efforts regarding software and hardware reliability estimation, significant challenges remain, and new methods are required that are specifically tailored to PCM-REL, providing adequate input metrics (such as software FOD probabilities) at adequate granularity levels (namely, distinguished according to FOD types and modelled PPOFs). The envisioned methods should consider the phase of application of PCM-REL (such as early design time versus system evolution) and the available information sources in each phase. An equally important effort should be devoted to the question how relevant statistical failure data can feasibly be collected during development processes and during a system's field operation, which can serve as a stable and comprehensive source of information for the required input estimations. In order to achieve credible results, the development of data collection and input estimation methods should take place in and be validated against the context of real-world industrial development processes.

The existing modelling capabilities of PCM-REL (b) could be extended in various directions. Typically, any extension requires the modellers to provide more input information, and it may also require advanced analysis methods to cope with the extended specifications. Hence, each possible extension has to be assessed against the potentially extended involved modelling and analysis efforts. According to the author's appraisement, the following extensions promise the most significant benefits:

- *Active components and asynchronous component interoperations:* These concepts are commonly found in event-based IT systems (and were also present in the Astaro ASG case study) but cannot directly be expressed in PCM-REL. An explicit support would enable a more direct and intuitive modelling of this class of systems. A corresponding extension could build upon existing recent work integrating event-based communication in the PCM meta-model [KRK11].

- *Reliability impacts through concurrency effects:* Many FOD occurrences in multi-user/multi-tasking systems are induced by concurrency effects such as race conditions, starvations and deadlocks. PCM-REL allows for modelling such failure potentials in an implicit way only, by creating custom FOD types related to concurrency and specifying PPOFs with corresponding FOD probabilities. More explicit modelling capabilities would be desirable to support software architects in foreseeing and resolving concurrency issues at the software architecture level.

- *Variance of input estimations:* To account for the uncertainty of PCM-REL's required input estimations, the approach could explicitly consider the involved variances, and it could calculate the corresponding variances of the resulting success and failure mode probabilities. One of the possible applications of this extension is the ranking of design alternatives with a known degree of confidence. While uncertainty analyses have been provided by related ASRP approaches, extending these analyses to a combined consideration of software and hardware failure potentials would constitute a new contribution to the field.

- *Stochastic dependencies between modelled failure potentials:* Failure potentials in PCM-REL are modelled as being independent, while interdependencies do exist in reality. Examples include physical interferences such as power outages affecting multiple hardware resources at once, as well as crash failures of software processes affecting all executed components. Likewise, multiple visits to the same PPOF during a usage scenario run may be stochastically dependent, with the result of the first visit strongly influencing the success and FOD probabilities of all further visits. Capturing such stochastic dependencies must be done with care to avoid overstraining modellers; still, the approach could benefit from corresponding extensions.

- *Time-dependent failure potentials:* A significant class of software-induced FOD occurrences refers to *aging effects*, which slowly degrade the service levels provided by the system's software components and are commonly tackled by measures of *software rejuvenation* [HKKF95]. A time-dependent specification of failure potentials such as software FOD probabilities could account for aging effects and would enable new kinds of analyses, such as the minimum and maximum system reliability within a given interval of the system's mission time.

- *Extended behavioural specifications:* PCM-REL's capabilities to express system behaviour could be extended to achieve more flexibility and higher expressiveness. Examples of possible extensions include parametric specifications of FOD probabilities using the *Stochastic Expressions* (StoEx) language [Koz08], multiple alternative paths between modelled actions (instead of sequences only), as well as loop conditions that may change dynamically within a loop's body behaviour.

Further future work potentials specifically target PCM-REL's analysis capabilities (c). To this end, the consideration of stochastic dependencies between multiple consecutive scenario runs would add further value to the approach. Especially (but not only) for hardware resource failures, longer periods of degradations or disruptions of system services can be expected, and the extent and frequency of such periods is an important information for the system's users (beyond the averaged success probability of an individual scenario run only). Moreover, the analysis could be extended to account for the possibility of multiple FOD occurrences during service execution. Such an extension would enable asking for the number of occurred FODs, rather than the individual failure mode probabilities only.

Another category of extensions refers to the support for automated evaluation of prediction results (d). As the case studies reported in the thesis have shown, a single Markov analysis run may produce a high number of individual results, and many variable model parameters may exist whose values additionally influence the results. Hence, finding the most significant parameters and deriving solid result interpretations constitutes a challenge. Systematic methods for automated selection of experiment runs and interpretation of the obtained prediction results would provide improved assistance for answering the relevant design questions with respect to the system under study. Such capabilities could be built upon existing research efforts for PCM-based multi-criteria optimization [Koz11].

The discussion of future work potentials is not limited to the aspects mentioned so far. From a long-term perspective (e), additional possibilities for extensions and transfers of scientific results to new problem domains arise. To this end, modelling a system's failure potentials does not only lend itself to reliability predictions as described in the thesis – it can also be a basis for the consideration of further dependability attributes, such as availability, safety and integrity [ALRL04]. In particular, the differentiation of multiple failure modes allows for considering the criticality of failure occurrences and performing risk analyses [GPHG$^+$03]. Such capabilities could be combined with existing PCM-based performance and cost predictions and corresponding trade-off analyses [Koz11] for a holistic support of system design activities. Furthermore, PCM-REL's separation of modelling concerns allows for supporting scenarios with strongly distributed design and development activities. For example, the reliability of service compositions could be predicted at composition time based on an automated synthesis of existing independent reliability models of the required basic services, taking into account the usage profile and execution environment of the composition. Also, the approach could be used to efficiently evaluate the different variants of a software product line [CN01], representing the common set of core assets through an equivalent set of core specifications that are reused across all variants. Finally, further contributions may be achieved by extending PCM-REL towards new system domains, including embedded systems and cloud-based systems.

8.4 Conclusions

The PCM-REL approach presented in this thesis tackles the fundamental challenge of predicting the reliability of IT systems with component-based software architectures, and it fulfils the initially formulated criteria of comprehensive reliability modelling and prediction. While being part of the field of architecture-based software reliability prediction (ASRP), PCM-REL overcomes weaknesses of existing ASRP approaches, including insufficient scope (such as neglecting FT capabilities of a system under study), missing differentiation (such as merging system behaviour and usage aspects in probabilistic model annotations) and an oversimplified view on real-world failure processes and circumstances (such as using the same modelling constructs for software and hardware failure potentials). Through its advanced modelling and analysis capabilities, PCM-REL achieves the following main benefits:

- *Improved decision support for software architects:* PCM-REL supports a comprehensive set of design decisions, covering changes in a system's software component structure, the component behaviours and their included FT capabilities, the usage of hardware resources by service execution, the physical distribution of the system to multiple computing nodes, the usage of system-external services, as well as the system's usage profile and its included usage scenarios. The approach realizes the decision support through providing explicit modelling constructs for all these architectural aspects. Furthermore, the analysis provides detailed prediction results for each evaluated architectural candidate, allowing for identification of critical parts in the architecture or processing steps during service execution.

- *Increased reusability of model artefacts:* Thanks to the differentiated modelling of individual architectural views and aspects through PCM-REL, multiple variations of architecture specifications can re-use significant parts of an underlying model base, lowering the overall effort and error-proneness of the modelling activity. Component types specified in a PCM-REL repository model can be instantiated within multiple system models, which in turn can be assigned to a resource environment in different ways through multiple allocation models. Moreover, different usage profiles are expressed through multiple usage models referring to the same system model.

- *Support of a truly distributed component-based development process:* The separation of modelling concerns provided by the approach allows for multiple envisioned developer roles in a distributed development process to independently contribute their respective parts of an architectural specification; each role provides only the information that it naturally possesses. Building upon the methodology of the existing PCM approach, the envisioned roles include component developers, software architects, component deployers and domain experts.

These benefits support the primary goal of PCM-REL to be applicable and relevant to real-world software development processes; further important features in this respect are the provision of a design-oriented modelling language readily understandable by software architects, the consequent assessment of system reliability from the user's point of view and the corresponding utilization of the failure-on-demand (FOD) concept, as well as the provision of comprehensive and ready-to-use tool support for reliability modelling and analysis.

From a broader perspective, PCM-REL contributes to the overall vision of a *systematic consideration of reliability throughout system engineering processes*. Such a systematic approach should replace the currently still prevalent best-effort strategies to eliminate as many failure potentials as possible until resource and budget limits are reached. An attitude is required accepting failure potentials as a natural part of an IT system rather than the result of failed development and production processes. Then, the impacts of such potentials can be quantified, predicted and set in relation to the system's architecture. As a result, system reliability will be much more plannable. Operators of IT systems and providers of IT-based services will be able to interoperate on the basis of contractually specified quantitative service reliability parameters. Quality assurance efforts will be allocated to those parts of a software architecture where they exhibit the highest benefits. Reliability targets of IT systems will be achieved more efficiently and with higher confidence, ultimately leading to a more sustainable support of businesses, communities and everyday life through these systems.

List of Figures

List of Tables

Listings

Bibliography

[AD94]   R. Alur and D. L. Dill, "A theory of timed automata," *Theoretical Computer Science (TCS)*, vol. 126, no. 2, pp. 183–235, 1994.

[AKL90]   J. Arlat, K. Kanoun, and J.-C. Laprie, "Dependability modeling and evaluation of software fault-tolerant systems," *IEEE Transactions on Computers (TC)*, vol. 39, no. 4, pp. 504–513, Apr. 1990.

[Alb79]   A. Albrecht, "Measuring application development productivity," in *Joint SHARE/GUIDE/IBM Application Development Symposium*, vol. 83, 1979, pp. 83–92.

[ALRL04]   A. Avizienis, J.-C. Laprie, B. Randell, and C. Landwehr, "Basic concepts and taxonomy of dependable and secure computing," *IEEE Transactions on Dependable and Secure Computing (TDSC)*, vol. 1, no. 1, pp. 11–33, 2004.

[Apa12]   Apache Software Foundation, "Apache Derby," 2012. [Online]. Available: http://db.apache.org/derby/

[Ape05]   S. Apel, "Software reliability growth prediction - state of the art," Fraunhofer IESE, Kaiserslautern, Tech. Rep., 2005.

[Ast12]   Astaro GmbH & Co. KG, "Astaro Security Gateway," 2012. [Online]. Available: http://www.astaro.com/products/hardware-appliances

[Aut08]   Automotive Industry Action Group (AIAG), *Potential Failure Mode and Effects Analysis (FMEA)*, 2008.

[AV-10]   AV-Comparatives e.V. (www.av-comparatives.org), "Anti-Virus Comparative Report No. 25," Tech. Rep., 2010.

[BBKR11]   F. Brosch, B. Buhnova, H. Koziolek, and R. Reussner, "Reliability prediction for fault-tolerant software architectures," in *International Conference on the Quality of Software Architectures (QoSA)*, 2011, pp. 75–84.

[BBKR12]   ——, "Reliability Prediction for Component-based Software Architectures," 2012. [Online]. Available: http://sdqweb.ipd. kit.edu/wiki/ReliabilityPrediction

[BDT⁺87]   S. J. Bavuso, J. B. Dugan, K. S. Trivedi, E. M. Rothmann, and W. E. Smith, "Analysis of Typical Fault-Tolerant Architectures using HARP," *IEEE Transactions on Reliability (TR)*, vol. R-36, no. 2, pp. 176–185, Jun. 1987.

[Bec08]   S. Becker, "Coupled Model Transformations for QoS Enabled Component-Based Software Design," Ph.D. dissertation, University of Oldenburg, Germany, 2008.

[BEFL00]   L. Briand, K. Emam, B. Freimut, and O. Laitenberger, "A comprehensive evaluation of capture-recapture models for estimating software defect content," *IEEE Transactions on Software Engineering (TSE)*, vol. 26, no. 6, pp. 518–540, 2000.

[BF93]   R. W. Butler and G. B. Finelli, "The infeasibility of quantifying the reliability of life-critical real-time software," *IEEE Transactions on Software Engineering (TSE)*, vol. 19, no. 1, pp. 3–12, 1993.

[Bir10]   A. Birolini, *Reliability Engineering: Theory and Practice*. Springer, 2010.

[BKBR10]   F. Brosch, H. Koziolek, B. Buhnova, and R. Reussner, "Parameterized Reliability Prediction for Component-based Software Architectures," in *International Conference on the Quality of Software Architectures (QoSA)*, vol. 6093. Springer, 2010, pp. 36–51.

[BKBR11]   ——, "Architecture-Based Reliability Prediction with the Palladio Component Model," *IEEE Transactions on Software Engineering (TSE)*, vol. Pre-Print, 2011.

[BKH09]   A. Beckhaus, L. Karg, and G. Hanselmann, "Applicability of Software Reliability Growth Modeling in the Quality Assurance Phase of a Large Business Software Vendor," *IEEE International Computer Software and Applications Conference (COMPSAC)*, vol. 1, pp. 209–215, 2009.

[BKR09]   S. Becker, H. Koziolek, and R. Reussner, "The Palladio component model for model-driven performance prediction," *Journal of Systems and Software (JSS)*, vol. 82, no. 1, pp. 3–22, 2009.

[BL08]   V. S. Barbu and N. Limnios, *Semi-Markov Chains and Hidden Semi-Markov Models toward Applications*. Springer, US, 2008.

[BMP09]   S. Bernardi, J. Merseguer, and D. C. Petriu, "A dependability profile within MARTE," *Software & Systems Modeling (SoSyM)*, vol. 10, no. 3, pp. 313–336, Aug. 2009.

[BZ09]   F. Brosch and B. Zimmerova, "Design-Time Reliability Prediction for Software Systems," in *International Workshop on*

Software Quality and Maintainability (SQM), 2009, pp. 70–74.

[CD09]   C. Catal and B. Diri, "A systematic review of software fault prediction studies," *Expert Systems with Applications (ESWA)*, vol. 36, no. 4, pp. 7346–7354, May 2009.

[CG07a]   V. Cortellessa and V. Grassi, "A Modeling Approach to Analyze the Impact of Error Propagation on Reliability of Component-Based Systems," in *International Symposium on Component Based Software Engineering (CBSE)*, ser. Lecture Notes in Computer Science.   Berlin, Heidelberg: Springer, 2007, pp. 140–156.

[CG07b]   ——, "Reliability Modeling and Analysis of Service-Oriented Architectures," in *Test and Analysis of Web Services*.   Springer Berlin / Heidelberg, 2007, pp. 339–362.

[Che80]   R. C. Cheung, "A user-oriented software reliability model," *IEEE Transactions on Software Engineering (TSE)*, vol. 6, no. 2, pp. 118–125, 1980.

[CL04]   X. Cai and M. R. Lyu, "An Empirical Study on Reliability Modeling for Diverse Software Systems," in *IEEE International Symposium on Software Reliability Engineering (IS-SRE)*, 2004, pp. 125 – 136.

[CLL78]   A. Costes, C. Landrault, and J.-C. Laprie, "Reliability and Availability Models for Maintained Systems Featuring Hardware Failures and Design Faults," *IEEE Transactions on Computers (TC)*, vol. C-27, no. 6, pp. 548–560, 1978.

[CLV05]   X. Cai, M. R. Lyu, and M. A. Vouk, "An Experimental Evaluation on Reliability Features of N-Version Programming," in *IEEE International Symposium on Software Reliability Engineering (ISSRE)*, 2005, pp. 161 – 170.

[CMRK10]   D. Cooray, S. Malek, R. Roshandel, and D. Kilgore, "RESISTing reliability degradation through proactive reconfiguration," in *IEEE/ACM International Conference on Automated Software Engineering (ASE)*, 2010, pp. 83–92.

[CN01]   P. Clements and L. Northrop, *Software Product Lines: Practices and Patterns*. Addison-Wesley Professional, 2001.

[COC12]   COCKTAIL, "Skalierbare, KMU-zentrierte Mashup & SaaS Diensteplattform," 2012. [Online]. Available: http://www.cocktail-projekt.de/

[Cox06]   D. Cox, *Principles of statistical inference*. Cambridge University Press, 2006.

[CRMG08]   L. Cheung, R. Roshandel, N. Medvidovic, and L. Golubchik, "Early prediction of software component reliability," in *International Conference on Software Engineering (ICSE)*. ACM, 2008, pp. 111–120.

[CSC02]   V. Cortellessa, H. Singh, and B. Cukic, "Early reliability assessment of UML based software models," in *International Workshop on Software and Performance (WOSP)*. New York, New York, USA: ACM Press, 2002, pp. 302–309.

[CW90]   T. Compton and C. Withrow, "Prediction and control of ADA software defects," *Journal of Systems and Software (JSS)*, vol. 12, no. 3, pp. 199–207, Jul. 1990.

[DDPH94]   J. B. Dugan, S. A. Doyle, and F. A. Patterson-Hine, "Simple models of hardware and software fault tolerance," in *Reliability and Maintainability Symposium (RAMS)*, 1994, pp. 124–129.

[DJP96]   T. Delong, B. Johnson, and J. Profeta III, "A fault injection technique for VHDL behavioral-level models," *Design & Test of Computers*, vol. 13, no. 4, pp. 24–33, 1996.

[DL93a]   J. B. Dugan and M. R. Lyu, "System-level reliability and sensitivity analyses for three fault-tolerant system architectures," in *International Working Conference on Dependable Computing for Critical Applications*, 1993, pp. 1–22.

[DL93b]   ——, "System reliability analysis of an N-version programming application," in *IEEE International Symposium on Software Reliability Engineering (ISSRE)*, 1993, pp. 103–111.

[DL95]   ——, "Dependability Modeling for Fault-Tolerant Software and Systems," in *Software Fault Tolerance*, M. R. Lyu, Ed. John Wiley & Sons, 1995, pp. 109–138.

[DS95]   J. Dolbec and T. Shepard, "A Component Based Software Reliability Model," in *Conference of the Centre for Advanced Studies on Collaborative Research (CASCON)*, 1995.

[DS97]   M. Diaz and J. Sligo, "How software process improvement helped Motorola," *IEEE Software*, vol. 14, no. 5, pp. 75–81, 1997.

[DT89]   J. B. Dugan and K. S. Trivedi, "Coverage modeling for dependability analysis of fault-tolerant systems," *IEEE Transactions on Computers (TC)*, vol. 38, no. 6, pp. 775–787, Jun. 1989.

[DW04a]   O. Das and C. M. Woodside, "Computing the performability of layered distributed systems with a management architecture," in *International Workshop on Software and Performance (WOSP)*, vol. 29, no. 1, 2004, pp. 174–185.

[DW04b]   ——, "Dependability modeling of self-healing client-server applications," in *Architecting Dependable Systems*, lncs ed. Springer Berlin / Heidelberg, 2004, vol. 3069, pp. 128–165.

[Ecl12a]   Eclipse Foundation, "Eclipse Modeling Framework (EMF)," 2012. [Online]. Available: http://www.eclipse.org/modeling/emf/

[Ecl12b]   ——, "Eclipse Rich Client Platform (RCP)," 2012. [Online]. Available: http://www.eclipse.org/home/categories/rcp.php

[Ecl12c]   ——, "Graphical Modeling Framework (GMF)," 2012. [Online]. Available: http://www.eclipse.org/modeling/gmp/

[EL85]   D. E. Eckhardt and L. D. Lee, "A theoretical basis for the analysis of multiversion software subject to coincident errors," *IEEE Transactions on Software Engineering (TSE)*, vol. SE-11, no. 12, pp. 1511–1517, 1985.

[Eve99]   W. Everett, "Software Component Reliability Analysis," in *IEEE Symposium on Application Specific Systems and Software Engineering and Technology (ASSET)*. IEEE, 1999, pp. 204–211.

[FGGM10]   A. Filieri, C. Ghezzi, V. Grassi, and R. Mirandola, "Reliability Analysis of Component-Based Systems with Multiple Failure Modes," in *International Symposium on Component Based Software Engineering (CBSE)*, 2010, pp. 1–20.

[Fin93]   A. Finkelstein, "Report of the Inquiry Into The London Ambulance Service," South West Thames Regional Health Authority, Tech. Rep., 1993.

[FN99]   N. Fenton and M. Neil, "A critique of software defect prediction models," *IEEE Transactions on Software Engineering (TSE)*, vol. SE-10, no. 4, pp. 675–689, 1999.

[FNM+08]   N. Fenton, M. Neil, W. Marsh, P. Hearty, L. Radlinski, and
            P. Krause, "On the effectiveness of early life cycle defect pre-
            diction with Bayesian Nets," *Empirical Software Engineer-
            ing (EMSE)*, vol. 13, no. 5, pp. 499–537, 2008.

[FZI12]   FZI Forschungszentrum Informatik, "The Palladio Ar-
            chitecture Simulator," 2012. [Online]. Available: http:
            //www.palladio-simulator.com/

[Gaf84]   J. Gaffney, "Estimating the Number of Faults in Code," *IEEE
            Transactions on Software Engineering (TSE)*, vol. 29, no. 2,
            pp. 459–464, 1984.

[GHK+99]   S. Garg, Y. Huang, C. Kintala, K. S. Trivedi, and S. Yajnik,
            "Performance and reliability evaluation of passive replication
            schemes in application level fault tolerance," in *International
            Symposium on Fault-Tolerant Computing (FTCS)*.   IEEE
            Comput. Soc, 1999, pp. 322–329.

[GI93]   K. Goswami and R. Iyer, "Simulation of software behav-
            ior under hardware faults," in *International Symposium on
            Fault-Tolerant Computing (FTCS)*, vol. 1, 1993, pp. 218–
            227.

[GL05]   S. S. Gokhale and M. R. Lyu, "A simulation approach to
            structure-based software reliability analysis," *IEEE Trans-
            actions on Software Engineering (TSE)*, vol. 31, no. 8, pp.
            643–656, Aug. 2005.

[GLT97]   S. S. Gokhale, M. R. Lyu, and K. S. Trivedi, "Reliability
            simulation of fault-tolerant software and systems," in *Pa-
            cific Rim International Symposium on Fault-tolerant Systems
            (PRFTS)*, 1997, pp. 167–173.

[GLT98]   ——, "Reliability simulation of component-based software systems," in *International Symposium on Software Reliability Engineering (ISSRE)*, 1998, pp. 192–201.

[GMS07]   V. Grassi, R. Mirandola, and A. Sabetta, "Filling the gap between design and performance/reliability models of component-based systems: A model-driven approach," *Journal of Systems and Software (JSS)*, vol. 80, no. 4, pp. 528–558, Apr. 2007.

[Gok05]   S. S. Gokhale, "Software reliability analysis with component-level fault tolerance," in *Reliability and Maintainability Symposium (RAMS)*, 2005, pp. 610–614.

[Gok07]   ——, "Architecture-Based Software Reliability Analysis: Overview and Limitations," *IEEE Transactions on Dependable and Secure Computing (TDSC)*, vol. 4, no. 1, pp. 32–40, 2007.

[GPHG+03]   K. Goseva-Popstojanova, A. Hassan, A. Guedem, W. Abdelmoez, D. E. M. Nassar, H. H. Ammar, and A. Mili, "Architectural-level risk analysis using UML," *IEEE Transactions on Software Engineering (TSE)*, vol. 29, no. 10, pp. 946–960, 2003.

[GPHP05]   K. Goseva-Popstojanova, M. Hamill, and R. Perugupalli, "Large Empirical Case Study of Architecture-Based Software Reliability," in *IEEE International Symposium on Software Reliability Engineering (ISSRE)*, 2005, pp. 43–52.

[GPHW06]   K. Goseva-Popstojanova, M. Hamill, and X. Wang, "Adequacy, Accuracy, Scalability, and Uncertainty of Architecture-based Software Reliability: Lessons Learned from Large Empirical Case Studies," in *IEEE International*

Symposium on Software Reliability Engineering (ISSRE), 2006, pp. 197–203.

[GPK03]   K. Goseva-Popstojanova and S. Kamavaram, "Assessing uncertainty in reliability of component-based software systems," in *International Symposium on Software Reliability Engineering (ISSRE)*, 2003, pp. 307–320.

[GPT01]   K. Goseva-Popstojanova and K. S. Trivedi, "Architecture-based approach to reliability assessment of software systems," *Performance Evaluation (PEVA)*, vol. 45, no. 2-3, pp. 179–204, 2001.

[Gra05]   V. Grassi, "Architecture-based reliability prediction for service-oriented computing," in *Architecting Dependable Systems*, lncs ed.   Springer Berlin / Heidelberg, 2005, vol. 3549, pp. 279–299.

[GRdL02]   P. A. Guerra, C. M. F. Rubira, and R. de Lemos, "An idealized fault-tolerant architectural component," in *Workshop on Architecting Dependable Systems (WADS)*, 2002.

[GT02]   S. S. Gokhale and K. S. Trivedi, "Reliability Prediction and Sensitivity Analysis Based on Software Architecture," in *IEEE International Symposium on Software Reliability Engineering (ISSRE)*, 2002, pp. 64–75.

[GWHT04]   S. S. Gokhale, E. Wong, J. Horgan, and K. S. Trivedi, "An analytical approach to architecture-based software performance and reliability prediction," *Performance Evaluation*, vol. 58, no. 4, pp. 391–412, Dec. 2004.

[GWTH98]   S. S. Gokhale, E. Wong, K. S. Trivedi, and J. Horgan, "An analytical approach to architecture-based software reliability prediction," in *IEEE International Computer Performance and Dependability Symposium (IPDS)*, 1998, pp. 13–22.

[HA08]   N. B. Harrison and P. Avgeriou, "Incorporating fault tolerance tactics in software architecture patterns," in *International Workshop on Software Engineering for Resilient Systems (SERENE)*, 2008, pp. 9–18.

[Hal77]   M. Halstead, *Elements of Software Science (Operating and programming systems series)*.   New York: Elsevier Science Inc., 1977.

[Ham92]   D. Hamlet, "Are We Testing for True Reliability?" *IEEE Software*, vol. 9, no. 4, pp. 21–27, 1992.

[Hap04]   J. Happe, "Predicting the Reliability of Component-Based Software Architectures," Master Thesis, 2004.

[Har87]   D. Harel, "Statecharts: A visual formalism for complex systems," *Science of Computer Programming (SCP)*, vol. 8, no. 3, pp. 231–274, 1987.

[HKKF95] Y. Huang, C. Kintala, N. Kolettis, and N. D. Fulton, "Software rejuvenation: Analysis, module and applications," in *International Symposium on Fault-Tolerant Computing (FTCS)*.   IEEE, 1995, pp. 381–390.

[HLL⁺05] B. Huang, X. Li, M. Li, J. Bernstein, and C. Smidts, "Study of the Impact of Hardware Fault on Software Reliability," in *IEEE International Symposium on Software Reliability Engineering (ISSRE)*, 2005, pp. 63–72.

[HMU01]   J. E. Hopcroft, R. Motwani, and J. D. Ullman, *Introduction to Automata Theory, Languages, and Computation*, 2nd ed. Addison-Wesley Longman, Amsterdam, 2001.

[HMW01]   D. Hamlet, D. Mason, and D. Woit, "Theory of software reliability based on components," in *International Conference on Software Engineering (ICSE)*, 2001, pp. 361–370.

[HWW+12]   P. Hazel, A. Williams, D. Woodhouse, G. Fowler, J. Jetmore, M. Haber, M. Cardwell, N. Metheringham, P. Bowyer, P. Pennock, T. Kistner, and T. Sheen, "Exim Internet Mailer," 2012. [Online]. Available: http://www.exim.org/

[IEE90]   IEEE Computer Society, *IEEE Standard Glossary of Software Engineering Terminology (IEEE 610.12-1990)*, 1990.

[IEE08]   IEEE Reliability Society, *Recommended Practice on Software Reliability (IEEE 1633)*, 2008.

[Imm06]   A. Immonen, "A Method for Predicting Reliability and Availability at the Architecture Level," in *Software Product Lines*. Berlin, Heidelberg: Springer, 2006, pp. 373–422.

[IN08]   A. Immonen and E. Niemelä, "Survey of reliability and availability prediction methods from the viewpoint of software architecture," *Software & Systems Modeling (SoSyM)*, vol. 7, no. 1, pp. 49–65, 2008.

[Int04]   International Electrotechnical Commission (IEC), *Reliability growth - Statistical test and estimation methods (IEC 61164)*, 2004.

[Int06a]   ——, *Analysis techniques for dependability - Reliability block diagram and boolean methods (IEC 61078)*, 2006.

[Int06b]   ——, *Application of Markov techniques (IEC 61165)*, 2006.

[Int06c]   ——, *Fault Tree Analysis (IEC 61025)*, 2006.

[Int06d]   ——, *Procedures for failure mode and effect analysis FMEA (IEC 60812)*, 2006.

[KB09]   H. Koziolek and F. Brosch, "Parameter Dependencies for Component Reliability Specifications," in *International Workshop on Formal Engineering Approaches to Software Components and Architectures (FESCA)*, ser. ENTCS, vol. 253, no. 1. Elsevier, 2009, pp. 23–38.

[Kie03]   J. Kienzle, "Software fault tolerance: an overview," in *Ada-Europe International Conference on Reliable Software Technologies*, ser. Ada-Europe'03. Berlin, Heidelberg: Springer-Verlag, 2003, pp. 45–67.

[KKB+93]   K. Kanoun, M. Kaaniche, C. Beounes, J.-C. Laprie, and J. Arlat, "Reliability growth of fault-tolerant software," *IEEE Transactions on Reliability (TR)*, vol. 42, no. 2, pp. 205–219, Jun. 1993.

[KKM03]   M. Kaaniche, K. Kanoun, and M. Martinello, "A user-perceived availability evaluation of a web based travel agency," in *International Conference on Dependable Systems and Networks (DSN)*, 2003, pp. 709–718.

[KKR01]   M. Kaaniche, K. Kanoun, and M. Rabah, "A Framework for Modeling Availability of e-Business Systems," in *International Conference on Computer Communications and Networks (ICCCN)*, 2001, pp. 40–45.

[KM97]   S. Krishnamurthy and A. Mathur, "On the Estimation of Reliability of a Software System Using Reliabilities of its Components," in *IEEE International Symposium on Software Reliability Engineering (ISSRE)*, 1997, pp. 146–155.

[KMT09]   D. Kim, F. Machida, and K. S. Trivedi, "Availability Modeling and Analysis of a Virtualized System," in *IEEE Pacific Rim International Symposium on Dependable Computing (PRDC)*, Nov. 2009, pp. 365–371.

[KOB00]   K. Kanoun and M. Ortalo-Borrel, "Fault-tolerant system dependability-explicit modeling of hardware and software component-interactions," *IEEE Transactions on Reliability (TR)*, vol. 49, no. 4, pp. 363–376, 2000.

[KOBMP99] K. Kanoun, M. Ortalo-Borrel, T. Morteveille, and A. Peytavin, "Availability of CAUTRA, a subset of the French air traffic control system," *IEEE Transactions on Computers (TC)*, vol. 48, no. 5, pp. 528–535, May 1999.

[Koz08]   H. Koziolek, "Parameter Dependencies for Reusable Performance Specifications of Software Components," Ph.D. dissertation, University of Oldenburg, 2008.

[Koz11]   A. Koziolek, "Automated Improvement of Software Architecture Models for Performance and Other Quality Attributes," Ph.D. dissertation, Karlsruhe Institute of Technology (KIT), Germany, 2011.

[KP00]   W. Kuo and R. Prasad, "An annotated overview of system-reliability optimization," *IEEE Transactions on Reliability (TR)*, vol. 49, no. 2, pp. 176–187, Jun. 2000.

[KRK11]   B. Klatt, C. Rathfelder, and S. Kounev, "Integration of event-based communication in the palladio software quality prediction framework," in *International Conference on the Quality of Software Architectures (QoSA)*, 2011, pp. 43–52.

[KRKB12]   A. Koziolek, R. Reussner, H. Koziolek, and S. Becker, "PerOpterix," 2012. [Online]. Available: http://sdqweb.ipd. kit.edu/wiki/PerOpteryx

[KSB10]   H. Koziolek, B. Schlich, and C. Bilich, "A Large-Scale Industrial Case Study on Architecture-based Software Reliability Analysis," in *IEEE International Symposium on Software Reliability Engineering (ISSRE)*. IEEE, 2010, pp. 279–288.

[LABK90]   J.-C. Laprie, J. Arlat, C. Beounes, and K. Kanoun, "Definition and analysis of hardware-and software-fault-tolerant architectures," *Computer*, vol. 23, no. 7, pp. 39–51, 1990.

[LG08]   M. Lipton and S. S. Gokhale, "Heuristic Component Placement for Maximizing Software Reliability," in *Recent Advances in Reliability and Quality in Design*. Springer, 2008, pp. 309–330.

[Lit05]   B. Littlewood, "Dependability Assessment of Software-based Systems : State of the Art," in *International Conference on Software Engineering (ICSE)*, 2005, pp. 6–7.

[LK92]   J.-C. Laprie and K. Kanoun, "X-ware reliability and availability modeling," *IEEE Transactions on Software Engineering (TSE)*, vol. 18, no. 2, pp. 130–147, 1992.

[LKBK91]   J.-C. Laprie, K. Kanoun, C. Beounes, and M. Kaaniche, "The KAT (Knowledge-Action-Transformation) approach to the modeling and evaluation of reliability and availability growth," *IEEE Transactions on Software Engineering (TSE)*, vol. 17, no. 4, pp. 370–382, 1991.

[LM89]   B. Littlewood and D. R. Miller, "Conceptual modeling of coincident failures in multiversion software," *IEEE Trans-*

actions on Software Engineering (TSE), vol. 15, no. 12, pp. 1596–1614, 1989.

[LN97]   P. Lakey and A. Neufelder, *System and Software Reliability Assurance Notebook.* Rome Lab, FSC-RELI, 1997.

[LR02]   C. Liu and D. J. Richardson, "RAIC: Architecting dependable systems through redundancy and just-in-time testing," in *Workshop on Architecting Dependable Systems (WADS)*, 2002.

[LW97]   B. Littlewood and D. Wright, "Some conservative stopping rules for the operational testing of safety critical software," *IEEE Transactions on Software Engineering (TSE)*, vol. 23, no. 11, pp. 673–683, 1997.

[Lyu95]   M. R. Lyu, Ed., *Software Fault Tolerance.* John Wiley & Sons, 1995.

[Lyu07]   M. R. Lyu, "Software reliability engineering: A roadmap," in *Future of Software Engineering (FOSE)*, Washington, DC, 2007, pp. 153–170.

[McC76]   T. McCabe, "A Complexity Measure," *IEEE Transactions on Software Engineering (TSE)*, vol. SE-2, no. 4, pp. 308–320, Dec. 1976.

[Mes04]   S. Mesure, "Sainsbury's supply problems lead to first loss in 135 years," 2004. [Online]. Available: http://www.independent.co.uk/news/business/news/ sainsburys-supply-problems-lead-to-first-loss-in-135-years/ 6157819.html

[MGC07]   Y. Ma, L. Guo, and B. Cukic, "A statistical framework for the prediction of fault-proneness," in *Advances in Machine*

Learning Application in Software Engineering. Idea Group, 2007, pp. 237–265.

[MGF07] T. Menzies, J. Greenwald, and A. Frank, "Data Mining Static Code Attributes to Learn Defect Predictors," *IEEE Transactions on Software Engineering (TSE)*, vol. 33, no. 1, pp. 2–13, 2007.

[MIO90] J. Musa, A. Iannino, and K. Okumoto, *Software reliability: measurement, prediction, application (professional ed.).* New York, NY, USA: McGraw-Hill, Inc., 1990.

[MKK03] M. Martinello, M. Kaaniche, and K. Kanoun, "Web Service Availability - Impact of Error Recovery," *Reliability Engineering & System Safety (RESS)*, vol. 89, no. 1, pp. 6–16, 2003.

[MMN⁺92] K. Miller, L. Morell, R. Noonan, S. Park, D. Nicol, B. Murrill, and J. Voas, "When Testing Reveals No Failures," *IEEE Transactions on Software Engineering (TSE)*, vol. 18, no. 1, pp. 33–43, 1992.

[MR07] H. Muccini and A. Romanovsky, "Architecting Fault Tolerant Systems," *Technical Report CS-TR-1051*, p. 62, 2007.

[MRKE09] S. Malek, R. Roshandel, D. Kilgore, and I. Elhag, "Improving the reliability of mobile software systems through continuous analysis and proactive reconfiguration," in *International Conference on Software Engineering (ICSE) - Companion Volume*, 2009, pp. 275–278.

[MSHT92] J. K. Muppala, A. S. Sathaye, R. C. Howe, and K. S. Trivedi, "Dependability modeling of a heterogeneous VAX-cluster system using stochastic reward nets," in *Hardware and software fault tolerance in parallel computing systems*. Ellis Horwood, 1992, pp. 33–59.

[Mus04]   J. Musa, *Software Reliability Engineering: More Reliable Software Faster and Cheaper*, 2nd ed. AuthorHouse, 2004.

[MZ08]   A. Mohamed and M. Zulkernine, "On Failure Propagation in Component-Based Software Systems," in *International Conference on Quality Software (QSIC)*, Aug. 2008, pp. 402–411.

[Obj07]   Object Management Group (OMG), *UML profile for Modeling and Analysis of Real Time Embedded Systems (MARTE)*, 2007.

[Ora12a]   Oracle Corporation, "GlassFish Application Server," 2012. [Online]. Available: http://glassfish.java.net/

[Ora12b]   ——, "The Enterprise JavaBeans (EJB) 3.0 Specification," 2012. [Online]. Available: http://java.sun.com/products/ejb/docs.html

[PA02]   H. Pentti and H. Atte, "Failure mode and effects analysis of software-based automation systems," Radiation and Nuclear Safety Authority (STUK), Tech. Rep., 2002.

[PDAC05]   P. Popic, D. Desovski, W. Abdelmoez, and B. Cukic, "Error Propagation in the Reliability Analysis of Component Based Systems," in *IEEE International Symposium on Software Reliability Engineering (ISSRE)*, 2005, pp. 53–62.

[PEO11]   M. Palviainen, A. Evesti, and E. Ovaska, "The reliability estimation, prediction and measuring of component-based software," *Journal of Systems and Software (JSS)*, vol. 84, no. 6, pp. 1054–1070, 2011.

[PPW⁺05]   A. Pretschner, W. Prenninter, S. Wagner, C. Kühnel, M. Baumgartner, B. Sostawa, R. Zölch, and T. Stauner, "One Evaluation of Model-Based Testing and its Automation," in *International Conference on Software Engineering (ICSE)*, no. 2, 2005, pp. 392–401.

[Pre03]   A. Pretschner, "Zum modellbasierten funktionalen Test reaktiver Systeme," Ph.D. dissertation, Technische Universität München, Germany, 2003.

[Pro03]   S. J. Prowell, "Jumbl: A tool for model-based statistical testing," in *International Conference on System Sciences (HICSS)*, 2003.

[PSMK03]   P. Popov, L. Strigini, J. May, and S. Kuball, "Estimating bounds on the reliability of diverse systems," *IEEE Transactions on Software Engineering (TSE)*, vol. 29, no. 4, pp. 345–359, Apr. 2003.

[PWB07]   E. Pinheiro, W.-D. Weber, and L. Barroso, "Failure trends in a large disk drive population," in *USENIX Conference on File and Storage Technologies (FAST)*. Berkeley: USENIX Association, 2007, pp. 17–29.

[Ran75]   B. Randell, "System structure for software fault tolerance," *IEEE Transactions on Software Engineering (TSE)*, vol. SE-1, no. 2, pp. 220–232, 1975.

[RBB⁺11]   R. Reussner, S. Becker, E. Burger, J. Happe, M. Hauck, A. Koziolek, H. Koziolek, K. Krogmann, and M. Kuperberg, "The Palladio Component Model," Karlsruhe Institute of Technology (KIT), Tech. Rep., 2011.

[RFKK08]   A.-E. Rugina, P. H. Feiler, K. Kanoun, and M. Kaaniche, "Software dependability modeling using an industry-standard architecture description language," in *European Congress of Embedded Real Time Software (ERTS)*, 2008.

[RKK07]   A.-E. Rugina, K. Kanoun, and M. Kaaniche, "A system dependability modeling framework using aadl and gspns," in *Architecting Dependable Systems*, 2007, pp. 14–38.

[RPS03]   R. Reussner, I. Poernomo, and H. Schmidt, "Reasoning about software architectures with contractually specified components," *Component-Based Software Quality*, vol. 2693, pp. 287–325, 2003.

[RRU05]   G. N. Rodrigues, D. Rosenblum, and S. Uchitel, "Using scenarios to predict the reliability of concurrent component-based software systems," in *International Conference on Fundamental Approaches to Software Engineering (FASE)*. Springer LNCS, 2005, pp. 111–126.

[RS07]   H. Ramasamy and M. Schunter, "Architecting dependable systems using virtualization," in *Workshop on Architecting Dependable Systems (WADS)*. Citeseer, 2007.

[RSP03]   R. Reussner, H. Schmidt, and I. Poernomo, "Reliability prediction for component-based software architectures," *Journal of Systems and Software (JSS)*, vol. 66, no. 3, pp. 241–252, 2003.

[SG07]   B. Schroeder and G. Gibson, "Disk failures in the real world: What does an MTTF of 1,000,000 hours mean to you?" in *USENIX Conference on File and Storage Technologies (FAST)*. USENIX Association, 2007, pp. 1–6.

[SGNG10]   K. Sharma, R. Garg, C. Nagpal, and R. Garg, "Selection of Optimal Software Reliability Growth Models Using a Distance Based Approach," *IEEE Transactions on Reliability (TR)*, vol. 59, no. 2, pp. 266–276, 2010.

[SL88]   K. Shin and T.-H. Lin, "Modeling and measurement of error propagation in a multimodule computing system," *IEEE Transactions on Computers (TC)*, vol. 37, no. 9, pp. 1053–1066, 1988.

[SLA12]   SLA@SOI, "Empowering the service industry with SLA-aware infrastructures," 2012. [Online]. Available: http://sla-at-soi.eu/

[ST06]   V. Sharma and K. S. Trivedi, "Reliability and Performance of Component Based Software Systems with Restarts, Retries, Reboots and Repairs," *IEEE International Symposium on Software Reliability Engineering (ISSRE)*, pp. 299–310, Nov. 2006.

[ST07a]   N. Sato and K. S. Trivedi, "Accurate and efficient stochastic reliability analysis of composite services using their compact Markov reward model representations," in *IEEE International Conference on Services Computing (SCC)*, Jul. 2007, pp. 114–121.

[ST07b]   ——, "Stochastic modeling of composite web services for closed-form analysis of their performance and reliability bottlenecks," in *International Conference on Service Oriented Computing (ICSOC)*, no. Figure 1. Springer, 2007, pp. 107–118.

[ST07c]   V. Sharma and K. S. Trivedi, "Quantifying software performance, reliability and security: An architecture-based approach," *Journal of Systems and Software (JSS)*, vol. 80, no. 4, pp. 493–509, Apr. 2007.

[Sta87]   G. E. Stark, "Dependability Evaluation of Integrated Hardware/Software Systems," *IEEE Transactions on Reliability (TR)*, vol. R-36, no. 4, pp. 440–444, Oct. 1987.

[STTA08]   W. E. Smith, K. S. Trivedi, L. Tomek, and J. Ackaret, "Availability analysis of blade server systems," *IBM Systems Journal*, vol. 47, no. 4, pp. 621–640, 2008.

[Szy02]   C. Szyperski, *Component Software: Beyond Object-Oriented Programming*, 2nd ed. Boston: Addison-Wesley Longman Publishing Co., Inc., 2002.

[TCD+08]   K. S. Trivedi, G. Ciardo, B. Dasarathy, M. Grottke, A. Rindos, and B. Vashaw, "Achieving and assuring high availability," in *IEEE Workshop on Dependable Parallel, Distributed and Network-Centric Systems (DPDNS)*. Ieee, Apr. 2008, pp. 1–7.

[TG83]   K. S. Trivedi and R. M. Geist, "Decomposition in reliability analysis of fault-tolerant systems," *IEEE Transactions on Reliability (TR)*, vol. R-32, no. 5, pp. 463–468, 1983.

[TP00]   W. Torres-Pomales, "Software Fault Tolerance: A Tutorial," NASA, Tech. Rep., 2000.

[Tri02]   K. S. Trivedi, *Probability and statistics with reliability, queuing and computer science applications*, 2nd ed. Chichester, UK: John Wiley and Sons Ltd., 2002.

[TST02]   M. Trapp, B. Schürmann, and T. Tetteroo, "Failure Behavior Analysis for Reliable Distributed Embedded Systems," in *International Parallel and Distributed Processing Symposium (IPDPS)*. IEEE Computer Society, 2002.

[TW99]   M. Thomason and J. Whittaker, "Rare failure-state in a Markov chain model for software reliability," in *IEEE International Symposium on Software Reliability Engineering (ISSRE)*, 1999, pp. 12–19.

[TWH⁺08]   K. S. Trivedi, D. Wang, D. J. Hunt, A. Rindos, W. E. Smith, and B. Vashaw, "Availability Modeling of SIP Protocol on IBM© WebSphere©," in *IEEE Pacific Rim International Symposium on Dependable Computing (PRDC)*, 2008, pp. 323–330.

[Uni06]   United States Army, "Failure Modes, Effects and Criticality Analysis (FMECA) for Command, Control, Communications, Computer, Intelligence, Surveillance, and Reconnaissance (C4ISR) Facilities (Technical Manual TM 5-698-4)," Washington, DC, Tech. Rep. September, 2006.

[UPL11]   M. Utting, A. Pretschner, and B. Legeard, "A taxonomy of model-based testing approaches," *Software Testing, Verification and Reliability (STVR)*, 2011.

[Vij03]   G. Vijayaraghavan, "A Taxonomy of e-commerce Risks and Failures," Ph.D. dissertation, Florida Institute of Technology, 2003.

[VM94]   A. Veevers and A. Marshall, "A relationship between software coverage metrics and reliability," *Software Testing, Verification and Reliability (STVR)*, vol. 4, no. 1, pp. 3–8, 1994.

[VM95]   J. Voas and K. Miller, "Software testability: the new verification," *IEEE Software*, vol. 12, no. 3, pp. 17–28, May 1995.

[VPMM05]   S. Vilkomir, D. Parnas, V. Mendiratta, and E. Murphy, "Availability Evaluation of Hardware/Software Systems with

Several Recovery Procedures," in *International Computer Software and Applications Conference (COMPSAC)*, 2005, pp. 473–478.

[WH07]   M. Wirsing and M. Hölzl, "Software-intensive systems: Report of the Beyond-the-Horizon WG6," 2007.

[Wol10]   K. Wolter, *Stochastic Models for Fault Tolerance: Restart, Rejuvenation and Checkpointing*. Springer, 2010.

[Woo97]   A. Wood, "Software reliability growth models: assumptions vs. reality," *IEEE International Symposium on Software Reliability Engineering (ISSRE)*, pp. 136–141, 1997.

[WPC06]   W.-L. Wang, D. Pan, and M.-H. Chen, "Architecture-based software reliability modeling," *Journal of Systems and Software (JSS)*, vol. 79, no. 1, pp. 132–146, 2006.

[WT05]   D. Wang and K. S. Trivedi, "Modeling user-perceived service availability," in *Service Availability*, lncs ed. Springer Berlin / Heidelberg, 2005, vol. 3694, pp. 107–122.

[WWC99]   W.-L. Wang, Y. Wu, and M.-H. Chen, "An Architecture-Based Software Reliability Model," in *IEEE Pacific Rim International Symposium on Dependable Computing (PRDC)*, 1999, pp. 143–150.

[Yan99]   J. Yang, "A comprehensive review of hard-disk drive reliability," in *Reliability and Maintainability Symposium (RAMS)*, 1999, pp. 403–409.

[YCA99]   S. M. Yacoub, B. Cukic, and H. H. Ammar, "Scenario-Based Reliability Analysis of Component-Based Software," in *IEEE International Symposium on Software Reliability Engineering (ISSRE)*, 1999, pp. 22–31.

[YCA04]   ——, "A Scenario-Based Reliability Analysis Approach for Component-Based Software," *IEEE Transactions on Reliability (TR)*, vol. 53, no. 4, pp. 465–480, Dec. 2004.

[YSP09]   I. Yusuf, H. Schmidt, and I. Peake, "Evaluating recovery aware components for grid reliability," in *European Software Engineering Conference / ACM SIGSOFT Symposium on the Foundations of Software Engineering (ESEC / FSE)*. New York, New York, USA: ACM Press, 2009, pp. 277–280.

[YSP11]   ——, "Architecture-Based Fault Tolerance Support for Grid Applications," in *International Conference on the Quality of Software Architectures (QoSA)*. New York: ACM, 2011, pp. 177–182.

[YST01]   L. Yin, M. Smith, and K. S. Trivedi, "Uncertainty analysis in reliability modeling," in *Reliability and Maintainability Symposium (RAMS)*, 2001, pp. 229–234.

[ZL10]   Z. Zheng and M. R. Lyu, "Collaborative reliability prediction of service-oriented systems," in *International Conference on Software Engineering (ICSE)*, 2010, pp. 35–44.

[ZNG+09]   T. Zimmermann, N. Nagappan, H. Gall, E. Giger, and B. Murphy, "Cross-project defect prediction," in *European Software Engineering Conference / ACM SIGSOFT Symposium on the Foundations of Software Engineering (ESEC / FSE)*. New York, New York, USA: ACM Press, 2009, pp. 91–100.